The HUMAN FACTOR

**MAXIMISING
TEAM
EFFICIENCY
THROUGH
COLLABORATIVE
LEADERSHIP**

Susan Jones

KOGAN
PAGE

First published in 1992

Kogan Page Limited
120 Pentonville Road
London N1 9JN

British Library Cataloguing in Publication Data
A CIP record for this book is available from the British Library.

ISBN 0 7494 0534 1

Typeset by BookEns Ltd., Baldock, Herts.
Printed and bound in Great Britain

Contents

Acknowledgements

I would like to give special acknowledgement to the philosophy and writings of W Edwards Deming and Douglas McGregor. Also to John Adair, Rosabeth Moss Kanter, Matthew Lipman, and Tom Peters.

Introduction

The 'secret' human resource message

The central theme of this book is: *the success of an organisation, whether in industry or education, rests ultimately on the way people are treated.* The central role of the human factor in achieving effectiveness and efficiency in both the learning and working environments is not a new discovery. But, from the increasing talk today about the need to bring in 'new' ways of doing things, new ways that 'value people as an organisation's most important resource' and that 'encourage team work', etc, you might be forgiven for thinking it so. However, at least as far back as the early 1920s, the 'Hawthorne' experiments, carried out at the Hawthorne Works of the giant Western Electric Company in Chicago, provided evidence to show that if factory workers are allowed to participate or 'collaborate' more in the decision-making process, morale, motivation and productivity increase markedly. And in the 1940s Lewin demonstrated the greater effectiveness of a participatory approach as opposed to the traditional authoritarian, lecture approach in an educational setting.

Over the intervening years there have been a wealth of findings within business and educational practice that illustrate the benefits of both worker and learner participation. Yet, despite the growing 'human resource/participation' rhetoric, their message has largely been ignored in practice by British industry and education. While in the 1950s the Japanese were beginning to take the human factor seriously in the running of their organisations, it was still being referred to as a 'pious hope' in the mid-1970s in America (McGregor, 1977), and incredibly in the early 1990s in Britain, industrialists and educationalists are still talking about the secret of Japanese success; and economists refer to the secret of getting both low inflation (with high efficiency/productivity), and high employment (with high growth), how it continues to elude us in the UK, and how it will need a *magic wand* to conquer. It is maintained that Japanese success, and the route to high efficiency and high employment remains a secret, continuing as we do to believe there is a trade-off between them, because we continue to see people primarily as a dispensable *cost* rather than as a central resource worth investing in. This is an attitude that has been highlighted in the latest British recession. Time and again we hear of job cuts in order to increase, or as a result of an increase in, efficiency/productivity through investment in machinery. But this leads only to short-term cost cutting and efficiency. The Japanese realise that the constant improvement in quality and innovation necessary for sustained, long-term efficiency and success is ultimately only achievable through the human resource, not machinery, high technology, buying-in consultants or any other factor. It is the generally poor attitude towards people and their value, therefore, that has caused the majority of British organisations in industry and education to either miss or ignore the human resource 'secret', and continue on the whole to be run under strongly non-participatory, hierarchical working practices.

The consequences

These are becoming increasingly evident. For forty years the Japanese, realising that organisational success depends on quality, and that 'quality control is about people not products' (*Nippon*, 28.10.90), have developed working and learning practices that centre more on people. These involve encouraging people's involvement in the working and learning environments through a group or team approach and investing heavily in people's education and training, and in developing their ideas, ie research and development (R&D). Their way of people working together cooperatively and helping each other's development is not restricted to within organisations. It also exists between organisations and their customers, suppliers, bankers and government. They have, in fact, developed a general *collaborative* way of doing things. So, to a certain extent, have many European countries. There is not, to the same extent, the 'them and us' mentality that exists here in Britain between manager and worker, teacher and pupil, manager and banker, and manager and government. It has meant that in Japan, and certain European countries, industry and education have roared ahead while in Britain, although there are pockets of good practice and success, generally there is relatively poor industrial and educational performance. Indeed so much so that many now talk about a 'crisis' in both industry and education. The figures are there to confirm it.

By neglecting the human factor there are poor personal relations between management and employees which lead to stress in the workplace; and bodies such as the Health and Safety Executive report that this is causing a high financial cost in both industry and education. This book considers how poor, 'non-collaborative' personal interaction is at the root of unethical working practices which undermine employee involvement and control, nurture judgemental performance appraisal and personal rivalry, and poor investment in people's training and R&D, all of which have a detrimental effect on efficiency, quality of employee performance, and therefore quality of goods and services. The effect is increased by a generally non-collaborative national culture, in which there is a lack of collaborative partnership between organisations and their customers, suppliers, investors and government. This means that factories, schools, businesses, hospitals, etc are finding it increasingly difficult to survive against the increased competition for customers and good staff imposed by more efficient 'people-centred' organisations, both at home and abroad. This competition is set to increase further after 1992 with the open European market.

Following the largest balance of payments deficit in British history in 1989 and 1990, the OECD reported in July 1991 that for the fourth year running Britain was bottom of the league of the seven most advanced industrial countries for growth, investment and job creation. This, and a continuing balance of payments deficit, despite the recession, is testimony to poor performance in the manufacturing sector. And the fact that nearly half of Britain's children leave full-time education without any qualification whatsoever, and only about a third continue with full-time education to the age of 18, compared to far higher numbers in many other industrialised countries, is testimony to poor performance in the educational sector. The point was driven home by the highest number of business failures for ten years in the first half of 1990, and a 71 per cent increase on this to over 33,000 business collapses in the first nine months of 1991.

The point is driven home further by the fact that while British organisations are having difficulties, the Japanese and Germans are increasingly setting up companies in Britain using British labour, and doing it more successfully. A similar crisis exists in other English-speaking countries, such as America. There, the demise of much of its electronics industry and shrinking manufacturing base faced with Japanese competition and reduced demand within its latest recession, vindicates the warnings of Deming who taught the Japanese about quality control many decades ago. The warning bells are increasingly being rung, and unless organisations learn the lessons of good practice now and change the way they go about things, the way they educate and train people, the way they build ideas through research and development, they will become uncompetitive and not have another chance to change in future. There is, therefore, an urgent need to learn the lessons, for the success of the country, the success of individual industrial and educational establishments, and for the well-being of people – on which it all pivots – who need to lead more meaningful and fulfilling lives. Why haven't we learned the lessons?

The reasons

Who is it in our schools, our factories, our businesses, etc, that is finding it so difficult to learn the lesson from all the evidence since the 1920s, and now from the successful Japanese and German companies on our doorstep? The lesson is that: *if people work collaboratively within and between organisations, then this will produce better motivation, better learning, better efficiency, better innovation, better quality and therefore more competitive goods and services.* Whose responsibility is it for there being a generally undervalued and marginalised frontline work-force – the shop-floor factory worker, the class teacher and lecturer, the ward nurse, the cleaner and laundry worker, etc – the only people who can deliver and guarantee a high quality of product and service; and the ones best placed to come up with ideas for improvement? In line with Deming's philosophy that it is the style of American management which is the basic cause of sickness in their economy, this book will consider the evidence to show that it is ultimately the underlying 'hierarchical' attitudes and values of top management towards people that makes them more concerned with short-term personal and financial gain rather than with long-term collaborative commitment to their employees and organisation, and that is the basis for poor technical and financial decisions and organisational performance. It also considers how, unlike our more successful competitors, the broader non-collaborative national culture imposes difficulties on individual organisations, both in industry and education, reinforcing short-term, non-collaborative attitudes in management. But it maintains that it is ultimately the interpersonal attitudes and skills of top management and whether they have a collaborative commitment to 'growing' their organisation through 'growing' their work-force that is the basis for effective financial and technical decisions, and therefore a central factor in the 'survivability' of an organisation against negative external factors. It points out that the underlying hierarchical attitudes that make it difficult for managers to lead others effectively are, at one and the same time, the attitudes that make it difficult for them to *learn* from others. The general inability to learn the lessons since the 1920s indicates the strength of these attitudes. Significantly, in contrast, it considers how Japanese managers who have more collaborative attitudes, are 'highly desirous' of learning.

The remedy

The unchanging attitudes of management in industry and education have meant that bureaucratic and hierarchical work practices predominate, with all the negative consequences summarised above. With the aid of examples, this book shows that top managers will need to take the lead in developing their collaborative interpersonal attitudes and skills. This is the only basis for the *genuine* implementation of more equal, horizontal, team structures throughout their organisations, replacing the present pyramidal, power structures, and handing over decision making and responsibility for quality to where it belongs – with every single employee. Only in this way will more ethical, less selfish, less personally acquisitive, and more caring *collaborative organisational cultures* be possible, providing less stressful, more motivating, more empowering, more creative, and more innovative learning and working environments. Only through such commitment from top managers will middle managers, supervisors, and teachers, etc, be truly able to develop their collaborative skills and work practices and translate the growing rhetoric for effective leadership and team work into practice. And only this way will a constructive, collaborative partnership be possible between industry, education, and unions.

Top managers who start this collaborative skills process will develop organisations that will be fitter and better able to meet and survive the challenges of the 1990s. They will have the flexibility and general work conditions to attract and meet the demands of good quality staff; to meet the needs of the non-traditional workers and students who will be increasingly required by organisations; to be able to work in constructive collaborative partnership with their

customers and suppliers; and to enable highly effective and cost-
effective skills training and development. As a result their fitness
and innovativeness will make them better able to produce leading
products and services within increasing competition and diminishing
resources. It will also make them better able to meet the increasing
public and government/EC demands for environmentally, ethically
and socially responsible practices, processes and products.

Finally, although the main obstacle to forming a collaborative
organisational culture, namely, the underlying attitudes of top management, has shown great resistance to the lessons of best
collaborative practice over many years, it is to be hoped that there
will be top managers with enough humility – faced with increasing
difficulties and competition in the 1990s, and the growing 'partnership' climate – to genuinely recognise the ineffectiveness of autocratic, hierarchical working practices and to realise it is now urgent
for survival that they learn those lessons. And it is hoped that this
book, by concentrating on the core interpersonal attitudes and skills
of collaborative leadership, and how to go about developing them –
put simply and in plain English, uncluttered by other aspects of management – will help busy top managers, middle managers, teachers,
supervisors, etc, to embark effectively on the learning process.

PART I

COLLABORATIVE LEADERSHIP AND ORGANISATIONAL SUCCESS

The view being put forward in this book is: *the survivability and success of an organisation rests ultimately on the way people are treated.* The first part looks at evidence from industry, business and education for making this claim, and points to *collaborative* leadership as the key to sound financial and technical decisions and successful employee performance. Part II lists the *core* skills of collaborative leadership, giving further evidence for their central importance – and the need for *everyone* to develop them – throughout the working and learning environments. Finally, Part III considers the nature of skills training, and provides a basic practical guide for developing the core collaborative skills.

1

The way people are treated and organisational success

Human relations and quality of performance

People in business and education are becoming increasingly aware of the central importance of *quality* and *innovation* if organisations are to survive and thrive against growing competition. Competition, which has been rising over the last fifteen years and is set to rise further in Europe after 1992, means that there is no longer any room for average products or services, in Britain or in any other of the 23 countries of the Organisation for Economic Cooperation and Development (OECD). This, for example, is pointed out by the American management guru Tom Peters, who warns that unless organisations 'add value' and 'do the service right', they are likely to 'bite the dust', as indeed many organisations, including giants, already are doing, or have done. (*In Business*, 13.3.91).

Organisations, whether in business or education, that do achieve high quality and innovation and are therefore able to survive and succeed against increased competition, will be those that have realised the following simple formula:

> **Success depends on quality and innovation**
> **quality and innovation depend on people**

The human resource, therefore, is an organisation's key resource for survivability and success. Perhaps the greatest testimony to the truth of this formula is provided by the outstanding success of many Japanese organisations where, as shall be considered in examples in this book, their so-called 'obsession' with quality and innovation is inextricably bound up with their people-centred work practices.

The weight of the evidence for this formula is slowly having an effect in Britain, and a growing number of industrialists, educationalists, management consultants and trainers are voicing the central importance of the human resource in the running of an efficient and successful organisation. The final chapter in this first part of the book gives a selection of comments on the 'human factor' theme from a wide range of people. Here are just two examples, one from the area of business, and the other from the area of education, linking quality with people. Adair maintains:

> The time is ripe to make a quantum leap forward in *the way people work together* in industry . . . The need for such [improvement] to raise *quality of performance* is growing more pressing. (1986, p202; my emphasis)

Essentially the same point has been made in the area of education:

> The union [NUT] believes education authorities and schools need to change *the way they work*. (Blackburne, 1990; my emphasis)

And according to Doug McAvoy, the National Union of Teachers' General Secretary, this is because:

> Schools are organised to run the education system of 1945 and not 1990. As a consequence they have become 'unhealthy' and *performance* – including academic performance of children – has been impaired. (Blackburne, 1990; my emphasis)

So, whether you are talking about industry or education, *the way people work* together, ie human or 'interpersonal' relationships, is of central importance to their quality of performance and so product or service quality. Which way, therefore, should people work, and whose responsibility is it?

Collaborative leadership, participation and motivation

Since the Hawthorne experiments of the early 1920s, there has been a great deal of evidence, both in the working and learning environments, to show that: *the more people participate in dialogue and the decision-making process, the more they are motivated to work and learn*[*]. This is shown most strikingly by many Japanese business organisations, and also in certain European and American organisations. Although there are examples in British business and education that illustrate the value of a *participatory* approach as will be considered below, as yet they represent a minority. They are, however, a growing minority, and the need for *active involvement* in the working and learning environments is endorsed by such leading bodies as the Confederation of British Industry (eg CBI 1989), and the Business and Technician Education Council (BTEC, 1989).

The responsibility for making *the way people work* more *participatory* is increasingly being placed squarely on management, both in business and education. For example Adair and McAvoy quoted above maintain:

> . . . we define that part of a manager's job concerned with getting the best contribution from those for whose work he is responsible as – *leadership* . . . The great leader is always aware of latent powers in people which can be evoked and harnessed . . . Generally speaking, the more members *participate in decisions*, the more they feel *motivated* to carry them out . . . (Adair, 1984, pp55, 16; my emphasis)

> School management has not kept up with the pace of change . . . A new management culture should mean teachers are *involved in decision making* and not excluded. (McAvoy, quoted in Blackburne 1990; my emphasis)

It is important, therefore, for managers to treat the human resource in such a way as will enable *participation in decision making* – the most effective way to enhance people's confidence, self-esteem and motivation to work and learn cooperatively, and so produce good ideas, good results, and high quality products and services. Managers will only be able to treat people in this way if they develop certain 'soft', interpersonal collaborative leadership skills. Part II will detail what these 'collaborative' skills are.

Rather than say these skills are needed to motivate people, it might be more apt to say they are needed to avoid *de-motivating* people. They *enable* and *empower* people to develop and fulfil their creative potential. The need to have collaborative leadership in order to enable participation as a basis for empowering human

---

* See, for example, Lewin, 1947; Bennett, 1955; Blumberg, 1968; Stenhouse, 1969; Chaney and Teel, 1977; Revans, 1978; Lipman *et al*, 1980, also teaching packs which incorporate the use of short 'philosophical' stories to catalyse group discussion, and teacher training which models the basic group/team format, *International Association for Philosophy for Children*, Montclair State College, New Jersey; Smith, 1983; Henry and Kemmis, 1985; Prideaux and Ford, 1988; Beck, 1989; Harber and Meighan, 1989.

potential, is strongly voiced by Michael Frye, for example, chairman of the successful B Elliott Group:

> So we need to be looking at a style of leadership, of culture and environment, whatever words you like, that is going to *encourage* people to participate, and part of that encouragement needs to be that *they* feel they can release, that they are going to develop, that they can realise their own potential. That's *every* work person, *every* person in the company – I mean *everyone*, the shop floor, the cleaner, *every* single person should have an opportunity to realise their own potential. (*Walk the Talk*, 28.4.91)

The leadership–quality–success 'chain reaction'

The reason why the way people are treated is central to organisational success can be spelled out as follows. It is the responsibility of those in management to develop collaborative leadership skills in order to involve people more, thus motivating them to give of their best. This will result in fewer delays, fewer mistakes, better ideas and better use of time, machines and materials. This, in turn, will produce good quality results and less re-work, improving efficiency/ productivity, as a basis for capturing the market with better quality, competitively priced, goods or services; which, in turn, will increase the chance of organisational survival and success. This 'chain reaction' is summarised in Figure 1.1 (adapted from Deming, 1986, p3).

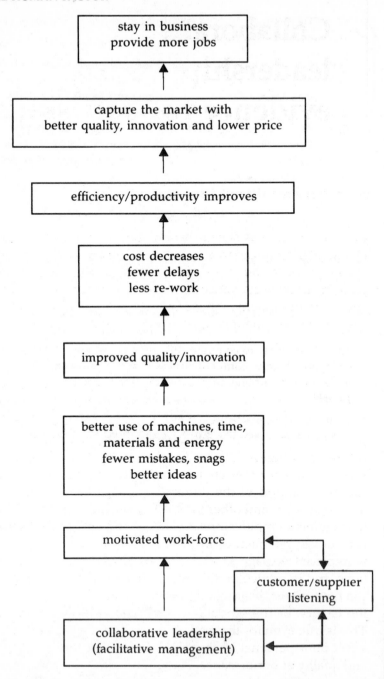

Figure 1.1 *The leadership–quality–success 'chain reaction'*

2
Collaborative leadership – hard evidence for soft skills

Successful reality not irrelevant idealism

In Chapter 1 it was stated that an increasing number of people in business and education are becoming aware of the importance of collaborative leadership – which involves everyone in the workplace in dialogue and decision making – in order to achieve motivation and therefore quality, innovation, efficiency, survivability and success. As management consultant Rosabeth Moss Kanter puts it:

> Today our ability to compete is based on capability . . . in this rapidly changing, highly competitive environment that we live in we're increasingly counting on people down on the floor. (*Business Matters*, 14.6.90)

But although there is growing awareness of this, the majority of people in business and education are still to be convinced of the central importance of 'people down on the floor' to organisational success – at worst they are unaware, and at best they are sceptical, of the major import of the human factor. Despite reports from business, education and other public organisations, which identify poor management-employee relationships and lack of involvement and control as key factors in stress and poor performance in the workplace (see page 33–4), there is a general belief that human relations, and in particular the way people are treated by management, can have no real bearing on the 'hard-headed' business of the office, the factory, or the school, etc. It is seen as irrelevant or idealistic. This is true even for the many individuals who are well aware of the effect poor personal interaction is having on their own motivation and quality of performance. Somehow it is explained away, possibly by seeing the problem as peculiar to themselves and the feeling that their work is insignificant to the organisation as a whole.

A typical viewpoint was voiced in a talk attended by the author in 1989 on the teachings of the management guru Tom Peters, who stresses the importance of employee (and customer) involvement in the workplace. The speaker, a managing director of an expanding garden centre business, used a videotape of actual examples from business and education where a 'people-centred' approach was paying off in terms of motivation and efficiency; and he himself was beginning to develop a group approach with employees in his workplace. His enthusiasm was unmistakable, but not contagious, at least for some of the audience of small business people present. At the end of the talk one audience member commented, almost indignantly: 'Why should we take any notice of these new-fangled ideas? It's just an American gimmick.'

A similar general scepticism towards group involvement exists in the educational sector. For example, one primary school teacher in a discussion conducted by the author on the value of group discussion and dialogue in the learning process, commented: 'But can we afford to be wasting time with the pupils in this way?' This view of group dis-cussion has been fairly widespread throughout education both within the classroom and beyond.

It seems the evidence, available since the 1920s, of successful practice that has centred on a participatory group or team approach has somehow passed these people by. Therefore, for those sceptics who have got this far in the book and who believe that human relations – the way people are treated – is an idealistic irrelevance in the workplace, it is important to be aware that the above view concerning worker and learner participation is not just the theoretical belief of academics, nor even the wishful thinking of some practitioners – it is actually the basis of highly successful practice in some organisations in this country today.

Some examples of success through collaborative leadership

In April 1990 it was reported on the national news that the Nissan UK plant at Sunderland, Britain's fastest-growing new motor manufacturing plant, was producing cars of a quality at least as high, and in some cases even higher, than that achieved in Japan. It was also reported that Nissan planned to invest £31 million in plant over the next two years for further expansion into Europe. A year later, as the latest British recession began to bite, media reports indicated that Nissan planned to double production in Sunderland. What is the basis for their past success and their future confidence? Their employment policy contains the answer. Here is a short extract:

If you can hire good people, train them well and get their commitment, *then give them real responsibility*, you are well on the way to success.

Thorough training and earning commitment through *an innovative management policy that actively encourages staff to become involved in every aspect of the running of the business* are the keystones to developing a work-force that has a well developed sense of team spirit and high levels of *motivation*.

The *motivation* to do the best possible job means not only that the quality of the end product is high; it also means that traditional factory practices such as clocking on and quality control inspections become unnecessary (Nissan, 1985, 'Employment', p1; my emphasis).

In short, the basis of their success is collaborative leadership. The managers know that leadership that *genuinely involves employees* and gives them 'real responsibility', will ensure motivation, innovation and so the high quality needed for success. They also know that obtaining quality through people in this way is more effective than any attempt to obtain quality through departments, quality controllers, traditional performance appraisal and even Quality Control Circles (see Chapter 8). There are no Japanese production staff. Treated the right way, therefore, people *will* produce top quality goods and services, and so bring organisational success.

Examples of successful junior schools cited in an Inner London Education Authority report identified 'purposeful leadership' by the head teacher and 'involvement of teachers' as key factors in those schools' success. Purposeful leadership was said to occur when the head was actively involved in the school's needs but was good at sharing power with the staff. He or she did not exert total control over teachers, but instead consulted them, especially in decision making:

In successful schools, the teachers were involved in curriculum planning and played a major role in developing their own curriculum guidelines . . . teacher involvement in decisions [on classes and spending] was important . . . schools in which teachers were consulted on issues affecting school policy as well as those affecting them directly, were more likely to be successful (ILEA, 1986, p35).

There was also more communication with, and less punishment of, the pupils; and more openness and involvement for parents. Success was shown in the positive gains in academic development and the improved behaviour of children.

The BM Group is an example of a British manufacturing organisation – with no Japanese connections – that has turned member companies around from loss to profit through a management approach that collaboratively involves *all* employees (*Walk the Talk*, 28.4.91).

The Rainbow General Stores in San Francisco is run as a highly successful business, with an annual turnover of $8 million, through a collective team approach where all decisions are made by groups, there are no managers who are over anyone else in the store, and everyone has a vote (*Where on Earth are We Going?*, 23.7.90).

Reported as the world's biggest maker of office furniture, Steelcase in Michigan has 'handed over' most decision making to teams involving *all* the work-force. A plant manager in the organisation relates how the new approach, begun in 1987, has taken a number of years to get the organisation 100 per cent covered with teams, so it is 'just getting started'. Yet, he maintains, already the approach has produced proposals and suggestions from the work-force that have resulted in savings of over $500,000, produced improved quality, and increased worker morale and commitment. He expects there to be a continuous and ever faster payback from the approach – 'more and more suggestions [are] coming all the time' – and believes this is: 'the *only* way we're going to survive in the future and still be that excellent office furniture manufacturer that we've been in the past.' (*Business Matters*, 8.8.91)

Collaborative leadership, family, and 'we're all in this together'

Dame Catherine's School in Derbyshire is another example of a successful educational organisation that is, perhaps to a greater extent than most others, run along participatory lines:

> There are no offices at Dame Catherine's, no staffroom . . . Staff and pupils are on first-name terms and *all school business is done in public*. An HMI visit is *discussed by everyone*, and even features on the timetable . . . It's not weird, strange or revolutionary, it's common sense. A way of teaching children properly (Gibbons, 1989, my emphasis).

The same openness that exists in Dame Catherine's School is characteristic of many Japanese organisations, and is expressed by Ian Sloss, personnel director of the Japanese-owned SP Tyres: 'we're all in this together so there is nothing confidential. The worker should know everything' (Murray, 1990). And an employee at the highly successful Sony plant in South Wales comments: 'you know where you are going with a Japanese company, there's not so many secrets at high level as there is with a British company' (*Business Matters*, 6.6.91). The reason for the contrast between the more open relationship between management and work-force in Japanese organisations and the more secretive nature of that in British organisations is explained by Jeremy Golden, Anglo-Japanese liaison officer with the Milton Keynes Development Corporation: '. . . the British manager feels a stronger identification with his board members, with the sort of horizontal class' (Murray, 1990, p43).

Why in general do Japanese managers, and managers of certain successful organisations in the West, operate less hierarchically and identify more with the work-force than do most British managers? It is based on differences in underlying attitudes towards people and their value – 'interpersonal' attitudes – Japanese managers having predominantly what this book refers to as 'collaborative attitudes and skills', as a basis for collaborative leadership, in contrast to the predominantly 'hierarchical attitudes and skills' found in British managers (see Part II).

The feeling that employees have of being 'in this together with management', of being part of an organisation, with everybody pulling in the same direction, is an outcome of collaborative leadership that values the work-force, keeps them fully informed, involves them in the decision-making process and is so essential for motivation, quality and success (see Chapter 5, Chapter 6, p83 and Chapter 8, p132). In fact, under collaborative leadership employee and management roles merge, not only through involving employees more in the decision-making process, but also through a greater flexibility in roles generally, where people interchange more between various jobs and activities (see also Chapter 4, p57 and Chapter 6, p.79). Included in the latter is the willingness of management to share in more menial tasks and to interchange with jobs 'lower down' the organisation if required. This occurs, for instance, in many Japanese organisations. For example, on a visit by the author to the Honda factory in Swindon, the plant manager and an associate manager talked of the way that 'everyone mucks in' on the various chores that need to be done, including occasionally management washing floors. Similarly, a team leader at the Toyota factory in Kentucky stays behind in his own time to clean and sweep his team area – 'it's worth it for Toyota . . . to give part of yourself to make the company work' (*The Midlands Report*, 25.10.90; see also p127). And again, the industrialist Sir Peter Parker, chairman of a number of British companies and also of Mitsubishi Electric UK, has noted 'the extraordinary interaction of the different levels of a Japanese company', which the British cannot so easily learn: 'The way in which you know, if the girl wants to go off to the loo the supervisor will take her place on the line' (*Open Mind*, 22.6.91). A greater interchange between management and employee roles is also encouraged under the participatory management programme being developed at the Beth Israel hospital in Boston, America. One aspect of the programme is the exercise 'nurse for the day', where top administrators are expected to volunteer for tasks on the wards (*Business Matters*, 13.6.91; see also Chapter 6, Example p90). And yet a further manifestation of collaborative leadership where everyone feels, and is, equally valued and involved, is job security, brought about by management commitment to give employees a job for life. This is a characteristic of Japanese organisations that is greatly appreciated by British employees. For example, a worker at the Nissan plant in Sunderland comments: 'I like working here. It's a company where I feel as if you do well for the company, you've got a steady job for the rest of your life.' (*Newsnight*, 29.10.91) A feeling of identification and commitment, which is rare, yet desperately needed, by most British employees, both in industry and education.

All of these are examples of moves that help create a more 'horizontal' 'single status' or 'classless' organisation, where people are truly 'all in this together', working towards the same goals, which is essential for effective teamwork. The examples given go further along that road by having generally single status facilities, such as dining area and car parking facilities. A further aspect of many Japanese companies is that everyone works under the same conditions of employment, the same holidays, the same pension, etc. Also, in Japanese manufacturing plants, *everybody*, from the top manager down, wears the same company-issued overalls. Some of these aspects might seem trivial, but they are all a sign that management are able to see the employees as equals and work together collaboratively with them; and this has a corresponding positive psychological effect on the employee. As Peters and Austin say, 'either you're part of a team or you're not part of a team', and for those managers who are unable to wear the same overalls, 'we wouldn't bet two cents on their ability to run a truly distinctive manufacturing operation' (1985, p212).

Concerning the collaborative approach, as one might expect, the reporter commenting on Dame Catherine's School refers to the 'extended family atmosphere and *glasnost* all round' at the school (pB₁). Similarly, Peters and Austin refer to the use of the terms 'community' and 'family' by what they class as 'excellent' head teachers, and they point out that in their investigations of business organisations: '. . . time and again we see the unabashed use of the word "family" among those who exhibit a passion for excellence. . . . In an effective family unit all members are full-scale partners.' (1985, p408)

This is also a key factor in the success of The Body Shop. In a lecture given by the founder and managing director, Anita Roddick, she implored the business and education people present in the audience to 'keep that family element' (Schumacher, 1990). She encouraged and enabled *all* of The Body Shop employees to participate in the compilation of a company charter, and again this emphasises the family element.

> We embrace everyone who works for The Body Shop and with The Body Shop as part of our extended family. We are all the company: it is up to us all to make it work. Enter into the spirit of partnership. We're all in this together!

Anita Roddick's collaborative leadership has brought about an internationally successful organisation, which continued to flourish through the latest British (American and Canadian) recession, and which is expected to flourish further in the future (NatWest 1991). It is the way she treats employees, the community, other species and the natural environment generally – her 'soft' leadership skills – that are the key to The Body Shop's success.

Soft collaborative skills – the bedrock of hard technical and financial skills

The underlying attitudes and skills of collaborative leadership that involve employees in decision making, and which will be listed in Part II, have two main aspects. Firstly, they enable a manager to hand over completely certain decisions to the appropriate groups or teams in the organisation. Secondly, they ensure that a manager never takes any decision independently, without considering and involving the work-force.

This is the way of operating, for example, in successful Japanese companies. Industrialist Sir Peter Parker points out that, although in the West we can learn about Japanese production technology – clean air, clean factories, etc – and are doing so, we cannot so easily learn the way people interact in a Japanese organisation – what this book refers to as the 'soft' interpersonal skills. He goes on, 'You feel a sort of internal democracy in the Japanese; you feel they are waiting to hear the messages from the bottom up' (*Open Mind*, 22.6.91). It means that no decisions, including technical and financial decisions, are made independently of the work-force, or the customer, or the supplier.

In truth, there is no such thing as a *purely* technical or financial decision taken independently of a manager's attitude towards people. The decision will always reflect the attitude, even if it is one of ignoring people and their needs and views. Interpersonal attitudes and skills, therefore, form the basis of the so-called 'hard' technical and financial skills; and examples within this book will illustrate how successful technical and financial decisions made by certain organisations have been based on underlying collaborative attitudes towards people. Here are two examples which illustrate the priority of collaborative leadership skills over 'technical' and 'financial' skills.

The priority of leadership skills – Example 1

The following was reported concerning the Channel Tunnel Project:

> Mr Neerhout has been installed to act as a buffer between TML [Transmanche-Link] and Mr Morton, *after the deterioration in relations which threatened the future of the £7.2 billion project*. The agreement,

which came after intervention from the Bank of England last week, was vital to secure more cash from the banks financing the project (Elliott, 1990, p12, my emphasis).

Discussing the problem that had arisen, a Transport and General Workers Union spokesman referred to Mr Alastair Morton's (the Channel Tunnel Group's Chief Executive) 'very abrasive management style', which was 'not conducive to high worker morale' (*BBC News*, 21.2.90). This example illustrates that it is the way a manager relates to the work-force, and his or her leadership skills that determines worker morale and so the success or otherwise of an organisation. However good a manager's financial and technical skills are deemed to be, they count for nothing if his or her collaborative leadership skills are lacking.

*The priority of leadership skills – Example 2**

The demise of the home furnishings empire Coloroll has been attributed to company chairman John Ashcroft's management style. It is this that is believed to have kept him out of touch with the economy, the market/customer (Chapter 9), and his own work-force (Chapter 8), and that led to faulty financial and technical decisions. As we shall see in Part II, the skills of effectively leading (motivating) people, include the self same skills of being able to *learn* from other people and situations. The following comments have been made concerning the management of Coloroll:

> He [John Ashcroft] comes across as being extremely aggressive, abrasive, perhaps a touch arrogant and very optimistic and I think very ambitious. (Kimlan Cook, retail analyst at Smith New Court)

> His [John Ashcroft's] own style is an expansive style, it enabled him to have the confidence to build up very rapidly, but also I think pushed him slightly over the brink. He was unable to stand back and accept that maybe he couldn't master the whole of the economy . . . (Donald Anderson, analyst with Hoare Govett Stockbrokers)

> The people that they brought in for management I don't think knew about furniture . . . some of our workers have been there twenty years – they could run the factory single handed, they know the busi-

*The quotations and factual data for this example are taken from *The Money Programme*, 4.2.90 and 16.6.91; the interpretations are this author's.

ness inside out, but they're not the ones that were running it. (Margaret Evans, factory worker at William Barratt Furniture Company)

Certainly the management style epitomised by John Ashcroft and Coloroll, so successful in the eighties, will have to change for the nineties. (Tom Maddocks, *The Money Programme* reporter)

It has been said that few businessmen boasted a better grasp of economics than John Ashcroft. In 1989, at the outset of the latest British recession, he publicly sounded the alarm. Concerning this a reporter from *The Money Programme* comments, 'It may seem strange that a man who took such a public interest in economics could leave himself so vulnerable to a downturn.' But of course it is not strange when it is realised that technical and financial judgements in the workplace do not depend on some remote academic grasp of economics, but are inextricably bound up with underlying inter-personal attitudes and skills (see also Chapter 14, p276–7).

John Ashcroft denies that the many acquisitions he made were responsible for his company's downfall, and he blames a 'freak economic wave' of deteriorating trading conditions. But not everyone goes bust in a recession (see Chapter 12), and even if his acquisitions were not responsible – which others would disagree with – his company's inability to deal with recession was an indication of poor decisions. Either way he cannot easily absolve himself from the accusation that he made poor financial and technical judgements – judgements that were the product of poor leadership skills based on non-collaborative attitudes towards employees and customers, which prevented him taking on board their needs and views.

Summary – the priority of leadership skills

In summary, it can be said that *if a manager has poor leadership skills, then this will undermine his or her financial and technical judgement – the skills of collaborative leadership form the bedrock of successful financial and technical decisions.* A manager with collaborative leadership skills will make technical and financial judgements that take into account the views and needs of the work-force (and the customer and supplier); decisions that will include directing resources to the employee in the form of training, and research and development (see Chapters 11 and 12).

There are many examples through the 1980s and early 1990s of top managers who did not act collaboratively in the best interests of their organisation and employees. Asil Nadir of Polly Peck International, John Gunn of British and Commonwealth Financial Group and Sir Ralph Halpern of the Burton Group, are just a few that hit the headlines. But they represent the tip of an iceberg of non-collaborative practice. They all exhibited a management style that has variously been described as 'flamboyant', 'dominating', 'unaccountable', and 'charismatic'. A major activity of these leaders was deal-making and the acquiring of new business, rather than developing their existing business and employees; and by over-extending they all led their companies into financial difficulties and in some cases to collapse (see also Chapter 11). Relating to this point of over-extending, Kanter observes that companies, such as Du Pont, that have focused on what they do well, have been much more successful than organisations that have invested money in diversification. She advises that organisations ought to be concentrating where they have skills that add value, and investing in R&D and training and development time for their people (*Business Matters*, 14.6.90).

The priority of collaborative leadership skills for effective technical and financial decisions is indirectly proclaimed by Peters and Austin when they point out that the 'superior customer service' and 'constant innovation' that are the key to success, are not dependent on any financial or technical wizardry, but on management having 'respect for the dignity *and* the creative potential of each person in the organization' (1985, p5). But it is not just certain management consultants who stress the priority of 'soft' social or interpersonal skills over other so-called 'hard' skills. Occupational psychologist Professor Cary Cooper, for example, states:

> The key thing that in my view is missing in the whole of work-life is to train bosses to realise that the most important thing they can do is not all the technical skills they have, but how to manage people properly. (*An Abuse of Power*, 2.5.91)

Collaborative leadership skills, therefore, are the key to the success, and the continuing 'long-term' success of an organisation.

Collaborative leadership, ethics and survival

The issue of business ethics has been highlighted by the increase in business and financial scandals that took place through the 1980s and into the 1990s, such as the conviction for fraud of the chairman

of Guinness, the charges of theft and false accounting against Asil
Nadir of Polly Peck, the charge of theft against Roger Levitt of the
Levitt Group, and charges against top people at the Bank of Credit
and Commerce International (BCCI), described as the world's
biggest ever banking scandal.

But such scandals are the tip of an iceberg of unethical work practices that are brought about by a predominantly non-collaborative
approach to management in the workplace. This undermines the
relationship between:

- managers and employees;

- organisations and supplier and customer;

- organisations and the environment.

The relationship between managers and employees

The predominantly non-collaborative relationship between manager
and employees:

- excludes people from involvement in decision making, the most
  effective basis of recognition, reward and motivation (see Chapter
  8);

- restricts people's discretion over their work – their control or
  autonomy;

- keeps people in the dark with secrecy, dishonesty and lack of
  openness;

- imposes performance appraisal with the fear of reprisal, including job loss (see Chapter 8);

- formulates technical and financial strategies around short-term/
  personal financial goals, rather than primarily directing funds
  towards employees, their training, ideas (R&D), and equipment,
  as a basis for long-term employee and organisational development (see above, and Chapters 11 and 12);

- perceives laying people off as a legitimate tool to counter financial hardship (see Chapter 12)

None of these acts are illegal – but all of them are unethical. Michael
Frye, managing director of the successful B Elliott Group of

companies, for example, refers to the 'barbarism' of management secrecy and lack of communication that limits people's involvement and personal growth (*Walk the Talk*, 28.4.91). Similarly, Freire maintains that to prevent people from being involved in enquiry and their own decision making is an act of 'violence' (1972, p58). And indeed such 'barbaric violence' has a devastating effect on the employee, producing:

- unfulfilled potential and demotivation;

- a reciprocal lack of openness, producing secrecy and dishonesty in the employee;

- a reciprocal lack of commitment by the employee;

- stress and ill health in the employee; all leading to:

- reduced efficiency, poor quality of employee performance and therefore poor quality of goods and services.

The situation is well summed up in a comment by Graham James, deputy head of the ACAS Work Research Unit. Recognising that the effectiveness of any organisation depends on the individuals that go to make up that organisation, he points out how poor treatment of employees by management alienates employees, producing the response:

> The organisation doesn't care about us, so why the hell should we care about the organisation? So things like concern with quality, for example, or productivity, tend to be down-graded. (*An Abuse of Power*, 2.5.91)

The extent of the above unethical, non-collaborative practices in business and education is reflected in:

- statistics relating to stress;

- statistics relating to the quality of goods and services;

- the predominantly negative and often dishonest attitude of employees.

Statistics relating to stress

Stress in the workplace, both in industry and education, is far more widespread than people care to admit, mainly because it is generally seen in terms of individual weakness rather than an organisational-management problem. The Health and Safety Executive estimate that stress costs British employers around £4 billion a year, and that relates to the cost of absenteeism only and does not include additional costs – produced by loss of efficiency (productivity), under-performance, early retirement, and recruitment and training costs when people leave their jobs as a result of stress (*The Money Programme*, 11.3.90). As far as individual firms are concerned, organisational psychologist Professor Cary Cooper estimates that poor management could cost anywhere up to 5 or 10 per cent of their profits (*An Abuse of Power*, 2.5.91).

Interestingly, a reporter from *The Money Programme*, commenting on the findings of a number of studies showing that blue-collar workers suffer from stress-related illness at a greater rate than white-collar workers, and that the further one goes down an organisation's hierarchy the higher the stress suffered by the employees, describes the findings as an 'upside-down stress effect'. Presumably this perception is based on the prevalent belief that the 'high-fliers', ie, the people with the highest status in an organisation, have greater responsibility and therefore suffer greater stress. But really it is the other way around. It will not be perceived as 'upside-down' when it is realised that stress is produced by the high responsibility, or at least high accountability, put on employees together with a lack of control through lack of involvement in decision making, and low job security – which are tied to low job status producing low job satisfaction – and these generally build up the lower down the organisational hierarchy we go. And lack of control in the workplace has been identified as a major cause of stress by a number of studies covering business, education and other public organisations (eg Anderson, 1991; NUT, 1990; HSE, 1990; see also Chapter 13, p258–9). This is the reason why stress counselling does not get to the root of the problem, a view held by Professor Ben Fletcher of Hatfield Polytechnic. He believes that, 'A sick person is a reflection often of a sick organisation . . .' and he maintains that if you do not change the organisational structure, the people, and the training, etc '. . . you elastoplast over one area and of course you get an eruption of the difficulty in another area, and that's no good at all' (*The Money Programme*, op cit).

All the studies cited here are recent, but in fact collaboratively involving people *equally* in the decision-making process, giving them control and autonomy, has been shown to be a key factor in employee health, morale and efficiency, at least since the Hawthorne experiments of the early 1920s (see, for example, Blumberg, 1968). Yet their message, as indeed has that of the people-centred working practices of many successful Japanese organisations since the early 1950s, has been largely overlooked in the West. With increased competition, the demographic downturn, and the skills shortage predicted for the 1990s, management, both in business and education, can no longer afford to overlook this central issue; and those that do so and continue to operate unethical, 'uncaring', non-collaborative working practices, risk their organisations going out of business before the end of the decade (see also Chapter 7, p116–17).

Bullying at work has been identified as a cause of stress, but there is a general resistance to accepting that it does occur in the workplace. There is an underlying feeling – perhaps wishful thinking – that bullying is a phenomenon that is left behind in the school playground, which results in a general disbelief and surprise – by those who have not been bullied at work – at claims of adult bullying. Yet there should be no surprise when it is realised that bullying is just the tip of the widespread unethical iceberg referred to above, where people are generally demeaned and robbed of self-esteem in the workplace by a lack of control and involvement in the decision-making process.

The wider significance of bullying to generally poor working relations between manager and employee in the workplace, is recognised by some of those dealing with problems at work (see *An Abuse of Power*, 2.5.91). Bill Greenaway, manager for Advisory Services of ACAS, finds that although people are willing to talk about problems of managing staff, etc, they rarely talk about someone being a bully, and that, he thinks, makes it difficult to tackle the problem. Professor Cary Cooper thinks that the 'bullying' label is emotive and likely to be rejected by senior managers, and recommends that people talk instead about the way the management style of executives and managers adversely affects not only the health and well-being of employees but also their productivity and performance. Psychotherapist and organisational consultant Neil Crawford makes the point most explicitly: 'Under the name of "bullying", it is allegedly not common, but under all sorts of other names, it is incredibly common.' Significantly, among the other 'commoner' names he and Professor Cooper include:

- envy of ability;

- not valuing the work of a subordinate;

- demeaning people;

- putting people down;

- making people do something that they do not wish to do;

- not listening to people's concerns – one of the worst forms of intimidation.

All these are characteristics of the ineffective non-collaborative leadership that has predominated in the workplace (see also Chapter 6, p78–9).

The poor personal relations between managers and employees that exist in the prevailing non-collaborative Western organisations contrast sharply with those prevailing in many Japanese organisations, and it is noteworthy that the Japanese, who are now longer-lived than anyone else, are less likely to die of stress-related diseases than Europeans and Americans. Michael Marmot, Professor of Community Medicine, reviewed all the major variables that might be affecting Japanese health (featured in *Medicine Now*, 9.1.89). He concluded that the dramatic increases in life expectancy over the past two decades could not be *completely* accounted for by factors such as increase in money spent on medical treatment, inheritance, and diet – although these were contributory factors. From his work in Britain, Professor Marmot maintains that the 'work environment is importantly related to people's health and status', and an important factor is: '. . . the degree to which people are in fulfilling jobs, in jobs that are not boring, repetitive, the degree to which they feel they have control over the work.' He speculates, therefore, that the penetration of automation in Japan and the elimination of boring, repetitive work, and its replacement by skilled jobs has led to a feeling of commitment in the workplace, and a feeling of control and involvement, with a consequent improvement in health. But he concludes from the fact that Japanese women have had the same increase in life expectancy, although their work is different from that of men, that the increase in automation is unlikely to be the *whole explanation*. One could have reached the same conclusion from the observation that increase in automation in Western organisations has not decreased stress and ill-health. As will be considered later in the book (Chapter 12, p240–1), automation *in itself* will not bring improvements in commitment, a feeling of control and involvement, and therefore health – some other aspect of Japanese organisation is achieving this. As Professor Marmot recognises, this is a characteristic of the Japanese national culture, namely: 'commitment to the group'. He found that people in Japan who live in supportive social networks had lower rates of heart disease than people who are living a more Westernised life-style, and concludes, '. . . it might be something about the commitment to the workplace, the commitment to the family, that is a protective against stress for example.'

He also points to the link between prosperity and health – poor people are unhealthier – and Japan is not only a prosperous nation, but also one in which income is distributed more equitably than in the West. This means there are fewer poor people and so less ill health as a result. However, this factor – a more equitable sharing of wealth – is again an outcome of the Japanese culture of collaborative group commitment. Significantly, Professor Marmot generally concludes that apart from diet, which is 'crucially important', the two other areas that need to be looked at are 'the economy and income distribution, and the work environment'; and he believes we need critically to ask ourselves what role these might be playing in Japan and 'what messages what's going on in Japan might have for European countries'. It is precisely these messages, and similar ones from successful organisations in the West, that this book attempts to pick up.

Statistics relating to quality of goods and services

The 1991 Annual Report of the Director General of Fair Trading recorded almost 700,000 complaints against poor goods and services for the year 1989–90; a 7.2 per cent increase over the previous year. This speaks for itself. Similarly in the area of education there is a general poor quality of service leading to poor performance and under-achievement. For example, Prince Charles, in his Shakespeare birthday lecture on 22 April 1991, expressed a feeling of profound sadness over damage already done by the under-education of children, and worries over how we will survive and avoid becoming the poor relation of the Europe of 1992 and beyond:

It is almost incredible that in Shakespeare's land one child in seven leaves primary school functionally illiterate . . . Perhaps most alarming of all, only a third of our 16–18 year olds are still in full-time education. Forty per cent of our children leave full-time schooling with no significant educational qualifications at all.

And he refers to the 'innovation fatigue' brought about by many changing policy initiatives and 'a teaching force which invariably feels underpaid and demoralised . . .' (see also Chapters 11 and 12 below).

The predominantly negative attitude of employees

The extent to which employees are foiled and frustrated by lack of involvement in decision making and by management secrecy and dishonesty, is reflected in the way they often spend a great deal of time and effort working against management and organisational goals (see eg McGregor, 1987, p129 ff, p152; also Chapter 7 below). McGregor, for example, refers to a situation where workers, when attempting to communicate errors in blueprints up the line, would be confronted with the stock answer 'Follow the blueprint'. Subsequently, when mistakes did occur, 'the workers took malicious pleasure in following the blueprint exactly, even though they knew they were making a costly mistake for the company' (p116). Anyone who has worked in a British organisation, whether in business or education, will doubtless be aware of many examples of similar events.

The negative and underhand attitude of employees might even extend to dishonesty in the form of petty thieving of an organisation's equipment or products. This contrasts sharply with the situation in collaborative, 'family' organisations (see also Chapter 6). An example of the latter is provided by the Japanese-owned JVC television and video factory near Glasgow (*Business Matters*, 11.7.91). The general manager at the factory is rightly sceptical about the value of a written code of ethics for an organisation. He believes:

> If there isn't one team and they [people] don't share this common purpose and goal, then ethics isn't going to instil that common purpose. If you write rules they can be broken . . . The culture has got to be right.

---

*Taken from the text of the Prince of Wales's Shakespeare birthday lecture

However, as the *Business Matters* reporter pointed out, 'TVs and videos are attractive items', and the company did lose stock from the stores at the start. But it turned out that JVC's staff were innocent, and the stealing was being done by a security guard from a private firm. The security firm was sacked and JVC employed its own security guards who became part of the 'company family'. The report continued: 'These days the stores are unlocked and JVC says nothing goes missing.' This is unusual. Most organisations, public or private, expect and budget for a minimum of goods and/or equipment being taken by staff. The general manager at JVC comments: 'I'm sure we have dishonest people, in six hundred there must be some who are basically dishonest.' But, of course, the facts belie this. Generally speaking individuals are not 'basically dishonest', and dishonesty in the workplace is usually a reflection of the way people are treated – the culture of an organisation. In general, if people are treated in a responsible way, they behave in a responsible way. If management are loyal and committed to people, then people will be loyal and committed to management. JVC, by involving people, treating them as responsible, and generally having a collaborative commitment to them, *have* got the culture right. No superfluous code of ethics is needed, ethics is inbuilt into the culture of personal relationships (Chapter 6).

Relating to the aspect of loyalty and commitment, Andrew Phillips, a City solicitor, points out that the rate at which companies are taken over reflects 'the wilting of loyalty . . . both board to employees and employees to board', which reduces the chances of developing a 'house morality' (*Business Matters*, 11.7.91). But as the example of JVC illustrates, the responsibility lies with management, since if loyalty is shown to employees – in the way it is in many Japanese companies, for example, where managers remain with an organisation for life, and employ workers for life – then it will be reciprocated by the employees. It is the mobility and corresponding non-collaborative attitudes of most British managers that are at the root of the problem. As Andrew Phillips points out: 'You know it's quite common these days for a large City corporation to have three chairmen in the space of eight or ten years.' In order to build a moral framework he says he would like to see every major manager, every decision-taker, have a compulsory course of business ethics, and concludes: 'I think I would almost teach that more than I would teach anything else.' Such a course, however, would not have to present ethics as an academic discipline to be learned 'at a distance'. This way, non-collaborative attitudes would remain intact. Rather, a course would need to provide a vehicle whereby managers can *do* ethics, by participating in a group/team approach, which will enable them to air their views, challenge, and be challenged on, underlying attitudes, beliefs and prejudices within an environment that encourages and develops collaborative attitudes and skills (see Part III).

The relationship between organisations and supplier and customer

There is also a predominantly non-collaborative relationship between organisations and supplier and customer, which is at the root of poor product/service quality and innovation (see Chapter 9); and which gives rise to unethical acts such as financial 'buck passing', undermining the well-being of the supplier or customer organisation, and ultimately the well-being of unethical organisations themselves (see Chapter 12).

The relationship between organisations and the environment

It is the generally non-collaborative relationship between organisations and the environment that has caused so much environmental damage. Depleting natural resources and environmental pollution will increasingly figure in an organisation's survival and success – and indeed in everyone's survival – and the link with collaborative organisations is dealt with in Chapter 10.

Summary – ethics, survivability and success

A non-collaborative disregard for the value of employees, private customers, supplier and customer organisation, and the environment, therefore, is the basis of widespread unethical practices, which, as considered above in the case of the employee, and below in the case of private customers, supplier/customer organisations and the environment, ultimately damages the health of the non-collaborative organisations themselves. In line with this, John Shad, ex-chairman of the Securities and Exchange Commission in the United States advises: 'I think it's smart to be ethical. I think that you win by having integrity and giving quality and being honest.' (*Business Matters*, 11.7.91) And specifically in the public service area, unethical, non-collaborative attitudes towards the customer, have a detrimental effect on the quality of service rendered. This, for example, is recognised by Jerome Mack, an American advisor running a training course for the British Police. He believes there is a significant minority of people in the Force who have prejudicial attitudes towards people of a different race and who let these attitudes show themselves in discriminatory behaviour. The police are now aggressively undertaking a training programme to change these attitudes, because, as Jerome Mack recognises: 'This issue is seen as a service-delivery issue. It is seen as a 'professionalism' issue, rather than something nice to do' (*Channel 4 News*, 26.7.91).

In summary, therefore, it can be said that an ethical regard for people, which sees them as a valuable, non-dispensable resource, and which collaboratively involves them in decision making and looks after their needs, will at one and the same time produce better ideas, greater efficiency, greater innovation, and the higher quality needed to survive and succeed against increasing competition. Non-collaborative leaders who believe they alone will be able to come up with all the answers and ideas for achieving efficiency and quality, are sadly and profoundly mistaken. Failing to consider the work-force's needs and views is not only unethical, but also inefficient and unprofessional, and represents a great waste of the potential of the most important resource in the working and learning environments. The people down 'on the floor' – the factory worker, class teacher/lecturer, nurse, etc are indeed the most important resource, not only because they, unlike other resources, are able to come up with ideas and solutions to problems, but also because, unlike management/senior management, they are the ones best placed to come up with the most effective ideas about how to innovate and improve efficiency and product/service quality, as examples within this book will illustrate. The same point can be made for suppliers and customers. An ethical regard for the employee, supplier and customer is precisely the basis of Japanese success. And it has been an ethical respect for the value of people and the environment that has been the cornerstone of certain organisations' success in the West, such as Anita Roddick's Body Shop.

Finally, here is an illustration of the fact that illegal unethical non-collaborative practices in the workplace are just the tip of the iceberg and do not essentially differ from other more widespread unethical non-collaborative work-practices – the difference merely being one of degree not of kind. Activities of top managers and other officers at BCCI included money laundering and using bank money to win political favours. This is illegal. Activities of top managers at the American Landmark Bank included using bank money for their private property businesses – insider lending, which was done without collateral. This is not necessarily illegal, but is at present a grey area (*In Business*, 10.4.91). Activities by top managers generally, in business and education, have increasingly included merging, the acquiring of new businesses and deal-making in order to boost share prices and/or their own salaries, and indeed directing funds directly towards their own salaries and dividends, rather than directing resources towards employees, training and research and development (see also Chapter 11). This is not illegal. All three kinds of activities, therefore, differ in legal status, but they all stem from the same underlying non-collaborative attitudes in management, attitudes that lead to a disregard for the well-being of the employee, the customer and the organisation, and a pre-occupation with personal gain. While we may safely sit back and get complacently outraged over the BCCI affair, we would do well to realise that, excluding the word 'blackmail', the following statement made by an ITN reporter about BCCI could be applied to the majority of organisations in the West: 'The power of money and blackmail seemed to be understood by many BCCI people, especially when it was put to use for their own huge personal gain' (*Channel 4 News*, 26.7.91).

The 'many BCCI people' referred to here do not include the majority of employees who were largely ignorant of the corruption. As a reporter observed, some individuals lower down the bank would have known about little frauds, '. . . but the big central fraud was obviously run from the top' (*Newsnight*, 2.8.91). A sign of the generality of the unethical, non-collaborative attitudes among top management that lay behind the BCCI affair was indicated by the manner in which the scandal spilled over to implicate the integrity of bank regulators, intelligence agencies, government ministers, and auditors both in Britain and America. There was the question over the delay in the authorities' response, when certain of the bank's employees, politicians and others had tried to alert them to the fraudulent activities years earlier; and over the *manner* in which the

Bank of England closed BCCI down – suddenly and seemingly without warning to the major shareholders in the Middle East, who had just completed a restructuring plan for the bank. These questions suggest a non-collaborative disconcern over the well-being of employees, customers and the organisation, by the various bodies, as well as by the organisation's top managers (see also Chapter 6, p83–4). Likewise, when a rescue package for the bank was announced in October 1991 to have failed, BCCI employees and depositors felt that 'the establishment' had worked against the rescue by not providing the necessary support.

The endemic inefficiency and suffering in organisations, of which BCCI represents an extreme example, contrasts with the exceptional and highly successful collaborative leadership of Anita Roddick:

> I think you can trade ethically; be committed to social responsibility, global responsibility; empower your employees without being afraid of them. I think you can rewrite the book on business (NatWest, 1991, p3).

Managers, in industry and education, need to take heed and rewrite their book on leadership.

In Part I some of the skills of collaborative leadership that are so vital for setting off the 'chain reaction' to organisational success (Figure 1.1) have been indicated. In Part II the main skills will be listed out. But first, here is a selection of comments from a broad spectrum of people in business and education that further point the way.

3

Comments from top executives, educationalists, management consultants, and health personnel etc, on the 'human' factor in success

The unsuccessful companies are also, in general, not noted for their degree of employee participation.

Walter Goldsmith, international businessman
David Clutterbuck, management consultant
(Goldsmith and Clutterbuck, 1984, p148)

... [higher education] staff [should] participate fully in decisions which affect them. ... Senior management should spend less time trying to 'manage' and more time relating to colleagues.

Michael Locke, lecturer in industrial studies
(Locke, 1989, pp6, 7)

---

*The positions indicated are those held at the time the statement was made.

... a structure of participation *creates* appropriate values, attitudes, and expectations ... the organisation that permits participation ultimately produces individuals who are responsible to participation.

Paul Blumberg, professor of sociology
(Blumberg, 1968, pp130, 109)

A key ingredient [in the successful businesses] was involving more people than average in business decisions ... the message is to promote and reward, to delegate and trust.

Mike Beck, management consultant, former Training Agency Unit Head
(Beck, 1989, p27)

Any situation in which some men prevent others from engaging in the process of inquiry is one of violence. The means used are not important; to alienate men from their own decision-making is to change them into objects.

Paulo Freire, educationalist
(Freire, 1972, p58)

In some cases, effective employee involvement has been a vital ingredient in turning businesses around.

David Nickson, President of the Confederation of British Industry
(McGregor, 1987, pxi)

First and foremost, there is the need to create more open, egalitarian and democratic structures within the schools. These reforms are needed both within the staffroom and in teacher-pupil relations.

Colin Lacey, professor of education
(Lacey, 1988, p22)

Individuals are now the only source of sustainable competitive advantage. Efforts must be focused on mobilising their commitment and encouraging self-development and lifetime learning.

CBI Training Task Force
(CBI, 1989, p9, p25)

Efficiency in industry and commerce depends upon the maximisation of the resources available – financial, technical and human. The
most important and most difficult is the maximisation of the human
resources, which, at its best, amounts to effective leadership.

Edwin Smith, (writing for the Industrial Society)
(Smith, 1969, p1)

What attracts me to [writing about] management is precisely that,
like a good novel, it is about people. It is not about mathematical
models, it is not about goods, it's about people at work together.

Peter Drucker, considered as the world's first management guru
(*Business Matters*, 5.9.91)

. . . an effective leader is one who motivates people, rather than simply
telling them what to do.

Mike Beck
(*op cit*, p26)

The only thing in commerce or industry that you spend money on
that doesn't depreciate and that *appreciates* are your human beings.

Sir Brian Wolfson, chairman, National Training Task Force
(*State of Training*, 29.9.91)

A company or organisation must operate as a genuine team. To enable
this Western management style needs total transformation; most
modern management (and political) strategies instead foster internal
competition and conflict.

W Edwards Deming, thought of as 'the father of quality control'
(Deming, 1988)

What is the essential element any successful leader absolutely must
have? I think it can be reduced to one word and a rather simple one
at that: caring . . . If people think you care, think you are emotionally
committed to them, they will go to great lengths, even extremes, to
get done what is necessary.

Colin Marshall, Chief Executive of British Airways
(Ritchie and Goldsmith, 1988, p172, 169)

Management is not just about controlling things, and counting
things, and organising things, and deciding things . . . it's first and

most importantly about infecting people . . . with energy, excitement, enthusiasm . . .

> *Charles Handy, management expert*
> *(Walk the Talk, 7.4.91)*

. . . really to listen to what their staff are asking of them, and be prepared to test out creative, novel, different ways of doing things – that's the real test of good management in the future, I believe.

LISTEN

> *Rhiannon Chapman, Director of the Industrial Society*
> *(In Business, 18.9.91)*

You cannot just say to people: 'You are our greatest asset', and then you behave as though your buildings, or your money, or the last quarter's profits are your greatest asset.

> *Frances Hesselbein, former director of Girls Scouts USA*
> *(Business Matters, 5.9.91)*

As we work in partnership with others more, they're not going to accept autocratic management, they're not going to accept imposition.

> *Michael Bichard, chief executive, Gloucestershire County Council*
> *(OU 1991c)*

When it comes to relations with one's work-force, paying attention to one's people, really listening to them, acting on what one hears, and treating them as full-scale partners, we are decidedly not going 'back' to basics . . .

> *Tom Peters, American management guru*
> (Peters and Austin, 1985, pxix)

. . . *please* think about how you relate to your staff. Please think about how you could enable them to speak to *you* and feel that they were being *listened* to.

> *Pamela Charlwood, Institute of Health Services Management*
> *(Public Eye, 10.5.91)*

High authoritarians are not comfortable, either as receivers or extenders of opportunities, to participate.

> *Victor Vroom, professor of industrial administration and psychology*
> (Vroom, 1960, p84)

'Great Man' styles of leadership . . . are, in gender terms, patriarchal
or masculine; that is they are dominating, authoritarian, elitist . . .
thrusting, dependency creating, lacking in finer feelings and dis-
regarding of weaknesses.

> *H L Gray, lecturer in educational research*
> (Gray, 1989, p129)

I have always found that the more power you give people, the more
responsibility they take. [The objective is to] create a school structure
that will increase the sense of community.

> *Bob McCarthy, principal of a tough American highschool*
> (Peters and Austin, 1985, p408)

The difference between cooperation and obedience is often the difference between profit and loss.

> *John Garnett, director of the Industrial Society*
> (Garnett, 1983, p10)

They [excellent principals] . . . facilitate the process of treating students
as adults by first treating the faculty as adults.

> *Tom Peters, American management guru*
> (Peters and Austin, 1985, p395)

Approximately 97 per cent of your people are creative, vigorous,
loyal, committed, caring and energetic – except for the eight hours
they work for you. And the serious question we've got to ask ourselves is: 'What kind of hell-hole have we created as managers that
has taken this talent and turned it into turned-off people?'

> *Tom Peters, American management guru*
> (Peters, 1989)

There is no traditional divide between 'management' and 'workers'
. . . Everyone works under the same conditions of employment . . .
Everyone uses the same car park and the same subsidised canteen
. . . There are no written job descriptions. There is no clocking on.
There are no salary deductions for lateness or absenteeism [which is
under 3 per cent] . . . There is a single union agreement between
Nissan and the AEU . . . [it is not] a No-Strike deal . . . There is no in-
process quality control . . . quality is the responsibility of each mem-
ber of staff.

> *Nissan's Policy – Britain's fastest growing new motor company*
> (Nissan, 1985)

For quite a few years I have been working as a management consultant, and . . . I must admit that I have faced a lot of people problems, and they were very, very difficult to solve. I think the reason is that we, in the Western world, are brought up to manage facts, all the things in the so-called bottom-line world. We are not brought up to manage feelings, things in the beyond bottom-line world.

Claus Moller, Dutch management consultant
(Business Matters, 1987)

I submit that much of our business leadership problem in this country stems from our justly famous educational system. . . . our university system supplies us with . . . analytical minds that have comparatively little understanding or empathy with the needs of other people.

Colin Marshall, chief executive of British Airways
(Ritchie and Goldsmith, 1988, p170)

It is widely acknowledged that the phenomenal success of the Japanese has been founded far more on the quality of their interpersonal relationships (in particular their ability to cooperate) than on the quality of their technical training, excellent though it is.

Martin Wenham, teacher
(Wenham, 1989, p14)

Good motivation will lift morale, will keep staff, will generate extra productivity, will lead on to a continual build up of productivity over the years of its operation, and will bring management and workers closer together.

Ian Arthur, a director of the KLP Group
(Money Box, 19.5.90)

. . . issues like human relations, work on problems of communication and of people understanding one another, which we used to think of as the frills of a business organisation, now become absolutely central.

John Adair, professor in leadership skills
(Adair, 1984, p233)

I believe most of us in the private sector are motivated – I certainly am – by a deep feeling of responsibility for the people in our organisation.

Sir John Harvey-Jones, chairman of Imperial Chemical Industries
(Ritchie and Goldsmith, 1988, p176)

The overriding mood amongst our employees is fear . . . In these circumstances . . . the power of management to implement change is at its greatest. However, raw power to act on one side and fear on the other are hardly the basis for a long-lasting productive relationship.

Richard Giordano, chief executive, BOC Group
(Ritchie and Goldsmith, 1988, p171)

Interpersonal skills courses are now recognised as an important part of management education. Managers spend on average three-quarters of their time in conversation with others.

Charles Margerison, Australian management consultant
(Margerison, 1988, p73)

The people are encouraged to make contributions wherever they are in the company, irrespective of their hierarchy or their seniority. If you have got a contribution to make, you are encouraged to make it.

David Pascall, British Petroleum 'Project 1990' team
(*The Money Programme*, 20.5.90)

. . . Leadership means vision, cheerleading, enthusiasm, love, trust, verve, passion, obsession, consistency, the use of symbols, paying attention . . . creating heroes at all levels, coaching, effectively wandering around. . . . Leadership must be present at *all* levels of the organisation . . .

Tom Peters, American management guru
(Peters and Austin, 1985, pp5–6)

Part I – key points

- Survivability and success depend on *quality* and *innovation*, quality and innovation depend on *people*. The human resource is therefore the most important resource.

- Human relations, or *interpersonal relations*, are central to *quality of performance* in industry, business and education.

- The nature of human relations is determined by the *way people are treated by management*.

- Management needs to develop *collaborative leadership skills* to enable people to participate in decisions – the most effective way to motivate people to work and learn together cooperatively and effectively.

- *The 'chain reaction'* – collaborative leadership leads to increased *motivation*, which leads to *improved quality and innovation*, which leads to better results and increased *efficiency/productivity and sales*, increasing an organisation's chances of survival and success.

- The evidence shows that 'soft' collaborative skills form the *bedrock* of effective 'hard' financial and technical decisions.

- Non-collaborative leadership has been the basis of widespread *unethical practices* in business and education, causing *employee and organisation ill health and poor performance*.

- Collaborative leadership means *good ethics*, means *good 'business'*.

PART II

THE CORE COLLABORATIVE SKILLS AND BUSINESS, EDUCATIONAL AND NATIONAL CULTURES

In Part I it was considered that the key skills for managing a successful organisation, whether in industry, business, or education, are not so much technical or financial skills as such, but 'human resource' or leadership skills. This part looks at what these leadership skills are and the *interpersonal attitudes* that underlie them; how they relate to team skills, needed by everyone for efficiency and effectiveness in the working and learning environments; and how interpersonal attitudes and skills permeate and determine the very fabric of a country's business, educational and national culture.

4

The core collaborative skills of leadership and teamwork

Three levels of leadership skills

The array of leadership skills given in the literature can present a daunting prospect to anyone wishing to develop their skills in this area. However, the prospect can be made less daunting if we divide the skills into three broadly different levels (Figure 4.1):

1. base *interpersonal attitudes*
2. underlying *interpersonal skills*
3. *functional skills.*

To undertake the general functional skills of level 3 effectively, requires the interpersonal skills of level 2. In turn, to employ the interpersonal skills of level 2 effectively requires the interpersonal attitudes of level 1. Levels 1 and 2, therefore, are the *core* attitudes and skills of effective leadership. If you develop these, the rest will follow.

It is the core interpersonal attitudes that are essential for enabling the core interpersonal skills, which, in turn, facilitate and encourage participation in decision making and *motivate* people to give of their best and work cooperatively with others – so initiating the chain reaction referred to in Chapter 1 (Figure 1.1). And it is because a major outcome of these attitudes and skills is people working together cooperatively and efficiently, that they are best described as the core *collaborative* attitudes and skills of leadership.

The separation between collaborative attitudes and skills is not clear cut, and the distinction made here is not meant to be definitive. The reason for making the distinction, however, is to draw attention to the importance of underlying interpersonal attitudes as the basis

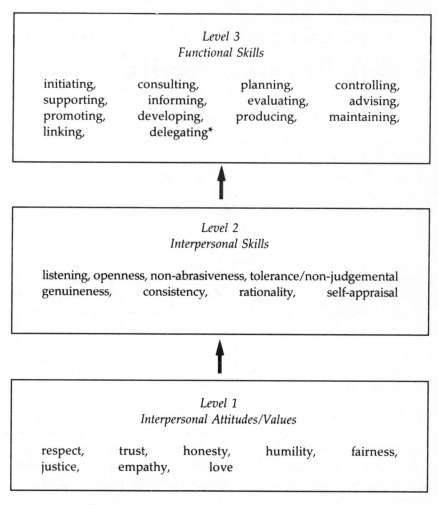

Figure 4.1 *Three levels of leadership skills*

of interpersonal skills. Also, it should be noted that the skills at level 2 are interdependent and overlapping, as are the attitudes at level 1.

The importance of underlying attitudes towards people, and the manner in which the various attitudes/skills shown here interrelate, can be illustrated in the case of the key collaborative skill, *listening*. It will not be possible to listen effectively unless one's underlying

---

*Mainly from Adair, 1984, p230; Adair, 1986, p122; Margerison and McCann, 1985, p10. The list for each level is not claimed to be definitive and comprehensive.

attitudes are ones of *respect* and *trust* in people, and their value and abilities, linked with a corresponding humility concerning one's own beliefs, views and abilities, and a corresponding sense of fairness and justice. These attitudes form the basis for dealing with people tolerantly, non-abrasively, non-judgementally and rationally – the basis of *genuine* listening. Conversely, a disrespect and distrust of people, and their value and abilities, linked with a corresponding lack of humility, arrogance concerning one's own beliefs, views and abilities, and a corresponding unfairness and injustice, will produce intolerance, abrasiveness, and a judgemental irrationality that will prevent genuine listening (see also Chapter 6, p77–8). Because of the overlap and interdependence of the interpersonal skills shown under level 2, they are in fact often grouped together under the heading *active listening skills* (cf Kendall, 1982; Margerison, 1987).

As an illustration of the point that the skill of listening rests on underlying collaborative attitudes, such as respect, notice the following claim by Goldsmith and Clutterbuck in their book on successful companies in Britain: 'If the greatest respect a manager can show to a subordinate is to listen to him, then many unsuccessful companies would fail the respect test' (1985, p153). A manager who is devoid of the collaborative attitudes at level 1, and therefore the collaborative skills at level 2, will be unable to harness effectively an organisation's most important resource, namely, people. They will be unable to involve employees in the decision-making process and consider and take on board their needs and views; and therefore they will be unable to learn from those needs and views. As a result, as considered in Part I, he or she will demotivate the work-force, blocking off the main spring of ideas for efficiency, innovation and quality, and setting the scene for faulty financial and technical decisions on their part.

The core collaborative skills of both leadership and teamwork

Books and training in the area of leadership and teamwork are usually thought to be the domain of managers/team leaders only, but in fact the core collaborative skills of effective leadership are the same skills that *all* people need in order to work cooperatively and effectively with others, in both the working and learning environments. This, for example, is recognised by Adair:

These [leadership] skills can contribute directly to your personal effectiveness, be you leader or team member. They will enable you to get things done as a colleague and as a subordinate as well as when you occupy the hot seat of a leadership role. (1984) p261)

The need for the roles and skills of managers and workers, team leader and team member to become closer, is also part of the philosophy of Michael Frye, chairman of the now successful B Elliott Group. He believes that over the next decade not communicating with everyone in an organisation will come to be seen as barbaric, and:

> Having too heavy a hierarchical structure will be seen as barbaric. People's skills and abilities, and we want them for the future, need to be raised, their status, their attitude . . . needs to be raised, *so that people see themselves as leaders, as part of the leadership of the business*. (*Walk the Talk*, 28.4.91; my emphasis)

And a manager at the Steelcase furniture company in Michigan, where they are successfully developing a team approach involving *all* employees in the decision-making process, says: 'we're all part of [the] management process' (*Business Matters*, 8.8.91).

In fact, it is important to develop the core attitudes and skills whether you are a top executive or a production worker, teacher or pupil, businessperson or employee, etc. They are the skills necessary for effectively relating to and motivating others, and they encompass the skills needed for effective decision making, self-development and self-directed learning, essential for *each and all* of these roles (see also Chapter 9). In short, *the collaborative interpersonal skills (and underlying attitudes) are the core skills of effective management, effective teaching, effective teamwork, and effective learning.* However, as was indicated in Part I, it is the responsibility of management to take the lead in developing these skills. The point is summed up by Adair:

> Virtues such as [honesty, integrity, courage and justice] in leader and member alike mean that the energies of the team are being spent on the task, not on in-fighting, politicking, back stabbing, intriguing and mutual suspicion. As with most things it is up to you as leader to set the example. (1986, p118)

The reason why the manager/leader, and in particular an organisation's top manager, needs to 'set the example', is further considered in Chapter 6 below.

The core collaborative skills and team roles

The distinction between the different levels of leadership/team skills is not made overt in the literature, but increasing weight is being put on the importance of the core collaborative interpersonal attitudes and skills at levels 1 and 2 in Figure 4.1 (eg Peters and Austin, 1985; Margerison, 1987; Beck, 1989). However, at the same time, a central plank of much of the literature and training courses in this area rests on the consideration of *team roles* (eg Belbin, 1981; Adair, 1986; Margerison and McCann, 1985). Broadly, it seems a person's 'role' is defined by the preference he or she has for undertaking certain of the work functions at level 3 (eg Margerison and McCann, 1985, p10, p16).

There is the risk, however, that too much emphasis on team roles at level 3, will result in people losing sight of the underlying core skills and attitudes that it is essential to develop if these roles are to be undertaken effectively (see also Part III, Chapter 14). It should be kept in mind that people may be unclear about or attach different meanings to the functional skills at level 3, and undertaking these skills according to some meanings will not necessarily lead to effective leadership and teamwork. Rather, it might be said, it is *how* the functions are carried out that is of significance. This is often referred to as the 'style' of management or leadership (eg Smith, 1969, p14; Adair, 1984, pp 230, 231). For example, it could be said to be possible to undertake most of the functions in an authoritarian or autocratic manner; but they will only be effective in *leading* people to work effectively if undertaken in a facilitative, coaching and enabling manner – ie, if the person has the core attitudes and skills of levels 1 and 2.

Others might object that this way of putting it is too much of a distortion – that it is a contradiction in terms to talk about 'authoritatively supporting', or 'authoritatively consulting', or 'authoritatively informing', or 'authoritatively delegating', etc. A better way of putting it might be to say that if you are authoritative and do not have the collaborative attitudes and skills at levels 1 and 2 (Figure 4.1), then it will just not be possible to undertake the functional skills at level 3 effectively and genuinely.

The collaborative approach – the need to be genuine

The final part of this book incorporates a practical guide to how to go about developing the core collaborative skills and attitudes. The core collaborative skills checklist given there indicates exactly what is involved in developing and carrying out these interpersonal skills effectively. But a brief word is needed here about the importance of the collaborative skill of *genuineness*. McGregor comments:

> Participation becomes a farce when it is applied as a sales gimmick or a device for kidding people into thinking they are important. Only the management that has confidence in human capacities and is itself directed toward organisational objectives rather than toward the preservation of personal power can grasp the implications of this emerging theory. (1977, p211)

The possibility of 'shamming' has meant that the 'Human Resource Development' approach is viewed by some with much suspicion, and the suspicion stems from the fact that the 'Human Relations' tradition, spawned in the late 1920s, was based on a particular interpretation by researchers and sociologists of work such as the Hawthorne experiments. This interpretation led to the belief that management decisions can best be achieved by obtaining the consent of employees through generally making workers feel important and satisfying their needs to belong; but it overlooked the central role of employee participation in the decision-making process for bringing about increased morale and efficiency (see eg Blumberg, 1968, p14ff; Stenning, 1989, p228).

There is a danger, however, in management using this approach to manipulate people dishonestly to get what they want. Deming, for example, refers to the superficial way in which American managers have attempted to 'soothe emotions' and 'boost lagging production':

> Workers now greet these management fads with skepticism . . . Background music and suggestion boxes and psychological counselling were tried and abandoned. These efforts are just naïve attempts, workers say, to get them to work harder. (1986, p147)

Most people in Britain will have experienced similar techniques. Another way of attempting to manipulate people is to substitute 'communication' for 'participation'. Admittedly, it is likely that good communication from management – in the form of discussions, information bulletins, etc, informing employees of decisions taken and the reasons for them – will result in people carrying out tasks a little more willingly (eg Reynolds, 1980). But, firstly, there is evidence that it is only through *genuine participation* in decision making that employees will improve their quality of performance (cf Bennett, 1955; Levinson, 1976). And secondly, if a 'communication strategy', such as the use of discussion meetings, is used as a way of deluding people that they are involved in setting objectives and making decisions, then they are soon likely to see through the dishonesty when management do not *act* on employee input. Deming, for example, talks about the way management, faced with people problems that they are unable to deal with, take refuge in forming quality-control circles, and groups for employee involvement, employee participation, and quality of work life. He refers to these as 'devastatingly cruel devices', which managers use to attempt 'to get rid of the problems of people'. They disintegrate within months and people become frustrated when they realise they are part of a 'cruel hoax', and no one in management will act on suggestions for improvement (1985, p85; see also p134–5). People must be genuinely respected, trusted and involved in decision making and see concrete results otherwise resentment, distrust and cynicism will grow, and this is likely to be counterproductive and lead to reduced employee performance.

Before leaving this chapter, notice in the above quotation (opposite, top) how McGregor makes the point that management will only be able to bring about genuine participation if it 'has confidence in human capacities', ie the collaborative interpersonal skill of 'genuineness' is dependent on the underlying collaborative attitudes of respect for, and trust in, people and their abilities (Figure 4.1 above).

5
Collaborative skills, management tasks and dealing with change

The core collaborative skills and the various areas of management

A manager who is developing his or her collaborative skills will begin to treat people as 'full-scale partners' (Peters, 1985, pxix). A central aspect of this will be the genuine enabling of employees to participate in dialogue and decision making, referred to in the previous chapter. In particular this requires, where appropriate and as much as possible, informing employees, and then listening to their experience and ideas concerning a situation/problem, *before* decisions are made. Such *consultation* is paramount to effective handling of most managerial activities, eg change management; conflict management; selection; appraisal/counselling interviewing; negotiating; committee meetings; team meetings.

In short, collaborative skills will enable managers to work together *with* their employees in all these areas. (See, for example, Adair, 1984; Kendall, 1982; Margerison, 1987.)

Collaborative skills and dealing with change

The situation can be exemplified in relation to change management. The need for constant change is becoming increasingly necessary as organisations, both in business and education, need to strive for constant innovation and incorporation of technological developments in order to meet the challenge of decreasing resources and

the increased competition brought about by globalisation, deregulation, and, after 1992, a single European market. However, it is
almost accepted as a law of human nature that nobody likes change
– people get used to certain ways of doing things, and they generally resist and fear new knowledge (cf Deming, 1986, p60). But this
is really a consequence of the kind of bureaucratic, hierarchical
organisations that mainly exist in industry and education. New
knowledge and procedures might reveal people's 'failings', but this
should not be a source of fear but of challenge, and would be so
under management with collaborative attitudes and skills. Fear and
resistance might also arise from a lack of confidence in learning
something new, especially amongst people who have been doing a
particular job for many years. Again, however, this is the product of
the kind of evaluative–judgemental systems in which most people
learn and work, which, amongst other things, develop in them a
strong fear of being punished for making mistakes (see Chapters 6,
7, and 8).

It need not be like this. As referred to in Part I, past evidence
shows that *the more people participate in dialogue and the decision-making
process, the more they are motivated to work and learn.* Finding things
out, learning about something new, different and better, being creative,
is an invigorating challenge in the right non-judgemental climate.
This will require managers with collaborative attitudes and skills
who, by respecting and trusting people, etc, will enhance their self-
esteem, give them confidence and security, and enable them to
participate, to ask questions, to innovate, to take risks, and to treat
mistakes as learning opportunities. This is the reason why
organisations where people operate collaboratively are sometimes
aptly referred to as 'learning' or 'developing' organisations (cf Beck,
1989; Davies *et al*, 1984). And this is why concern for people, treating
them collaboratively, leads to innovation, quality and success.

The response to change, therefore, would be quite a different
matter if people become the architects or 'owners' of change by
being consulted and involved from the outset, rather than having
change autocratically *imposed* on them. This is borne out by many
Japanese organisations. They are the masters of consultation. A
manager in the Japanese Fuji Film organisation, for example, refers
to the Japanese 'reserve' or 'holding back', which makes them 'reluctant to impose' themselves on others in the group. The reason they
exercise this reserve, he says, is 'to try to understand each others'

feelings' (empathy), and he adds: 'But we also try to suppress our own will so that we don't shatter the unity of the group.' (*Nippon*, 2.12.90)

This particular manager had worked thirteen years in Germany, a culture that has a more consensus approach than Britain (see Chapters 11, 12 and 13). Yet, although he says he could not do everything according to his own convenience, he was able to act more individually there. In Japan, he says, attitudes are different and he has 'to take *everyone's* views into account *far* more'. It is this which gives him 'a much stronger sense of working as part of the company' compared to working abroad. This point about the group and people feeling part of an organisation – the 'we're all in this together' aspect referred to in Part I – is crucial. If managers in the West were aware of the importance of this aspect to the well-being of an organisation, and that it is shattered each time they impose their will, they might be more reluctant to impose that will autocratically, and more willing to take on board the views, ideas and needs of employees.

The difference in attitudes between Japanese managers and their Western counterparts is recognised by some Western managers. It is the Japanese reserve, their reluctance to impose on employees in the group and their need to try to understand each others' feelings, that is the reason for Sir Peter Parker's observation, referred to in Chapter 2 (p28), that Japanese managers 'are waiting to hear the messages from the bottom up'. He continues:

> They give plenty of *time* for that – you know. *Nemawashi* is the word . . . of root binding, if you want to move the tree, you've got to be very careful consulting each little individual root of an idea, then you can move it . . . (*Open Mind*, 22.6.91)

The Fuji manager quoted above also talks of this process of 'preparing the ground or digging round the roots'. And, as Sir Peter Parker recognises, although they take a long time in consultation, when a decision is reached they then 'go like hell'. A fact also recognised by American robot pioneer, Joseph Engelberger:

> And there isn't anybody knocking the effort down once it's been decided to go . . . It may take a while, but boy, when they get going it's altogether now, and we're going to succeed. (*Nippon*, 25.11.90)

So consultation gets the commitment of workers. It also gets the best ideas. This is recognised, for example, by the vice president of nursing at the Beth Israel Hospital in Boston, USA, who believes that their development programme of 'participatory management' will result in better decisions, because:

> . . . those who are at the *closest* point of the delivery of service *know best*, know more than any of us who are far removed from that, what really needs to be done to make changes . . . (*Business Matters*, 13.6.91)

The Western way of managers not consulting with the work-force but of deciding first and then trying to get people to act on that decision is, quite simply, inefficient. In short, it is the genuine and constant consultation of employees, ie their constant involvement in the decision-making process – a characteristic of many Japanese and some Western management – that makes people feel part of an organisation, and is the basis of them working together to achieve the efficiency, constant innovation and quality needed for success. In contrast, it is the lack of genuine consultation of employees – a characteristic of most Western management – that alienates people from an organisation, and is the basis of them resisting and working against management, and a general demotivation that undermines the efficiency, constant innovation and quality needed for success. In a word, to be effective, constant change/innovation requires constant consultation.

The following examples illustrate the centrality of consultation in effectively dealing with change.

Collaborative skills and dealing with change – Example 1*

The introduction of the Japanese Just in Time approach to production in British organisations has been revealing of the predominant way management deal with change. Put very briefly and simply, Just in Time (JIT) is an inventory control system that ensures that components arrive in the production process only when they are actually needed, literally just in time. It means that materials are never lying around at rest, taking up space and collecting storage costs, etc. Organisations that successfully use the approach have reaped considerable financial savings, and have a work-force that shows a positive attitude to the approach since it enables more local control and

---

* The quotations and factual information for this example are taken from *The Money Programme*, 21.4.91, unless otherwise stated. The interpretations are this author's.

makes life more predictable. On the surface, therefore, one would expect there to be no problem introducing the JIT approach.

The reality in Britain has been different. Often there has been fierce resistance to the introduction of JIT. The attempted introduction of JIT at Ford's caused a strike at its Dagenham plant in 1988, and the workers' slogans strongly attacked the 'Japanese way' of doing things. More recently, in 1991, the attempt to introduce JIT at the Belling cooker factory in London has not been plain sailing, and it produced a lack of enthusiasm and a certain amount of resistance from the work-force in the first two months. In contrast, Austin-Rover maintain they have been following the approach successfully for several years, saving at least £40 million a year (JIT, 1989).

Why the differences? The operations director at Austin-Rover comments: '. . . we pay, have to pay, much greater attention to *communication and bringing our work-force along with us* than perhaps earlier generations had to.' (JIT, 1989; my emphasis) On the other hand a worker at the Belling factory complains: 'But the management never come down to us and ask us what we think, or they haven't in the past.' The fact that this latter comment was made in a meeting arranged by the production director at Belling, does indicate that some attempt was being made by management to communicate with the work-force. But the comment clearly indicates the one-way nature of that communication up to that time. In this, as with the practice in so many organisations, it was the lack of true involvement of employees in the decision-making process *from the outset* that was at the root of their apathy, lack of enthusiasm and anxiety when the change was introduced. In fact, the change at the factory was initiated by a statement of intent that was passed down the line, and literally read out to the work-force. This lack of true involvement, and the related lack of information employees receive, causes a fear and distrust of management; and the fact that at the Belling factory there had been redundancies and short-time working in the months prior to introducing JIT, will have added to that fear and distrust. As one Belling worker put it: 'If only people didn't frighten the work-force. They're very unsure of themselves, they're unsure of their selves and the management.'

The production director, in reply to the above worker's comment concerning lack of involvement and consultation of the work-force, acknowledged that was something which management has 'got to change', and adds 'hopefully we are doing . . . hopefully you've got an input in the new line layout'. He does acknowledge to the workers: 'I've got to delegate to people, the supervision's got to delegate to people, we've got to get you involved. You know you've probably got more information about problems on the line.' Fine words, but up to that point no more than words, as shown by the apathetic response to them by the work-force. An attitude survey of the work-force indicated that only 45 per cent of the respondents said they believe what they are told by management; and the response to the survey – over 40 per cent of the staff did not return the question-naire, and even less of the shopfloor personnel – perhaps gives the loudest message. However, there was an acceptance by manage-ment that communication needed to improve, particularly at the level of middle management (see Chapter 7), and a training pro-gramme was introduced (but see Chapter 7, p112). After two months of introducing the new system, the company was reported to have saved £400,000 by cutting work in progress, and £5 million by reducing its finished goods stock.

Put briefly, the difference between the three examples considered was that the management at Austin-Rover collaborated with and involved all the employees in the introduction of the new system; the management at Ford imposed the new system on the workers without any consultation; and the management at Belling also began by first *telling* the work-force about the new system and decisions already made about it by management, although they did have some meetings with workers and were aware of the need for man-agement to learn to delegate and to involve workers more in the decision-making process.

Although the Belling company had some success after two months of introducing JIT, management acknowledge that they would need to develop the approach further. According to Professor Chris Voss, however, only about 5 to 10 per cent of the British companies who have introduced JIT have been able to apply it totally successfully. His findings show that 60 per cent have some initial success, but they quickly reach a plateau and do not progress any further. A closer look at what the JIT approach involves reveals the reason. It is more than just an inventory system as it requires for its success, for example:

- effective working – more quality and less scrap as there is no back-up safety stock;

- the involvement of workers in operating decisions, monitoring of quality, performance, planning, etc;

- cooperation and teamwork at all levels to ensure evenness and smoothness between the various steps of work;

- flexibility of workers and suppliers;

- high motivation and trust between workers, workers and managers, organisation and its suppliers and customers – these relate to quality and delivery.

In other words, it requires management and workers to be interacting *collaboratively*. The JIT system, therefore, is not a mere inventory system to be tagged on to existing work practices, but requires a fundamental transformation of those work practices. It requires both sides, management and work-force, to develop the collaborative attitudes and skills outlined in Figure 4.1. The following comment by an independent management consultant sums up the change involved for employees, indicating how their role will need to come closer to that of managers – a characteristic of the collaborative approach (see also Chapter 2, p25; Chapter 4, p57):

> They've always been motivated in the past in many companies simply by things like piece rate and a kick when they get things wrong. *You're now asking people to respond almost as managers themselves*, part of a team, trying to make good quality product, first time at lowest cost, efficiently. You're asking them to think, and they've not been asked to do that before.

And in turn, to achieve this change in workers will require what Deming calls 'a cultural revolution' in management. Without this managers will just be deceiving themselves and workers, and procedures such as JIT and quality control circles will not be totally successful, and are likely to be harmful (see also Chapter 4, p59–60 and Chapter 8, p134–5). This was the case for the plastic tubing company Raychem at Swindon. Their manufacturing costs shot up and orders were delayed on introducing JIT. As one commentator put it ' "Just in time" seemed to magnify everyday problems causing confusion and frustration on the shop-floor' (JIT, 1989). It was not until they introduced daily meetings and began to develop a team approach that they were able to begin to cut waste and increase efficiency.

In short, the introduction of change – and especially procedures such as JIT and quality control circles, which require collaborative teamwork – will only be totally successful if management becomes *actively* involved in the process of change by beginning to act as advisors and facilitators, rather than autocratically imposing a new system – usually by handing the job over to others to impose – on to existing work practices. Management will need to ensure that *informal* team meetings become a part of the work process, and allow projects, and how to proceed, to be initiated and decided by the member workers, rather than have formal meetings where the project is *imposed* by management, as is usually the case in British organisations. The management practice of formally imposing decisions and goals on the work-force, not only makes it difficult to introduce change, but also ensures a continuing block on a totally successful implementation of new systems such as JIT and quality control circles.

Two months after the move to introduce JIT into the Belling factory, communications between management and the work-force were reported to need improving still, and not surprisingly, therefore, the production director refers to the difficulty management had in 'actually persuading the people on the shop-floor that we're very serious in what we intend to do'. Amongst other things, therefore, the work-force were still not able totally to trust the management, indicating that management were not yet genuinely attempting to apply a collaborative approach (see also next chapter). As a reporter from *The Money Programme* poignantly observed, if Belling, and what is left of Britain's industrial base, are to be saved, 'so much depends on winning the hearts and minds of ordinary people'. But this, in turn, depends on management developing collaborative attitudes and skills, which would enable them to realise the simple but fundamental truth expressed by the union convenor at Belling, that if: 'the company took the union into its confidence and put its cards on the table, I think you could get along better, and I think we could be more helpful to the company.' Invariably workers are eager to be involved and helpful. *They are only unhelpful when they are not truly involved.* The inventor of JIT, Taichi Ohno, soon learned this fact: '. . . unless I spoke to the worker right on the shop-floor, it was difficult to get things to change.' (*Nippon*, 18.11.90)

Collaborative skills and dealing with change – Example 2

In contrast to the negative response of workers where managers *impose* change, change has been accepted and successfully implemented by workers within the B Elliott Group of companies, thanks to the delegatory collaborative lead from the chairman, Michael Frye, and the managing directors of the individual companies. The foundry foreman in one of the companies comments:

> In the middle of last year the management style has changed. Instead of the management telling us what to do, they have asked us to sort the problems out for ourselves. All the best ideas I believe, and the shop-floor believe, come from them. (*Walk the Talk*, 28.4.91.)

And this was made possible by the management developing the collaborative attitudes of respect for, and trust in, the employees (see also Chapter 7, p111). These attitudes and skills enabled the managing director and other senior management to implement 'project teams for *all* of the 230 employees, capitalising on the fact that the individual employee has more knowledge of his particular activity than anybody else in the company, and giving the opportunity through these project teams for everybody to contribute'. Chairman Michael Frye says the company went from making losses to being 'extremely profitable'. Successful innovation and change, therefore, rest on management developing collaborative attitudes and skills as a basis for effectively involving all employees.

Collaborative skills and dealing with change – Example 3

Today in primary, secondary and higher education, there is increased government imposition of changes in structures, conditions of service and funding arrangements. Far from dealing with this necessary change collaboratively, however, some local educational managers have been accused of compounding 'the misery by engaging in additional and unnecessary reorganisation' (Lawrence, 1990, p29). Be that as it may, not consulting people and keeping them in the dark and imposing decisions on them, is a general characteristic of management, both in business and education, and this in itself gives rise to apathy and opposition from employees. Concerning reorganisations at Leeds and Sheffield Polytechnics, for example, it has been reported:

> It is near impossible to find an ordinary worker . . . whether lecturer, technician, secretary, administrator, porter, gardener or cleaner, who believes the current reorganisations are necessary or desirable. (Lawrence, op cit)

Similarly, the following comments were made by staff to this author at the end of many months of reorganisation resulting from a merger between two colleges of higher education:

> Why? Why are we merging? Why is it necessary? (Lecturer)

> Everything is being reorganised, but they're not asking our opinion – just telling us what is decided. (Senior technician)

> We're all nobodies really. I've got fed up with people not listening. I feel battered and bruised. (Lecturer who subsequently left the institution)

The third comment here surely must be one of the saddest and most damning indictments any organisation could receive. It should be of no surprise to hear that the principal of that organisation, in a lecture to a group of staff shortly after taking on the job, boasted: '. . . I usually get what I want.' And it is the same attitudes of lack of respect and humility, etc that make such managers unable to listen and consult, and also make them deaf to the frustrations, disaffection and anxieties of employees that inevitably follow.

If managers were less autocratic, less secretive, more open, and involved employees in discussing problems and deciding outcomes, then frustrations, fears and anxieties would be dispelled, and apathy and resistance turned into enthusiasm and commitment to the change-innovation process. Genuine collaborative management in the school or college could do a great deal to avoid the build up of resentment and lack of morale that is presently occurring in the education profession, by enabling genuine employee involvement in decision making within the immediate teaching environment (see also Chapter 13).

Collaborative skills and dealing with change – Example 4

A clear example of the effectiveness of involving everyone in the process of change and development is provided by Kanter (*Business Matters*, 21.6.90). She refers to the Japanese company Komatsu who 'came from nowhere to challenge Caterpillar for world dominance of the earth-moving equipment industry'. They did not even have the support of the Japanese Ministry of Trade and Industry (MITI). There were a series of overall goals – focusing first on learning the technology, then on quality, then on costs, etc – and the management 'got *everybody* involved' in the learning process and in projects relating to the various goals. The projects were 'transmitted to the lowest level' and 'understood' – there were 'specific projects and activities that *everybody* down the line could engage in, and they could all pull together in a common focus'. As Kanter points out: '. . . it wasn't the Japanese government that gave them advantage, in part it was leadership.' Although, this author would slightly qualify her statement and say '*in whole* it was leadership'.

Summary – dealing with change

Change within organisations is not restricted to take-overs, mergers and restructurings – it also needs to be an on-going characteristic if organisations are going to achieve the efficiency, constant innovation and quality necessary to survive and flourish against increasing competition and decreasing resources. In business and education people generally oppose new ways of doing things. This is not so much because of anything lacking in themselves or the new ways, but management response to this opposition usually manifests itself in terms of a lack in the employee, and terms like 'old guard' and 'Luddite' are often used. However, in truth opposition to change usually occurs because of the *manner* in which that change is introduced.

Effective change cannot be autocratically *imposed* on employees, as this creates apathy, anxiety and resistance, causing demotivation and leading to poor ideas and reduced efficiency. Employees need to be involved in decisions and goals – they need to be the architects of change. This would ensure not only greater commitment from employees, but would also motivate them and enable the ideas and creativity necessary for efficient and innovative change. Further, to survive and succeed, increasingly organisations are going to need to work in collaborative partnership with individual customers and customer-supplier organisations (see Chapter 9), and these increasingly are not going to accept autocratic management and imposition. The key to effective involvement of employees, customers and other organisations is having management that develops collaborative attitudes and skills that will make them reluctant to impose on others, and that will enable them to consult, listen to, and involve everyone in the decision-making process from the outset. Only this way will the following ideals of Peters' be achieved:

I don't like the whole idea of *managing* change. I like the idea of creating institutions where large numbers of people are organised so that they can *deal* with opportunities or bad news as the case may be (*In Business*, 13.3.91).

We literally must learn to love change as much as we hated it in the past (Peters, 1989).

6
The organisational culture – the central role of top management

Differing views on the influence of top management

The point was made in Chapter 4 that, although *everyone* needs to develop collaborative interpersonal skills to be effective in the workplace, management, and in particular top management, needs to take the lead. There are, however, a number of apparently conflicting viewpoints on this in the literature, sometimes within the same work. McGregor, for example, writes:

> If the initial steps are taken by a manager toward the top of the organisation, the growth of the idea may be more rapid, *but the process can start anywhere* (1987, p76; my emphasis).

But later, commenting on the way many rigid and hierarchical levels of a centralised organisational structure limit individual growth, and the consequent need for decentralised organisations, he points out that there still may be severe limits to growth if there exists a tight system of control:

> If [a manager's] superiors keep him under constant surveillance by means of detailed reports on his behavior, *he has no real freedom of action* (p195; my emphasis).

Beck concludes his article on a number of successful companies in the US with the prescription:

> . . . open up the opportunity for dialogue in any organisation about the sorts of issues I have covered, and I reckon something useful would come out of it (1989, p28).

But it is not clear whether he is necessarily directing this to top management, and it appears from his earlier statement that he is not, although it does indicate the importance of top management in enabling dialogue and participation to occur.

> Having sounded notes of caution, there are some conditions which help, including commitment from top management, their personal involvement and stamp of authority on any cultural changes that are desired (p26).

Kanter, at the end of a lecture to European managers on bringing about a more cooperative team approach in the workplace, gives advice on how to get started:

> . . . how you do it, what do you do if not everybody supports it, what do you do if you don't have top management behind you, what do you do – well, my answer is you just *do* it . . . try it, and explain later (*Business Matters*, 21.6.90).

However, earlier in her lecture she draws attention to the important fact that, '. . . people have gotten punished for taking responsibility in the classic bureaucracy' (op cit). And she generally indicates that the majority of organisations in the UK and the US are still run along bureaucratic hierarchical lines.

Top management's attitudes, the knock-on effect and organisational culture

There are certain basic considerations that suggest that it is generally unrealistic to expect any individual employee, either in education or industry, to be able to *effectively* develop their collaborative skills and introduce a collaborative approach into their workplace, without the genuine support of the top manager. The main considerations stem from the fact that:

The attitudes, the habits, the expectations of the subordinate will be either reinforced or modified to some degree as a result of every encounter with the boss (McGregor, 1987, p200).

It follows from this that no individual employee, whether in a position of management or not, can be considered in isolation – there will be a knock-on effect throughout an organisation. The point is put graphically in a book by Andrea Adams to be published by Virago on adult bullying, about the extreme abuse of power possible in hierarchical institutions. One of the victims of bullying which Adams refers to is well aware of the fact that for everyone who kicks you, there is someone above kicking them. A middle manager makes the same point: 'There were people going home after having a belting from me, in tears, and I was just doing to them what was happening to me' (*The Money Programme*, 11.3.90). This is from a television programme considering general stress in the workplace with no specific reference to bullying. The points being made, however, are indistinguishable, indicating that bullying is just an extension of generally poor personal relationships in the workplace as referred to in Chapter 2.

The above viewpoints indicate that no particular superior-subordinate relationship, can be considered in isolation from the organisation as a whole. McGregor makes the point that it is the manager's attitudes and beliefs about people and management that determine the 'psychological climate' of the superior–subordinate relationship (1987, p141 ff). It therefore follows from the above that it will ultimately be the attitudes and beliefs of the top manager which determine the general 'psychological climate' of an institution – the *ethos* or *culture* of that institution.

The view that people's behaviour is strongly influenced by the culture of an institution, and that that culture is determined by top management, is illustrated by the following two examples. accordingly

A top manager's attitudes set the organisational culture – Example 1

In the forthcoming book by Adams on adult bullying referred to above, she cites someone who behaved as a bully in the workplace. When asked whether he thought the structure of the organisation in which he worked had influenced his behaviour, he unhestitatingly replied that it had, as he believed an organisation's ethos reinforced one's tendency to behave as a bully. He realised that when one

works in an authoritarian environment which has a disrespectful
attitude to people, and perceives them as idle and in need of coer-
cion, then it is unlikely that one would change one's behaviour. He
claimed that many other managers in the organisation were acting
in similar ways and were getting promoted despite acting in those
ways – it might be more accurate to say *because* they were acting in
those ways. As he said, the message was clear. In this same text, a
director of human resources for a large corporation, was asked
whether he thought that the kind of behaviour that is thought
acceptable in an organisation – ie the culture – actually comes from
the top. Despite a hesitancy based on a concern for the phrase
'comes from the top', he had to admit that there is no doubt that it
cascades down.

A top manager's attitudes set the organisational culture – Example 2

One of the television programmes in a series on good management by
the management consultant Charles Handy, featured the changes that
took place on the appointment of a new director at the Kelvin
Grove art gallery and museum (*Walk the Talk*, 21.4.91). The new
director, Julian Spalding, started his job by writing to *all* the staff
asking them 'how do we make this service more interesting to the
public?' He then *immediately* arranged meetings with all the different
sections, and spent the first week or two seeing people, talking to
them, talking about ideas; and the following two weeks involving
people in making decisions. This immediate action will have shown
employees that the original letters were not a mere exercise in rhetoric
and PR, and that the new director was genuinely committed to
involving employees. Within the programme Charles Handy
observed:

> The first bubbles of change seldom come from the top. They come
> from new people in the organisation, they come from . . . bubbles
> from the bottom you might say, or at least from the middle.

It is important not to misunderstand this point. Certainly, and
understandably, the best ideas about improving a job come from
the people who know most about that job, ie the people actually
doing that job. This is recognised by an increasing number of man-
agement/supervisory personnel (see eg Chapter 5, p64 and 69),

including Julian Spalding: 'they aren't my ideas . . . because almost every idea has come from here [the employees]'. But ideas from people lower down an organisation will not necessarily take hold and lead to practical change. For example, an employee at the Glasgow art gallery and museum, who has been part of making the recent 'bubbles' that have led to change, reminisces:

> I seem to remember in the early days of being here that I was full of bright ideas as new people sometimes are about changing it . . . then you get into a sort of way of thinking which remains the same, so I got used to [the ways things were].

So why did her bubbles burst then and not now? What is the difference between 'the early days' and now? The main difference no doubt is that now her ideas, and those of others, are enabled and supported by the new person at the top. Those with new ideas wanting to make changes need his support, particularly the junior members of his staff, against people more entrenched in non-collaborative, hierarchical practices, as he clearly recognises:

> So I've got clear evidence that the heads of those two departments are *not* working together, that on a junior level a couple, possibly more, are working together and are doing ideas, and are coming to me for *help* really, saying, look, how can we get this somehow aired?

Without his support they would have been helpless to bring about the collaborative dialogue and trust needed to implement the effective and innovative change that occurred – their bubbles and probably those of future new employees they came in contact with, would not have seen the light of day. It has been the new director's collaborative attitudes, such as *respect* for, and *trust* in people and their abilities, which encouraged, empowered, and enabled effective ideas on efficiency and innovation from employees; which enabled him to *listen* to these new ideas and *act* upon them; and which set the culture to gradually encourage others to begin to work together more collaboratively within the organisation.

Hierarchical as opposed to collaborative attitudes and skills

An authoritarian top manager will have 'hierarchical' attitudes and skills that are in direct contrast to the collaborative ones listed in Figure 4.1 (Chapter 4; see, eg Peters and Austin, 1985, pp 354–7).

Hierarchical interpersonal skills

poor listener – good talker; secretive; abrasive; intolerant/ judgemental; insincere (manipulates, improvises, equivocates); irrational; unpredictable; incapable of self-appraisal.

Hierarchical interpersonal attitudes/values

disrespect; mistrust; dishonesty; arrogance; unfairness; injustice, unsympathetic; dislikes/loathes people.

As in the case for the collaborative attitudes and skills listed in Figure 4.1, the separation between hierarchical attitudes and skills is not clear cut and is not meant to be definitive; and the hierarchical skills are interdependent and overlapping, as are the hierarchical attitudes.

Authoritarian, 'hierarchical' managers who lack respect for, and trust in people, and their abilities, have an arrogant and inflated view of their own abilities, while at the same time fearing being 'shown up' by competent subordinates (see, eg McGregor, 1987, p201; Freire, 1972; also Chapter 7 below). For example, organis- ational psychotherapist Neil Crawford maintains that people who operate in an authoritative way are (probably) the victims of past judgemental authoritative treatment, making them always fright- ened that they are going to get things wrong. As a result, they are 'rather ineffectual people' who have been unable to find 'a mature adult way of relating', and who therefore see somebody who is better at their job, or more popular, or more amusing, as: 'Intolerable. Not just a threat; intolerable. Absolutely intolerable, because it reminds you of all the things that you are not and would like to be' (*An Abuse of Power*, 2.5.91).

In contrast, Peters and Austin refer to a school principal who is thought to have been able to encourage autonomy among his staff because of his own 'deeply rooted self-confidence'. A relatively new member of his staff commented: 'He is the most secure principal I have ever known. He likes to see strength, not weakness, in the people who work for him' (1985, p407).

Mistrust and fear at the top is highly contagious – it cascades down the line and is made manifest in organisational policy and procedure. It has created the hierarchical bureaucratic cultures that still mainly dominate the workplace today, both in industry and education, with all the harmful effects on organisational and employee well-being already considered.

A collaborative organisational structure

If people are going to be able to develop their collaborative attitudes and skills, there needs to be a structure in place (or in the process of being put into place) that will support and encourage such development, and it will need to include the following changes to what Kanter calls 'the classic bureaucracy':

1. Removal of management layers and generally fewer levels of the hierarchy and fewer or no job classifications.
2. All people working in informal flexible teams, making decisions on projects and how to divide up tasks, and having responsibility for outcomes.
3. A system of interchanging people between teams, including the use of informal interdepartmental meetings, conferences and councils.
4. Reward and recognition for learning skills and achievement on objective criteria (not numerical goals – see 5 below) – rather than for status, position, ladder climbing and promotion politics, sometimes based on merit rating systems which can reward favourites irrespective of true merit.
5. Reward and recognition for ideas and collaborative involvement, and (if managers) for collaboratively developing and enabling subordinates – rather than for people doing as they are told and managers giving orders (see also Chapter 8 on reward and recognition).
6. Self/team-appraisal and evaluation, and team reward systems – rather than management appraisal and evaluation, and individual reward systems, which are divisive and stifle teamwork (see Chapter 8 and Part III);

7. Quality through the responsibility of all employees and not through a separate quality control department (see Chapter 8, p134).

8. A system of evaluation and feedback (decided collaboratively) making it right for management to be criticised – rather than it being unacceptable to criticise, or even question, management (see below, Chapter 7, Chapter 8 and Part III).*

A collaborative horizontal structure of this kind, if genuinely implemented from the top, creates and promotes a participatory and cooperative spirit among people. It is *essential* if embedded hierarchical attitudes and practices are to be countered in those people who are unsympathetic to collaborative procedures, and if collaborative attitudes and skills are to be further developed and not eroded in those employees who are sympathetic to collaborative methods.

All the points above are closely linked and necessary ingredients of a true collaborative team culture. For example, people are more likely to be able to adopt a truly cooperative team approach and be committed to concentrating on work issues (point 2) in an organisation where there are few levels of the hierarchy and few or no job descriptions (point 1), and there is a system of self-team appraisal (point 6), so that people are not directing their energies into competing with others (see Chapters 7 and 8). The flexibility aspects of points 2 and 3 link with point 7, and are the basis for improved customer response and care (Chapter 9, p153). Piecemeal changes or additions to hierarchical structures to incorporate one or two aspects of the above collaborative structure, therefore, should be viewed with suspicion – they are likely to have limited effectiveness and possibly backfire (see Chapters 4 and 8).

Hierarchy vs flexibility – Example 1

The general concern in most British organisations with defining roles and job classifications (point 1 above), is a sign of the rigid, hierarchical structures that predominate. In contrast, a lack of concern with job classifications is an aspect of a flexible, collaborative

---

* Compiled and adapted from: Beck, 1989; Deming, 1986; Kanter, *Business Matters*, 14/21.6.90; McGregor, 1987.

organisational structure (although it can also be an aspect of hierarchical, non-collaborative management as a way of imposing additional work without more pay). Sir Peter Parker relates the following interchange between himself as chairman, and the managing director of Mitsubishi Electric UK, when the latter wanted to appoint a marketing director:

> I said: 'Please put down the specification.'
> He said: *'I don't like specifications.'*
> 'Why don't you like specifications?'
> *'We don't like them in Mitsubishi.'*
> 'Why not?'
> *'Because if I write it down and that's all he does, maybe that's all he'll do. I want him to come to do what I want and maybe bring something else.'* (*Open Mind*, 22.6.91)

Sir Peter rightly sees this as an indication that 'there's a kind of spirit at work . . . something freer there that's on the move'; and it is clear how this freer spirit, this flexibility, is the basis for a fuller development of human potential and creativity than is possible in more rigid structures.

Hierarchy vs flexibility – Example 2

A lack of job descriptions and a related greater flexibility in roles is a characteristic of many Japanese organisations. People are expected to interchange between various jobs and roles, and this is essential for effective teamwork. At the Honda factory in Swindon, for example, there are no job descriptions, and there are no special craftsmen, no work-study engineers, and no industrial engineers. Teams of workers themselves write their own work systems (Honda, 1990).

Hierarchy vs flexibility – Example 3

Flexibility is the main theme in a training programme being developed between the Champion Sparking Plug Company and the Prospect Centre training consultancy in London. The company's future is seen in terms of small teams to handle manufacturing and assembly, and also to integrate functions now undertaken in separate departments (Golzen, 1991; cf points 2 and 3 above).

A genuine collaborative culture

Because of the overriding influence of top management, it is extremely unlikely that the above collaborative structure will be introduced into an organisation where top management has embedded hierarchical attitudes about people and management. There is the further concern that, with the increasing awareness and lip service paid to the importance of collaborative techniques for motivating employees, there will be an increasing likelihood that top management will formulate organisational policy statements along collaborative lines in order to delude people into thinking they are important. It is possible that they may go as far as formulating a structure similar to the above, although it is more likely to be a watered down version of this, or just a general mission statement about organisational values, containing buzz words such as: 'open', 'listening', 'liberal', 'liberating', 'caring'. However, it is *how* policy statements are administered, or whether they are administered at all, that is of utmost importance (cf Chapter 4, p59–60; also McGregor, 1987, p133; Peters and Austin, 1985, p34). Where top management retains underlying hierarchical attitudes and values towards people, the statement or policy will remain at the level of rhetoric. It is even possible in these cases that the deception is extended to themselves, and there are many examples where top managers: '. . . *think* they are doing well, they *think* they are listening, to their people, but they've simply not provided any forum' (Kanter, *Business Matters*, 21.6.90).

Mere good intentions, therefore, are not enough, and *action* is needed. This, for example, is recognised by Jeremy Golden, Anglo-Japanese liaison officer in Milton Keynes: 'Even if the British manager has got good intentions and wants to do things the Japanese way, the way he says things can tend to be antagonistic' (Murray, 1990, p3). The good intentions need to be genuine if action is to match them. Only those top managers who are able to recognise the ineffectiveness of an authoritarian, hierarchical approach *and* who have enough humility, honesty and self-appraisal genuinely to recognise their own hierarchical ways, together with a related amount of respect for and trust in the ability and value of others, will truly be able to commit themselves to begin genuinely to act to put collaborative procedures into practice – to begin to make moves to develop their own collaborative attitudes and skills, genuinely to listen to others, and to enable and support others to develop collaborative skills and procedures (see also next section and Chapter 7). Without a certain degree of humility, therefore, this process will not be able to get off the ground. But it is only through this process that a manager's actions, including 'the way he [or she] says things', will become cooperative, supportive and constructive rather than antagonistic and counterproductive. And it is only in this way that it will be possible to have a *genuine* policy or mission statement – a genuine *common* purpose – arrived at, and deployed, by consulting employees, their needs and their views (Chapter 5), removing the inbuilt conflict and employee resistance in hierarchical structures, and enabling *everyone* to pull together in the same direction to achieve organisational and individual development where *everyone* gains.

In summary, *a collaborative 'structure' (in the form of organisational policy statements) does not guarantee a collaborative culture.* This rests ultimately on the underlying interpersonal attitudes and skills of top management.

Organisational policy vs organisational culture – Example 1

The futility of such things as policy or mission statements, or codes of ethics – not to say deception and dishonesty in many cases – is provided by the extreme example of the BCCI affair. At the time of the bank's closure, media reports related how the founder had religious convictions and saw the enterprise in terms of a religious mission. The company agenda refers to the organisation forming:

> . . . a bridge where all peoples of the world come together on a single platform joining hands in mutual respect, creating a bold future embodied in one world, one nation, one bank.

Fine words. Regrettably the action was different. The founder and chief executive were indicted by the New York Grand Jury of defrauding depositors, accused of bribes, kick-backs, and theft as well as fraud, and of operating the bank as a criminal organisation throughout its entire 19-year history. To the House of Commons Treasury Select Committee, the governor of the Bank of England maintained: 'the *culture* of the bank is criminal', and at the time of writing it was believed that many more charges would be brought against criminal activities alleged to have occurred worldwide on a massive scale.

Not much 'mutual respect' there for the majority of honest and loyal employees and customers, who stood to suffer devastating personal losses on the closure of the bank. A clear case of a collaborative organisational statement – which deceived many people into thinking the organisation had a collaborative structure – existing alongside a decidedly unethical, criminal, non-collaborative culture.

Organisational policy vs organisational culture – Example 2

Jim Levine, the director of the Work and Family Institute in New York, is one who has noticed the discrepancy that often exists between organisational policy and organisational culture. Through the 'Fatherhood Project', which he heads, he is involved with men who take 'career breaks' from work to look after their young families. He points out that all of the men have some kind of apprehension that there might be some set-back for taking time off, because: '. . . no matter what the corporate policy is officially, corporate culture is another thing' (*In Business*, 18.9.91). For example, he has come across several people who, although their career break was officially endorsed, felt that when they returned to work they had set-backs, they have not been looked at in the same way by others, they have been considered to be less committed and loyal to the organisation, and their bosses and supervisors do not look at them 'as such a star' as before. The example shows that it takes more than rhetoric and written policy (or even good intentions), to overcome and change underlying non-collaborative attitudes, and the judgemental intolerance and irrationality they bring.

Introducing a collaborative approach – a caution

What is the message for anyone who wishes to introduce a collaborative approach into his or her work environment? Well each individual will be aware of the 'culture' of his or her work environment, regardless of organisational policy statements, from the nature and tone of the personal relationships between people generally. This is particularly so in extreme cases, even for outsiders. For example, a business analyst commenting on an organisation in the B Elliott Group that has been genuinely developing a team approach involving 'everybody', says how 'You can *feel* it as you walk round, everybody feels part of it' (*Walk the Talk*, 28.4.91). And similarly, in the case of the other extreme of a rigid, autocratically run organisation, any outsider can 'feel' the oppression, the non-collaborative alienation, and the mental stagnation, almost as soon as he or she walks into that organisation.

It is possible that there are organisations that do not have a collaborative structure in place, but nevertheless relationships between people are generally cooperative and trusting, where the top person, although sympathetic to collaborative procedures and not hierarchical: '. . . goes into work everyday and is swamped in the paper work, and is thinking about the big financial decisions, and *forgets* to do it' (Kanter in *Business Matters*, 21.6.90). In these circumstances it would be possible for any individual down the line to begin to try and develop collaborative procedures without resistance or risk of censorship from the top. But it would be difficult without *active* support from the top if there is resistance elsewhere (see below). The fact is that it is unlikely that a *genuinely* sympathetic top manager will not have found time enough to implement his or her own collaborative 'tactics' (cf McGregor, 1987, p75), especially given the general increase in awareness of its importance.

In reality most people, both in industry and education, are part of a hierarchical institution, where cooperation and trust between people is not the norm, and top managers have underlying hierarchical attitudes and skills. If these latter are deeply embedded, then the organisation will be autocratically run, rigid and inflexible. Individual employees would need to be wary about trying to introduce collaborative procedures into their workplace within this kind of culture. If the top manager's hierarchical attitudes are not so deeply embedded, then there is potential for some cross-over to attitudes of respect, trust and humility, and there is likely to be more lee way for individuals lower down the line wishing to develop a collaborative approach. The following case exemplifies how it all ultimately depends on the underlying attitudes of the top manager.

In 1977 Frederick Chaney and Kenneth Teel published an article describing their four years of experience implementing and applying participative management techniques in a large manufacturing company in America. It centred on training supervisors to employ a participative group approach with their employees. Chaney and Teel reported that the overall programme was successful and maintain that:

> It helps, but participation doesn't have to start with the boss . . . successful implementation [of participation techniques] occurred from the bottom up, rather than in the more traditional top-down direction (1977, p229).

But despite this claim by Chaney and Teel, a consideration of the way in which they think 'it helps' to start from top management, and of other findings and claims they make, point to the ultimate importance of top management. 'A top-down programme' they say 'undoubtedly would have been faster' and possibly 'more effective', and they continue:

> . . . but it might also have had only token acceptance, which would have died out as soon as another management technique received the blessing of top executives (pp229, 230).

Here they seem unknowingly, to be indicating the ultimate influence of top executives – techniques 'die out' without their blessing. And earlier, referring to the fact that all the participating supervisors found that their superiors did not initially adequately support the use of participative techniques, and that some expressed doubts about their value, they conclude:

> This finding clearly demonstrated that more effort was needed to orient higher levels of management before any attempt to introduce participative management at lower levels (pp226, 227).

Significantly, after a programme of 'orientation' for the managers to whom the supervisors taking part in the programme reported, for a small minority who did not become committed to supporting the programme, 'no further attempt was made to implement the programme in the managers' bailiwicks' (p227). And perhaps most significantly, immediately after their conclusion that successful implementation of participative techniques had occurred from the bottom up rather than top down quoted above, Chaney and Teel add in parentheses:

> Of course, the management orientation at the outset established at least a hands-off, wait-and-see management commitment to what the supervisors were about to try (p229).

This statement goes right to the core of the matter. The 'hands-off, wait-and-see commitment' they refer to in the higher levels of management illustrates that they had at least a certain amount of humility concerning authoritarian technqiues they were likely to be using; and a certain amount of respect and trust in the supervisors' abilities to test the new technique effectively. In other words, there already existed in the higher managers a certain level of the collaborative interpersonal attitudes referred to above, and these were the basis for the collaborative skills of openness, tolerance and self-appraisal that they exhibited. If, on the other hand, they had been totally arrogant about the use of authoritarian techniques, and distrustful of the supervisors' abilities to do anything effectively, then it is unlikely that they would have enabled any programme to get started in the first place. This is indeed what happened with a small percentage of the higher level managers. The fact that most of the 'higher management level' exhibited a 'hands-off, wait-and-see commitment' indicates in turn that the top manager also had a hands-off, wait-and-see outlook. Again, if the top manager had been totally arrogant concerning authoritarian techniques, and distrustful and disrespectful of others, then he or she would have given the higher management no real headroom for them to exhibit openness and tolerance down the line. Rather, a top manager with hierarchical attitudes would have adopted very much a 'hands-on' style, be unable to delegate down the line, and would be likely to rule out from the start any attempt to bring in practices that oppose authoritarian ones.

Within the mainly hierarchical nature of organisations, any individual wishing to introduce a collaborative approach into their working environment will inevitably face some kind of opposition. They are likely to experience opposition from above and from colleagues on the same level who, embedded in authoritarian ways of doing things, might criticise the value or merit of the approach (eg S Prideaux and Ford, 1988, p20; Meighan and Harber, 1986, p171; see also Chapter 7 below concerning resistance from employees). In order to win through this opposition, therefore, people will need the *active* support and backing of top management. Brian Burdsall, the Director of 'Quality Through People', British Rail's five-year quality initiative launched in 1989, recognises this in his reply to the question whether it is possible to change the internal culture of a giant like BR:

> I believe you can if the commitment is there, and the commitment has to be there at the top of the industry . . . I'm talking about the new chairman, I'm talking about the chief executive. I work for the chief

executive . . . and you need consistent leadership from him, and that means consistent leadership when the going gets tough (*Business Matters*, 11.10.90).

Those in management or teaching positions might also experience opposition from the employees or students below them. The latter may either hold authoritarian beliefs and attitudes, such as 'boss knows best', 'teacher knows best', and 'it's his decision, that's what he's paid for'; or are likely not to trust the genuineness and/or efficacy of the manager or teacher:

Those designated as participants will not respond if they . . . feel the offer is an empty gesture or if they are members of a culture where it is not customary for workers or subordinates to do anything but take orders. (French et al, 1960, p19)

As was considered in Chapter 4 (p59–60) above, if the teacher or manager is not genuine, then people will soon see through him or her and react negatively (cf Chaney and Teel, 1977, p229; also p127). But the genuineness of any individual teacher or manager is not enough. *Unless top management are actively behind them*, not only is their genuineness likely to be undermined – eg they may be unable to *act* on a decision made by their group because of opposition from their colleagues and people above them – but also the authoritarian culture of the rest of the organisation is likely to reinforce hierarchical attitudes and beliefs in their subordinates (see also Chapter 7 regarding resistance from employees lower down the hierarchy). The ultimate importance of top management is recognised by Local Education Authority inspector Jeff Jones in the area of education:

The importance of the headteacher as the initiator and supporter of innovation generally, and staff development in particular, has been referred to in much of the existing literature. The evidence . . . suggests that it is invariably the headteacher who takes the initiative in the introduction of innovation, change and improvement within the school. *Even where this is not actually the case, his or her support is vital for any development proposed by staff members to prosper* (Jones, 1990, p27; my emphasis).

The overriding influence of the top manager – Example 1

The world's biggest maker of office furniture, Steelcase, based in Michigan, USA, has been developing a collaborative team approach since 1987 (featured in *Business Matters*, 8.8.91). Most of the decision making has been 'handed over' to teams involving all of the workers. For example, a press operator who had worked with the company for 22 years, talks about the way they now have a 'big degree' of freedom about what sort of things should be done, and that, for instance, an idea his team came up with to move into a new area was thought to be a good idea by management and they were given the go ahead. The press operator compares it with what happened before the team approach was introduced when they tried to suggest ideas to management: 'No. They'd say no, everything is going good the way it is, why spoil something that's working? But now it's working better.' The team leader of that particular team acknowledges that they still have to ask the permission of the supervisors and higher management to be able to do things, but: 'The real difference is before we were told, you know, what's going to move, and what's not going to move. Now we were the ones actually making the decision.'

So why has this 'real difference' occurred? Why has the decision making been 'handed over' to the employees' teams, when for so long before it was solely the domain of management? The reason is the underlying collaborative attitudes of the top manager, president and chief executive officer, Frank Merlotti. He shows humility concerning management's abilities, and a deep-seated respect for workers' abilities, as the following comment reveals:

> It always struck me that whenever there was a problem on the floor . . . you called the engineer from the office . . . nobody ever asked the people who were doing the job . . . but all my life, you know, I also told the managers, the supervision 'talk to the people, they know more about problems on the line than you do, ask them to fix it'.

And he says there is nothing magical about the approach, it just needs 'trust' and 'recognising that everybody's got something to contribute if you let them'. Most organisations, he adds, do not let people contribute, bosses must tell people what to do – but instead they should 'encourage and empower people'.

He relates how, as he got into positions of plant management, etc, he always tried to promote the idea of getting the people involved, 'but we really never have done it on a formal basis like this'. Try as he might, therefore, as the comments of the two workers quoted above testify, he only had a limited effect, and a non-collaborative approach generally prevailed. It needed him to reach the very top position before a truly team approach could begin to develop through the organisation. And through his underlying attitudes and beliefs, and his commitment to the idea, there was a general requirement on *action*: workers should form teams and attend compulsory meetings to discuss problems and come to decisions (which used to be the management's preserve). If it had been voluntary and left open for individual managers and supervisors to form teams, then it would not have happened (see Example 2 below). The reason being that the majority of middle managers/supervisors often have more deeply entrenched hierarchical attitudes and skills than employees lower down an organisation's hierarchy, and generally feel threatened by, shy away from, and oppose, collaborative practices (see Chapter 7, p119).

A great deal of time, effort and training has been needed at Steelcase to develop the new team approach. It would not have been possible without commitment and active support from the top.

The overriding influence of the top manager – Example 2

The Beth Israel hospital in Boston, USA, is an example of an organisation that is developing a 'participatory management' approach (featured in *Business Matters*, 13.6.91). It involves, for the first time, workers who are doing a particular job being involved in the decision-making process concerning that job; and it involves all senior management doing a certain amount of sharing of the menial tasks on the ward, in their 'nurse for the day' exercise. The vice president of human resources at the hospital refers to some good success they have had, of patients wanting to come back, employees wanting to stay there, and financial objectives being met; and she believes this is due to the way the community, employees, managers and doctors, work together in 'a focused collaboration and an atmosphere climate of respect and listening and teaching . . .'

So how did this 'focused collaboration' start to develop? Certainly not with the doctors and consultants, it seems, who were reported as 'one level . . . where the project has *not* gone down well'. In fact, it has all come about due to the commitment of the hospital president, Dr Mitchell Rabkin, and he himself recognises the central role of the person at the top:

Any programme which tends to re-work significant aspects of a company simply won't work without the *commitment* and understanding of the top level of administration, and that includes the CEO, there's just no question about it.

And he continues to say that it is no good the top person saying that ideas, such as Deming's, seem marvellous ideas, and then sending somebody off to do it and to report back in three months – 'it will not work, it will not work'.

Without the *active* involvement and support of the top manager, underlying hierarchical attitudes will remain lower down the line and determine working practices. This, for example is illustrated by the situation of the Royal Free Hospital in London, also featured in *Business Matters* (13.6.91).

The *Business Matters* commentator reported that the Royal Free Hospital, who sent a delegation of managers and doctors to the Beth Israel, have not so far imported the concept of 'nurse for the day' for senior managers, or the participatory management approach of making sure that *all* the staff are represented in working parties. His suggestion of the former to a ward sister and the chief executive at the Royal Free initially produced embarrassed laughter. When pressed the ward sister said she thought it would be a good idea, and the chief executive thought it could be introduced if people thought it interesting – although he quickly added 'I have to say it's not been discussed.'

The commentator had to press even harder concerning the idea of people who actually work on a job, such as laundry workers, taking part in the decision-making process. Interestingly, the ward sister, who believed that it would be a good idea for senior management to come down to ward level so that a ward sister's problems might be better understood by them, did not seem to believe it was her responsibility to involve laundry workers so that she could understand their problems. When asked whether there had ever been a working party where the people who actually work in the laundry are present (as occurs at the Beth Israel hospital) she referred to a Sisters' Group, which 'invited' the laundry manager to go along to discuss their problems 'and why we have such problems at ward level, and they are aware of it and hopefully will be acting on it'. When pressed further as to whether they have any committee where 'people who *actually work* in the laundry come along and try to solve these problems', she replied, 'The manager, the manager. That's where it stops at, the manager.'

Her replies suggest that there has been little thought or concern for the workers' problems and suggestions. Their role, through their immediate manager, is to be aware of problems at ward level and act on it. To the same question of finding the views of the people who are doing the job, the chief executive passes the responsibility to individual managers lower down the line, 'That's the part of the management. I would expect our managers to be doing that.' It is little wonder, therefore, that it was not generally occurring at the Royal Free Hospital, as that would have required the active commitment of the chief executive. That is not to say that anybody wishing to introduce a collaborative approach will necessarily be opposed by the top manager in this situation – and consequently there may be pockets of collaborative practice, or developing collaborative practice. For example, this seems to be the case with the relatively separate pharmaceutical unit at the Royal Free, which is headed by someone who 'values' his staff, producing 'eager' and 'motivated' staff. But more generally, in less isolated situations in the hospital, people wishing to introduce a more participatory approach are likely to be opposed by the underlying attitudes revealed by the ward sister quoted above, unless they have the active support of the top manager. Notice the difference in attitude of the general manager at Lucas Aerospace Engineering and Heating Systems Division shown by the following comment of his – although at first glance it may also seem to shun responsibility:

> . . . we wanted to indicate as management that we were going to change the culture, but we wanted the work-force to change the culture for us (*State of Training*, 29.9.91).

It does in fact indicate a definite supportive commitment to change, and a wish for that change to be 'owned' by the work-force rather than imposed by management. Not surprisingly, therefore, they have successfully begun to develop a collaborative team approach.

Even with the active support of the top manager, the process 'isn't simple', as pointed out by the human resources vice president at the Beth Israel, but it takes a great deal of 'very, very committed work', which is not always appreciated nor does it produce immediate gratification. The president at the Beth Israel estimates that the participatory management programme, begun about 15 months previously, will take another four or five more years 'to become enmeshed in the warp and the woof of the organisation'. But, as the president observes, their programme, which thanks to his active commitment is *genuinely* developing a collaborative approach, '. . . seems to have a lot more stability and stamina than the vast bulk of these quality things that are going on . . .'

The overriding influence of the top manager – Example 3

There are examples of schools that are beginning to develop a more collaborative approach (see Chapter 2, p23). For instance, the author was informed by a member of staff at one large primary school in Birmingham that they have been making efforts to develop what they call a 'collegiate' approach to management. Staff meetings are held weekly, and smaller 'phase meetings' consisting of two or three teachers, a non-teaching assistant, and one of the two deputy head teachers, are also held weekly to discuss textbooks that the teachers would like to use and to forge a common pattern.

Although not every teacher believes in the value of the meetings, and one or two complain that they are 'a waste of time' (see also Chapter 2, p22; and Chapter 7, p117), the teacher comments: 'I believe they have value in inculcating a sense of cohesion and common purpose . . . Teachers are not all working behind closed doors . . . It is much better to have grumbles out in the open.' She also points out how 'the school fund committee is a new departure' – teachers in each 'phase' submit ideas for exenditure on non-teaching items for the school.

But how has this general 'new departure' come about? Why has the school begun to develop a new 'collegiate' approach? The answer is given in what this particular teacher goes on to point out next. 'Under the last head no one knew anything about the school fund.' It was the new headteacher, therefore, with his particular attitudes and skills, who had enabled a new, more democratic approach to begin to develop. Without that attitude change at the top, people down the line would have been powerless to make such changes. The greater involvement of the teachers that that change had brought about would be beneficial for everyone; and the obvious inefficiencies of the previous culture, such as the case where money was spent on a reading scheme that 'nobody uses', would be safeguarded against.

Summary – introducing a collaborative approach

The cautionary message is, for industrial worker, teacher, office worker, lecturer, salesperson, student, line manager, etc, etc – in fact everyone excluding the top manager – without the *active* support and backing of top management it would be difficult to develop an effective collaborative approach in your work environment. If you try, always be wary, polite but assertive, and be prepared for – and harden yourself to – opposition. You may be lucky and have a sympathetic and supportive top management.

Learning the collaborative way

In Part I evidence was considered to show how collaborative leadership skills are necessary for successful technical and financial management decisions. In this part it has been considered that it is ultimately the underlying attitudes of the top manager towards people, ie their interpersonal attitudes (Figure 4.1), which are the first and biggest obstacles to them developing their collaborative skills, and their organisation becoming a collaborative culture. A main theme of this book, therefore, is that if an organisation gets into extreme difficulties, then it is ultimately the underlying attitudes of the top manager that are at fault. This might seem harsh. However, it is not to deny that there are factors outside a top manager's control that impose problems. Managers often invoke factors such as high interest rates, the value of the pound and competition, etc, as the reasons for their difficulties, and these are indeed valid reasons (see also Chapters 11 and 12). But it is believed that managerial skill is the major factor determining whether an organisation sinks or swims against external pressures (cf Peters and Austin, 1985, p4).

There are many who propound this view. Former head of ICI and now management consultant Sir John Harvey-Jones, for example, responding to the comment: 'I can blame competition from other manufacturers, I can blame the pound . . .' made by a concerned managing director, replies: 'But at the end of the day the salvation is in your hands, it isn't in anybody else's.' (*Troubleshooter*, 30.9.90). The same view has been voiced by company liquidators and administrators. For example:

The majority of situations that come across my desk are in some way a function of management problems . . . the majority of UK management is still not a patch on its German or its Japanese rival (Company liquidator in *The Thatcher Audit*, 4.9.90).

From my experience, I found that there's really only one reason why companies fail, and that is through mismanagement (Company administrator in *The Money Programme*, 28.10.90).

An example of a company manager who holds this view is Ian Sloss, manufacturing and personnel director of the Japanese-owned SP-Tyres, formerly Dunlop Rubber Company. The company has been turned round from 'chronic losses to regular profit through imaginative but extremely basic changes in management style' (Murray, 1990, p40), and Sloss maintains, '. . . most of the problems out there have nothing to do with the workers – 85 per cent are simply management problems' (op cit, p43). This view has also been voiced by union officials, such as the following comment by a union official at Philips concerning that company's problems. 'The central problem within Philips is the way the concern is managed and organised. That's the fundamental problem' (*The Money Programme*, 2.12.90).

Significantly, relating to the central importance of management, it has been reported concerning Toyota's new plant in Britain that:

> Toyota plans to supply over half its components from companies in mainland Europe – they're judged technically more capable and managerially more competent (*The Thatcher Audit*, 4.9.90).

Poor management, both in industry and education, is the central theme of Deming's philosophy, the American statistician who taught the Japanese quality control after the war. He writes:

> The causes usually cited for failure of a company are costs of start-up, overruns on costs, depreciation of excess inventory, competition – anything but the actual cause, pure and simple bad management (1986, pix).

Deming, who stresses the human element in achieving quality and therefore success, claims that there needs to be a complete 'transformation' in Western management style. He also points out that managers seeking to transform need to *learn* how to change, and this transformation requires *long-term commitment to new learning and new philosophy* (1986, px).

Learning new ways can be a long haul if opposing attitudes are deeply rooted. From the fact that British management has largely ignored the wealth of evidence, since at least the Hawthorne experiments of the early 1920s, that worker and learner participation improves motivation, learning and efficiency, it would seem that, in the main, underlying hierarchical attitudes have been deeply rooted. The success of Japanese and German industry and education since the 1960s has not greatly affected these attitudes. The existence of best 'collaborative' practice on their doorstep, with the growing number of Japanese and German 'transplants' in Britain, is not yet having any great impact on British management practices.

It was noted in Chapter 4 above how the collaborative interpersonal attitudes and skills of effective leadership – trust, humility, listening, self-appraisal, etc – are the self-same attitudes and skills of effective learning. It is not surprising, therefore, that British managers, both in industry and education, with predominantly hierarchical attitudes and skills, have found it difficult to learn the lessons since the 1920s. Hierarchical attitudes, such as arrogance and distrust, close people off to listening and self-appraisal, etc, and therefore to learning.

The inability of British managers to learn is a cause for concern among some industrial commentators. For example, the following two statements were made by a professor of engineering and a professor of Japanese studies, respectively:

> If you start *learning* from them [German companies in Britain], their management practices, the way they carry out their R&D, the way they train people – if we can *learn* from them . . . it [having German companies on the doorstep] has been the right thing to do . . . No, I don't think I can see universal signs of [the opportunity] being seized (*Newsnight*, 25.10.90).

> . . . we will lose many more sectors of industry to the Japanese as we have done in the past. And the reason for it is that we are *stupid*, that we are *inflexible*, that *we do not want to learn the lessons*, and this in a very competitive international environment will cost us a lot . . . (*The Thatcher Audit*, 28.8.90; my emphasis).

And it is not only industrial managers, but also educational managers and government who do not want to learn the lessons of the more successful educational and industrial systems, both in Europe and Japan (see Chapters 12 and 13).

In contrast, Deming has said of the Japanese managers he taught after the war, 'They took note, they remembered, they listened, asked me to come. They were highly desirous of learning' (*Nippon*, 28.10.90). The seeds of humility, trust, and self-appraisal, were already present. Eric Holbeche, an Austin production engineer in 1953, also found the Japanese eager to learn and persistent. He recalls that if he was unable to give a precise answer to their question, they would repeat it, ask again during the next day or two, and finally come out with: 'Mr Holbeche, we must learn from the West, please can you answer this question' (*Nippon*, 18.11.90). The same eagerness, and humility, was shown by Eiji Toyoda, Toyota's manager in 1945. He spent several weeks in Ford's Detroit factory after the war. When he was asked why he was so 'greedy', why he was asking so many questions, he replied, 'I understand, but because Toyota is such a little company, we managers have to be involved in all the manufacturing areas. So please help me' (*Nippon*, 18.11.90). He wrote home to his company newspaper, 'There's much for Toyota to learn here.'

The Japanese managers and engineers were not too proud and arrogant to say they did not know or understand something, and to ask humbly for help. They had humility. They were also not ashamed or frightened to say they did not know or understand something – it is not perceived judgementally, as a *personal* fault or weakness as it often is by British people and some other Westerners. Instead, they see it as part of the learning process and maintain respect for the learner's abilities and value (see also Chapters 7 and 8). This no doubt stems from the fact that their organisational cultures in education and industry are less hierarchical and so less judgemental than ours (see also Chapter 13).

Collaborative interpersonal attitudes, such as humility, and collaborative interpersonal skills, such as self-appraisal, explain the ability and eagerness of the Japanese to learn. Their eagerness to learn about industrial automation reveals another collaborative interpersonal attitude. In line with the findings of other Europeans and Americans, Joseph Engelberger, robot pioneer in 1967, found the Japanese eager and receptive:

> Here in the United States I was able to get maybe eight or ten people to listen. And they [the Japanese] brought something like 600 engineers and scientists and executives to hear my lecture (*Nippon*, 25.11.90).

Gensuke Okada was the manager of Kawasaki in 1967, the company that bought the licence from Engelberger to build the first industrial robot in Japan. He told Engelberger, who could not understand the difference in response between the Americans and the Japanese, that Americans were not interested to learn about robots because, unlike Japan, America still had 'cheap labour to do the dirty work' (*Nippon*, 25.11.90). The fact is that the Japanese's eagerness and ability to learn about robots, and the technical and financial decisions taken by managers concerning automation, *were strongly tied to their respect for, and commitment to, the work-force*. It was their respect for the work-force that determined the *collaborative manner* in which they implemented automation. People were taken into consideration – automation was introduced to relieve people of laborious, heavy and dirty jobs, freeing them for more creative work, and to increase efficiency to save jobs not to cut them (see also Chapter 12, p240); and people's views were taken into account, as noticed by Engelberger: '. . . they may have controversy at the outset, but they don't proceed until they have consensus' (*Nippon*, 25.11.90).

The possible 'controversy' Engleberger refers to should not be confused with the conflict and confrontation produced by management imposition, so common in Western organisations. It is the 'controversy' of *healthy and open dialogue and discussion*, generally welcomed by Japanese managers. It is the way they can listen to, and learn from, the work-force. And, as considered in Chapter 5, this people-centred consensus approach where all employees are respected, trusted and fully involved, is the reason why they constructively 'knuckle under' – the secret of Japanese success in quickly and effectively implementing change.

It was their underlying collaborative interpersonal attitudes and skills, therefore, that were behind the fact that automation was introduced more rapidly in Japan than in any other country. The fact that in 1980 there were 14,000 robots installed in Japan, compared to only 4000 in the United States, and a few hundred in Britain (*Nippon*, 25.11.90) reflects on the underlying 'non-collaborative', 'non-learning' attitudes prevailing in the latter countries.

Often the Japanese have been accused of stealing Western ideas, but, in line with the point being made here, Kanter observes:

> . . . that's really what Americans say when the Japanese learn better than we do. We call it stealing, but they're really learning from things that were perfectly well available to them [the Americans] (*Business Matters*, 21.6.90).

And they have been able to learn better than Westerners, because of their underlying collaborative attitudes and skills.

Learning through collaboration not conflict*

Although here it has been said that the 'controversy' the Japanese have – the dialogue and discussion – should not be confused with conflict and confrontation, one American management guru, Richard Pascale, does use the term 'conflict' to describe the successful Japanese approach. This author maintains, however, that the broad meaning of the word 'conflict' directly opposes the situation that holds in successful Japanese organisations, and it is therefore misleading to apply it as such. If it is used in this context then it should only be with clear qualifications. For example, Pascale applies the term to describe the work processes in the Honda of America plant, which he has studied. But this is how the plant manager at Honda perceives the situation:

> It's not an adversarial [thing] that I want to hurt or destroy or over-run you. It's a conflict in the fact that we have different individuals that should have different ideas that should be expressed and explored and discussed; and from that discussion we find the best solution.

He uses the term 'conflict', therefore, to describe the open expression, exploration and discussion of different ideas. The 'non-adversarial' aspect he refers to means that people are not *personalising* the process and seeing each other as enemies or opponents. Within the broad meaning of conflict, however, is the notion of a struggle or a battle, including the hostile struggle or battle between people. The use of the term could be qualified by referring to a conflict of ideas, but without this qualification the personal connotations of the term 'conflict' mean that it is misleading and confusing to apply it as such to the Japanese approach. It is the lack of a personal element in the Japanese approach that makes open discussion and criticism possible and acceptable. Coming up with different, new and opposing ideas and criticisms is not perceived, or used, judgementally as a personal

---

* The quotations and factual information for this and the next sub-section are taken from *Business Matters*, 26.9.91, unless otherwise stated. The interpretations are this author's.

attack – just as not knowing or understanding something, or making a mistake, is not perceived as an inbuilt personal weakness. People are not personally judged in any way and not punished in any way – they are totally secure. Everything is perceived 'non-personally', at the level of ideas, as part of the learning process. This, for example, is borne out by a comment the plant manager of Honda in America makes about the group meetings they have: 'The discussion is about the *idea* not about *people*, so it can become very passionate, it can become very emotional'. It is the lack of a judgemental, intolerant, personal element in the Japanese organisational culture that enables new, different and opposing ideas, and creates the enthusiastic, motivated *learning* organisations that the Japanese have.

The opposite is generally true in the prevailing non-collaborative, hierarchical organisations in the West. There is a strong personal element running deep through hierarchical cultures. This is an outcome of a strong judgemental element based on attitudes of arrogance, disrespect and distrust of others. It makes people from the top down, operate individually and competitively, rather than as a group, vying for personal rewards, promotion and power (see also Chapter 8, p131–2); it makes them fear new, different and opposing ideas and perceive them as a personal attack (particularly if the opposing ideas come from subordinates (Chapter 7, p119)); and it makes them fear proposing new, different and opposing ideas (especially if they are subordinates), and making mistakes, for fear of being personally judged and punished (Chapter 8, p128). In contrast to collaborative organisational cultures, in hierarchical cultures new, different and opposing ideas *are* often perceived, and used, judgementally as a personal attack, just as admitting to short-comings or mistakes is perceived as an inbuilt personal weakness. People *are* personally judged and punished for mistakes or having different ideas – they are not secure. The personal level predominates over the level of ideas, the judgemental, intolerant, personal element disenables new and creative ideas, and motivation and learning – the key to survivability and success – is stifled.

So it is this element of personal fear and rivalry that characterises the conflict that takes place in hierarchical Western organisations, and that inhibits the open expression, exploration and discussion of different ideas that the Honda plant manager refers to. It is therefore misleading to apply the same term 'conflict' to both situations, as Pascale does. It is misleading to talk about conflict being 'part of the company culture' at Honda, and to say 'Honda has engineered conflict throughout the company'. What he means by conflict here is conflict of ideas, and it should not be confused with the kind of hostile personal conflict that generally takes place in Western organisations. In fact Pascale goes on to say after the latter comment: 'There's a restlessness. It encourages *all* of its people to question *all* of the time.' The very opposite of the conflict situation in hierarchical organisations that stifles questioning. He also says that: 'the most successful Japanese companies have mastered the art of disagreeing without being disagreeable' – in other words, the art of having, and encouraging, the conflict of ideas without having personal conflict. Again, the very opposite of the situation prevailing in Western organisations. And this Japanese 'art' is based on underlying collaborative attitudes towards others, which involve people equally, so enabling an open culture of cooperation rather than one of rivalry, personal power and gain.

> We ask a lot of questions . . .
>
> Here you're able to say what's on your mind . . . you're not criticised for what you say. They do take it in their stride. If there's something that has to be resolved, they do try to get a solution for it. You're able to talk to your peers and not feel that they're above you and you're below them, it seems like it's equal (Production associates at Honda).

Surely the antithesis of Western organisational conflict? Perhaps it is a product of underlying hierarchical attitudes that Pascale uses the same term to refer to 'expressing, exploring and discussing different ideas' as to 'personal conflict' – after all, attempting to express, explore and discuss different ideas in hierarchical cultures does cause personal conflict.

A perfect summation of the difference in approach between collaborative and hierarchical cultures is given by McGregor towards the end of his book (1987, p232ff). He asks what distinguishes effective groups from less effective groups, and his list includes:

> *an effective group*
> informal, comfortable, relaxed atmosphere, with people interested in the task; discussion in which virtually everyone participates, and is kept to the point; discussion and agreement on objectives; people listen to each other, every idea is given a hearing, and people are not afraid

of appearing foolish by suggesting creative and extreme ideas; disagreement is open and comfortable, conflict [of ideas] is not suppressed or overridden to keep things on a plane of sweetness and light, reasons are carefully examined and resolved rather than dominating the dissenter; likewise dissenters do not express hostility or try to dominate the group, and their disagreement is a genuine difference of opinion which they expect to be fairly considered; most decisions are reached by a true general consensus as any individual opposition is not kept private; criticism is frequent, frank, and comfortable, there is little evidence of personal attack, either open or hidden, and it is dealt with constructively; people are free in expressing their feelings as well as ideas; there is little pussyfooting and few 'hidden agendas'; there is little evidence of struggle for power – the issue is not who controls but how to get the job done.

an ineffective group
formal, stiff, antagonistic, hostile atmosphere with indifference and boredom of some members to the task; a few people dominate the discussion, often going off the point; confusion over group task and objective, with different private and personal objectives which different people are attempting to achieve in conflict with each other; people do not listen to each other and ideas are ignored and overridden, the discussion jumps around with little coherence or progress, there is talking for effect – people make speeches to impress someone else rather than address the task at hand; some people feel that their contribution is being constantly judged and evaluated by others, so they are careful and fail to express ideas or feelings for fear of being criticised and regarded as silly; disagreements are either suppressed or may result in open warfare and consequent domination by one subgroup over another, they may be 'resolved' by a vote where the majority remain unconvinced and accede to an aggressive subgroup for peace and to get on with the task; generally only aggressive members' ideas are considered, less aggressive people keep quiet or give up after a short ineffectual attempt to be heard; decisions are taken before real issues are examined or resolved, but people who dislike the decision and fail to speak remain resentful and uncommitted to it after the meeting; confusion over action – who is going to do what, or doubt over deployment when assignments of responsibility are made; criticism is embarrassing, tension-producing, and uncomfortable, and often involves personal hostility which members are unable to cope with, criticism of ideas tends to be destructive – so no one is willing to stick their neck out; personal feelings are hidden rather than out in the open, the general attitude is that these are inappropriate for discussion and too explosive.

Pascale maintains that 'we as Westerners are notoriously bad at dealing with conflict'. If he means by conflict here the expressing, exploring and discussing of different ideas, then it is true we are bad at dealing with that. In the first place, as discussed above, we do not enable it because the underlying personal conflict that goes through relationships in organisations stifles it. And, although our institutions generally create personal conflict, we are bad at dealing with that also since, by definition, personal hostility is unmanageable – although in one sense we are good at 'managing' it, by being able to breed it continuously and control it through suppression. The best and only way to deal properly with this kind of conflict, in fact, would be to remove it altogether by forming more collaborative cultures.

The way the situation is confused by Pascale's use of the term 'conflict' to describe successful Japanese organisations, is illustrated in his comparison of Honda of America with British Petroleum. He comments: 'While BP's managers are *learning* how to manage conflict, at Honda it's part of the company culture'. As considered above, the kind of 'conflict' that exists in successful Japanese companies is quite different from the conflict that generally exists in Western organisations, and this is encapsulated in the following two comments, the first by a senior coordinator at Honda, and the second by a systems manager at BP:

> . . . it doesn't matter if you're the President or you're the youngest guy there, you're listened to and respected . . . we throw out [ideas] that can be so 'off-the-wall', that it's amazing. But at the same time, by throwing them out, everyone's thought processes get involved and pretty soon we come to an idea, we all start to focus down, and we come to the solution to our problem.

> So we spent two and a half days bullshitting on basically going round and round this problem. And I just got to a certain level of frustration . . . and I went up like a rocket . . . The important thing that should be said . . . is that we actually achieved the actual object – I *got* what I wanted.

Although the last sentence was accompanied by laughter from the systems manager and the rest of the BP group, there was a serious side to it. Significantly, the memory of another member of the BP group was that the meeting had ended in total deadlock, and she recalls how the group: 'are all tired of the subject matter . . . and people are *all* talking, nobody really is taking the lead as to what we

ought to do . . .' These kinds of adversarial stances in non-collaborative 'teams' are captured precisely by McGregor's list referred to above.

The difference between the approach of successful Japanese organisations and that prevailing in Western organisations is well illustrated by these two situations. Also, it is significant that the task of the particular Honda meeting referred to in the above quotation related to solving the problem of a leaking car window, whereas the BP meeting was trying to agree on big budget cuts. It reflects the general preoccupation with financial considerations and personal advancement by non-collaborative top managers in the West, rather than with solving problems and human and organisational development (see Chapter 11); and this sets the culture where everyone is preoccupied with financial considerations and personal advancement, rather than mutual development (Chapter 8, p131–2). It is not surprising, therefore, that the BP people each acted individually and competitively 'to get what they wanted', and were unable to solve the problem rationally and collaboratively as the Honda people did (but see Chapter 7 regarding BP).

In a word, the 'equal' collaborative culture centres on learning and looking for solutions, the 'unequal' hierarchical culture centres on personal conflict and struggle for power. The superior creative outcome of collaborative cultures is plain to see.

Learning cultures – collaborative not impositional top management

The observation by Richard Pascale that successful Japanese companies 'have mastered the art of disagreeing without being disagreeable' is in line with characteristics such as openness and tolerance claimed for Japanese organisations in this book and by others. However, he also maintains that effective Japanese companies 'combine the directive with the participative', which is out of step with claims made above in Chapter 5 concerning the general Japanese culture of not wanting to impose on others. It also seems out of step with the following example he cites from the Honda plant that he has studied in America.

Don English, assistant vice president at the plant, refers to their practice of asking the employees themselves who are on the job, questions such as: 'What do you think? How can this be improved?

Why does it matter that we do it this way versus some other way?'
He says that although it is by no means a Utopia, they do work very
hard at it; and he admits that he found in previous experience that it
was easier to make decisions without input from the employee, as it
takes time to ask the question 'What do you think?' It is easier in
hierarchical cultures, because of prevailing attitudes of disrespect, etc
for others, and arrogance about one's own abilities – there is no
wish *to waste time* gathering ideas from below when one can impose
one's own superior ideas. In collaborative cultures, however, such
as in many successful Japanese organisations, attitudes such as
respect for others and their abilities, and a corresponding humility
about one's own, makes it difficult for people to operate in this
impositional way. For them it is easier to ask questions and listen to
other people's views and ideas – and to encourage others to question –
because they are eager to find solutions and learn better ways. It is
not difficult but automatic. The assistant plant manager at the
Honda plant in America says:

> If you keep asking yourself why?, why?, why?, you ultimately get to
> the root cause of a problem. *What* we're doing, *how* we're doing it,
> *why* we're doing it – and *never* accepting it's always been done that
> way, always asking, why?, why?, why?, and why? 'Why' is not a negative
> term.

But as considered above, to ask 'why?' in hierarchical cultures and
to come up with new, different, and opposing ideas, is often seen,
and used, negatively, as an attack against a person; and is often perceived as 'rocking the boat', making things difficult for people, or
even being impertinent when asked by subordinates of their superiors
(if they dare do it), even though it may be a genuine, totally imper-
sonal query. This is why, in the main, British managers neither
question things constructively in this way, nor enable and empower
others to do so. It is not part of hierarchical cultures in which people
are preoccupied with competing for personal advancement at the
expense of looking for solutions and improving effectiveness and
efficiency through a collaborative learning process with others. And
linked with this, it is not expected of them, they are not rewarded
for it (quite the contrary), as the reward system is set by top managers
with underlying hierarchical attitudes that also neglect personal and
organisational growth, instead centring on status, position, ladder
climbing and promotion politics (see p79–80). It is a vicious circle –

2 cultures

hierarchical top managers motivated by personal gain create a culture where employees are motivated by personal gain and whose performance is judged by hierarchical top managers. In contrast, collaborative cultures centre on the group, the problem, empowerment, learning, ideas, improvement – not personal advancement and power.

The attitude change needed to go from a hierarchical to a collaborative culture does not happen overnight, even if a person is working under a collaborative top management (Chapter 7), and Don English says he and his senior manager colleagues are still learning the importance of asking questions, at least of the employees. Unable to shake off completely the old hierarchical ways, they came up with what they thought was a better title for their maintenance associates – within an hour of the decision 30 associates were at his desk asking why he had not asked for their input. Despite his explanation that it was done with good intentions to improve things, they insisted: 'But you didn't ask us.' He continues: 'The next day I changed it back, and that was just another . . . opportunity for me to better understand – *never* leave the associates out of the decisions we make.'

Generally it seems that Japanese managers do not leave their employees out of the decisions they make, and always take into account their views and needs. In this sense, therefore, it seems out of step for Pascale to talk about them combining directives with participation, as though the directives are separate from the participation. He talks about 'the inescapable tension between the need to give orders from above and to tap in from the collective talent from below'. But really it is the predominantly hierarchical Western attitude that sees orders from above as needing to be separate from the consideration of employees, and which cannot marry a 'directive' with prior consultation with the work-force. He also says that Japanese companies 'expect [the] empowered worker to also be a loyal and obedient follower'. This author would say that the employee is loyal *because* he or she is constantly consulted and empowered, and does not resist when a final decision is made *because* his or her views have been listened to and taken into account. In the words of Drucker, the Japanese manager earns 'followership', something that you cannot 'demand' or 'command' (*Business Matters*, 5.9.91); but it seems misleading to use the word 'obedient' which suggests being *imposed on* rather than being *listened to* and taking part in the formulation of the 'directive'; and it would be more accurate to use terms such as 'unresistant' or 'cooperative'.

Collaborative questioning, learning and 'followership' – Example

In most non-collaborative, hierarchical, non-learning, Western organisational cultures, people are afraid to openly question the boss's ideas and decisions. As Deming says: 'The game becomes one of politics. Keep on the good side of the boss . . . Be a yes man' (1986, p108). Industrialist, Sir Peter Parker, well versed in the 'fear' politics of a typical Western organisational culture, said he had found the openness at Mitsubishi Electric UK when he began his job as chairman there *'quite* startling'. He relates the situation where he sat in on a discussion when the visiting top man came to London. The younger men running the companies were around the table and there was a debate about an investment. He continues: '. . . my managing director was *very* forthright, and *very* aggressive with this very senior chap, who was *very* senior'. At the end of the debate Sir Peter said to the managing director that presumably he would be ringing his wife to tell her, 'don't buy the curtains, because I think we're on the move'. Sir Peter thought that because if that happened in any Western company he would be expecting the head man at the end of the day to say, ' "Ah fine, you have your opinions, you take them away" '. The managing director had replied to him:

> Not at all. He wants to hear my view. He'll make his decision and I'll follow his decision. (*Open Mind*, 22.6.91)

No fear there on either side. The top man had the humility and rationality to treat the dissension and different viewpoint as a learning opportunity. The words that Sir Peter Parker uses in his assessment of the situation are interesting: 'Now there was a degree of liberty within the security which was *quite* startling.' But, of course, the liberty that exists is an outcome of the security – the security of a collaborative 'learning' culture which does not personally judge and punish people for enthusiastically coming up with new, different and opposing ideas.

Summary – Top management and the organisational culture

With rapidly growing competition, and the consequent need for improved efficiency, innovation and quality, British managers in industry and education will come under increasing pressure to adopt a more collaborative approach if their organisations are going to survive, let alone flourish, in the 1990s and beyond. The extent of the resistance to this pressure, and whether or not a particular organisation will ultimately adopt genuine collaborative procedures, however, depends on how deeply embedded hierarchical attitudes are in the top manager. The point is contained in the comment by Belbin: 'The quickest and surest way of changing the fortunes of a firm is to replace the man at the top' (1981, p50).

Despite the general resistance of British management to collaborative procedures in the past, it is to be hoped that there are top managers whose hierarchical attitudes are not so deeply rooted as to make them continue to be impervious to the now urgent need to learn and develop more collaborative work practices. They need to take heed of warnings such as that given by Jean Irvine (director of information technology with the Post Office), when she refers to the need for: 'Getting to changing the culture or you're dead' (*State of Training*, 29.9.91). And to Professor Dan Jones who maintains that the only salvation for British industry is its adoption of Japanese working practices, 'giving the responsibility and the opportunity *back* to *every single* worker . . .' (*Newsnight*, 29.10.91).

It is to be hoped that there are top managers, both in industry and education, with at least a certain level of the collaborative attitudes of *humility*, *respect* for, and *trust* in people, which will enable them to take active heed of such warnings and to begin the process of developing their collaborative leadership/team skills. This development by top management is the only basis for developing genuine collaborative organisational cultures, and it would provide the real (as opposed to lip-service) support needed for middle managers, teachers, supervisors, etc to develop their collaborative attitudes and skills and therefore their effectiveness and efficiency. Part III provides two basic aids to help people in the learning process.

An example of an organisation where top management does have the humility to recognise the inefficiency of traditional hierarchical working practices compared to more collaborative approaches, and the need to learn from those approaches, is provided by Rover Cars. ITN has reported that managers at the Rover plants in Britain: 'are trying to push through radical new plans to boost efficiency', based on Japanese working practices, in order to compete and survive in the 1990s (*News at Ten*, 25.10.91). The proposed change, said to be accepted by the unions subject to discussion of details, will include: single status terms for all, with the scrapping of distinctions between white and blue collar workers; more emphasis on team-work, with an end to demarcations between jobs; and streamlined trade union negotiations, with one body and one voice representing all (op cit). As discussed above, for these good intentions to succeed and such a collaborative structure to be applied genuinely and effectively, the top managers will need to begin the process of fur-ther developing their own collaborative attitudes and skills. The alternative is uncompromisingly summed up by the ITN reporter: 'If they don't succeed [in making sweeping changes to working practices], the Japanese will be able to wave goodbye to the British car industry' (op cit).

In short, organisations will only survive if the people within them develop collaborative working practices; and people will only be able to work *truly* cooperatively in teams and start *effectively* devel-oping their collaborative skills, *if the top manager is actively committed to developing his or her collaborative attitudes and skills, the only basis for a true collaborative organisational culture.*

7

Collaborative top management – the caring culture

Harnessing the most important resource – from rhetoric to action

Today an increasing amount of lip service is paid by top managers to the idea of the 'human resource' being the most important resource, and the need for cooperative teamwork in order to harness this resource effectively. But, as discussed in the previous chapter, a genuine commitment by top managers is not just a matter of them being aware of, and merely giving verbal allegiance to, the idea. It means those top people *acting* and getting *involved* in the process of changing their own attitudes, developing their own interpersonal skills, and changing their own work practices.

The need to go from rhetoric to action is acknowedged by Robert Horton, for example, the chairman of Britain's biggest company, British Petroleum. Shortly after his appointment he began the process of attempting to dismantle what a *Money Programme* reporter described as the company's 'male dominated', 'bureaucratic', rigid hierarchical structure, which had been 'strangling' people's decision making, and trying to develop a more collaborative 'team' culture. Robert Horton realises, however, that:

> . . . it does mean that we have got to start rethinking the way in which many of us have spent most of our lives in BP . . . I am going to have to resist the temptation of picking up that telephone every time the price of petrol goes up and asking the guy responsible for the United Kingdom why he has put it up (*The Money Programme*, 20.5.90).

Among other things, therefore, the top person will need to delegate more and *trust* people more to make their own decisions. He or she will also need to be non-judgemental and have the *tolerance* to give people time to develop a different approach, and allow them to make 'mistakes'.

In addition to the top manager being actively involved in trying to develop his or her own collaborative attitudes and skills, another indication that he or she has gone beyond rhetoric and genuinely wants to develop a collaborative organisational culture, is when she or he introduces a training programme for senior and middle management – ideally with the top manager taking part in the training programme. The importance of 'top-down' training is recognised, for example, by Michael Frye, chairman of the B Elliott Group. Talking about one of the organisations in the group that had successfully gone from loss to profit, he comments:

> They started in the way that I like, which is training managers from, if you like, top down first of all, because what you must do is create the atmosphere and the culture in which the senior managers will listen to the shop-floor and everybody else (*Walk the Talk*, 28.4.91).

This collaborative skill of *genuinely listening* so that it influences action, is crucial. As Michael Frye recognises, there is nothing more 'frustrating' and 'demotivating' for people at shop-floor level or any level, than for management first to get them enthused and then the level directly above them, ie their supervisor or line manager, to block their enthusiasm and decision making (see Chapter 4). The company, he continues, have been able, by using top-down training, effectively to 'cascade the approach out', and work on the process of 'having it cascade, in return, in the feedback coming from the shop-floor all the way up'.

In summary, the main indicators that a top manager is serious about going from rhetoric to action in trying to harness the human resource, include him or her:

1. actively taking the lead to develop his or her own collaborative attitudes and skills through training (see point 3), and developing a team approach with senior managers, where he or she *acts* on decisions made 'lower' down;
2. instigating a team structure throughout their organisation enabling everybody to be involved in the decision-making process, (eg Steelcase and Beth Israel examples in Chapter 6);
3. instigating a 'top-down' training programme (including him or

herself) in collaborative interpersonal attitudes and skills (eg B Elliot Group referred to above).

These three actions are inextricably linked. For example, a training programme for managers and supervisors (3) will not necessarily be of benefit in the workplace if the training is not 'work-based' and there is little flexibility to change the structure of working practices. A genuine obligation from the top to form a team structure throughout an institution (2) needs to go hand in hand with training, otherwise training can deteriorate into nothing more than a remote and costly academic game (see also Chapter 11, p178). For example, the training to improve communication skills in middle managers instigated at the Belling factory (Example 1, Chapter 5), was reported to include them giving presentations to senior colleagues, and playing team games. In this way they began to learn that to solve problems effectively they needed to listen and cooperate with others, but there was no guarantee that they would apply this 'down the line', outside of the training exercise. Indeed, without a culture where the top manager sets the example of using a team approach himself, and also where he requires that there be a team structure that involves all employees, it was unlikely that they would.

The following are examples of success achieved by top managers who, from the outset, went beyond rhetoric to a genuine collaborative commitment to the most important resource – people.

Commitment to the most important resource – Example 1

An exception to the rhetoric is provided by Anita Roddick, managing director of The Body Shop. She claims 'we walk the talk in this company' (*Walk the Talk*, 7.4.91), and talks about 'leadership that isn't rhetorical, but is behaviour' (Schumacher, 1990). A major activity of the company is concerned with the personal development and empowerment of employees. There is no marketing department, for example, but instead the money is spent on a training department which is really an education department. Roddick believes it is important for managers to address questions such as:

- How do you deal with your staff?

- Are they empowered?

- Are they part of decision making?

- Do they determine their own wages? (Schumacher, 1990).

Employees were asked to write their own company charter – *everyone* was involved. Among other things, the charter calls for 'honesty', 'integrity', 'caring', 'treating *everyone* equally', 'mutual trust and respect', 'respect and care for humans, animals, the planet', 'a spirit of partnership between everyone who works for the company'. Concerning the charter, Roddick says:

> The work-force constantly police the charter. They are not working for me but this new concept of business. Directors are questioned constantly . . . The sense of hierarchy is abolished in our company. (Schumacher, 1990)

From the start of the business, her attitudes towards people and the environment, her respect for their value and their needs, and her commitment to honesty, have predominated and have not been squeezed out by purely technical and financial considerations. Rather, her 'soft' collaborative interpersonal attitudes and skills have formed the basis of her successful financial and technical judgements (see Chapter 2, p27). And from the start, these 'human' attitudes and skills have ensured that her *action* puts people, and the environment, before profits, which in turn ensures motivation, quality and success.

Commitment to the most important resource – Example 2

An example of an organisation that employed a collaborative approach with people from the outset, and pulled through difficulties by doing so, is provided by Seabait Ltd, a ragworm farm featured in, and an eventual winner of, the £10,000 award in the *Radio Times* Radio 4 *Enterprise 90* competition (31.10.90).

Firstly, the managing director Peter Cowin formed a collaborative agreement with the adjoining private power station, Alcan, to use their cooling water outflow. Both sides gained – Seabait by getting a supply of heated water, the cost of which would otherwise have made their farming process uneconomic, and Alcan by showing that their water was not polluted, which was 'clearly a good thing for [them]', according to their director. He also voiced a deeper collaborative attitude when he added another reason for them being involved in the Seabait project – it would provide employment for young people: 'I think we've *all, all* managers, have this responsibility'.

And, as he said, the project cost his company nothing, 'just co-operation'.

Secondly, the co-founder and research director at Seabait, Peter Olive, formed a collaborative agreement with Newcastle University, where he also works. Again, both sides gained; as the research director says 'it's really a two-way exchange'. Seabait gets help from the university concerning information on breeding cycles, etc, and the university benefits not only by receiving a royalty for that help, but also from the fact that it 'has a member of staff who now has *real* understanding of the commercial world', the world that most of his students will go to work in.

Thirdly, both the managing director and research director showed a collaborative commitment to the work-force when the company hit difficulties in its first year. Because of 'teething troubles' in the farm's design and operation procedure, a bacterial infection killed 80 per cent of the stock of ragworms. Remarkably, despite the fact that 'everything [the managing director and research director] owned was mortgaged for Seabait' – both their houses were on the line, and for the managing director the previous five years of research and what little money he did have, was all at stake, and interest rates were rising – they did not let it affect employees. The research director recalls:

> Throughout this time the staff came with us – if we believed that we could get through the problem they would come with us. We *never* laid anyone off even though we were not generating the money that we thought we would in that first year.

This collaborative act meant, again, that both sides gained. The work-force, of course, by not losing their jobs, but the company also, by virtue of the fact that all the staff at Seabait, 'right down to the people involved on the YTS level', bought shares in the company. It is not surprising, therefore, that the management found that 'the staff came with us' in this way, and believed and trusted the management when they said they believed they could get through the problem, after the collaborative treatment they had received from management. And one way the management were able to keep on the work-force in these difficult times was by not wasting money on 'unnecessary frivolities like smart offices with fancy swivel chairs in them'. The staff could see that they were more of a priority. Again, therefore, it is not surprising that this collaborative management gained the commitment of employees. When asked whether he was making sacrifices, taking pay cuts, etc, investing for the future, Jonathan Land, who had begun working there over three years before on the YTS scheme, and was then taken on full-time, replied: 'We haven't taken pay cuts, no. But I am a shareholder in the company, and that gives me a personal interest in the welfare of the company, obviously.'

Seabait's collaborative management, therefore, had created an enabling and empowering 'developing' culture, which, in turn, had produced a highly motivated work-force. The above employee showed great enthusiasm:

> It's definitely on the up and up. I mean, we're moving forwards and upwards, we're making improvements, and understanding a lot more how to look after the worms and it's getting better.

If the managing director had done what usually happens when an organisation gets into difficulties, namely, started by cutting employees' pay and jobs, then the lifeblood of the organisation would have been sapped, and these regenerative and creative forces stifled. Instead, the collaborative action of top management brought about employee commitment and motivation, supporting survival, and resulting in a quality product, which, despite the fact that the price was double the price of wild worms from Ireland, already in 1990 could not keep up with demand. The company also then started to export.

Collaborative caring

In all, as Figure 4.1 illustrates, in order to develop their collaborative interpersonal skills, top managers will need to develop and exhibit their ability to respect and trust people and their abilities, to be honest, humble, have a sense of fairness and justice, be empathetic, and love people. It could be put into a single word by saying employers will need to develop a *caring* attitude towards people. This, for example, was clearly shown by the two top managers at Seabait.

If a top manager has these collaborative attitudes then he or she will have the manner and the interpersonal skills that will, among other things, make them approachable by employees – an important factor in employees feeling 'cared' for. And this approachability or 'common touch' figures highly with Peters and Austin, who believe that perhaps the biggest indicator of whether a top manager is truly involved and truly respects people and their work, etc, is the extent to which he or she practises MBWA (Managing By Wandering Around). That does not just mean occasionally gliding through a work area like visiting royalty. Peters and Austin refer to the comment of a general manager which indicates what is needed: 'If *I* don't go to the field, if *I* don't treat the field as important, . . . then why should I expect people in the field to think that they're important?' (1985, p208). By genuinely getting involved in people's work, genuinely listening, etc, this particular top manager turned the company around in just 18 months.

Because of the tight labour market, there is increasing talk today of the need for organisations to be 'caring' in order to attract and retain good staff (eg *Money Box*, 19.5.90; *Business Matters*, 21.6.90). Employers with the above collaborative attitudes (and related interpersonal skills):

- will *care* enough to respect, listen to and collaboratively involve employees in decisions that affect them (see Chapter 8);

- will *care* enough to recognise and reward employees for their performance (see Chapter 8);

- will *care* enough to invest in training and developing their employees' skills, and researching and developing their ideas (see Chapter 11);

- will *care* enough to try to maintain people's pay and employment through difficulties, and look for other ways out (see Chapter 12);

- will *care* enough to listen to and work collaboratively with customers (see Chapter 9);

- will *care* enough to listen to and work collaboratively with other organisations they have dealings with (see Chapter 9);

- will *care* for the environment and other living species, inextricably bound up with human and organisational well-being (see Chapter 10).

It is predicted that, with the demographic downturn and skills shortage, 'everybody is going to compete for people in the 1990s' (eg *Business Matters*, 21.6.90), and caring for people in this manner – providing a secure, non-stressful, flexible work environment; giving people autonomy, reward and recognition; enabling them to develop skills; and showing a social responsibility to the community and the environment – is going to be a way that organisations will be able to entice and retain good staff in the limited pool available. In the past the general belief has been that caring for the employee, the customer, and the environment, costs money and reduces profit. But caring is not incompatible with profit. Indeed, because it produces motivation, innovation and quality, it increases efficiency and profit. As stated in the early chapters of this book, collaborative, ethical, 'caring' organisations are the ones most likely to survive and succeed into the 1990s and beyond (see for example Chapter 2).

If top management does these things it can be said to be truly *committed* to the collaborative approach. And it is only when the rhetoric of top management is translated into such actions that collaborative practices will pass down the line and permeate through an organisation – making it a more attractive, more flexible, more motivating work environment, increasing efficiency, innovation and quality.

Hurdles for caring management

Employee apathy to participation?

Having a truly committed top management will not guarantee that an organisation's transition to a more collaborative culture will be problem free, and it is likely that he or she will be faced with certain difficulties. Employees lower down the hierarchy might resist change to more participatory procedures. It is often maintained that most people are apathetic and just not interested in participating in decisions and learning about the broader aspects of an organisation; they believe that it is the job of others who are paid for it and/or are more capable. But that is only the case under existing hierarchical, non-participatory cultures. The strong evidence is that most people do quickly get involved and want to participate *if given a genuine chance* to have an influence over their environment (see below; also cf Blumberg, 1968, p133; White, 1983, p14ff; *Business Matters*, 14.6.90).

Employee apathy to self-appraisal

Employee apathy to self-appraisal – a requirement of the collaborative process – is again a consequence of current hierarchical work cultures, and would be removed under *genuine* collaborative leadership (see Chapter 8).

Employee opposition – animosity, lack of self-confidence, etc

The claims that people will not adapt to, and benefit from, a collaborative approach, either in work or education – because they are apathetic, don't want to participate in decisions, and are opposed to self-appraisal – are invalid. There may be an initial reaction to the introduction of participatory procedures linked with 'the need to release bottled-up animosity and the need to test the superior's sincerity' (Likert, 1961, p245). There may also be an initial lack of confidence given the fact that they will be used to being told what to do both in school and at work. But both these responses would be easily overcome by a top management that genuinely and skilfully introduces collaborative procedures. In general, employees lower down the hierarchy are less likely to resist change than those in management positions. Most employees after all will be gaining involvement, autonomy and recognition (see also Chapter 8), and with management support and the flexibility that teamwork requires and enables, will welcome the change.

Employees' need for genuine collaborative involvement

The introduction of a team structure at Steelcase considered in Chapter 6 (pp88–90), involving *all* employees in the decision-making process, first met with some resistance from the workers (featured in *Business Matters*, 8.8.91). A main reason given was the fact that workers, who were on piecework, lost money when they attended team meetings. The reason why this concern of workers was overcome, was expressed slightly differently by a manager and a worker. According to the manager it was because workers realised that although they lose incentive money during meetings, in the long term it would mean the company doing better, being better managed, as that involved the workers, driving down costs and increasing their bonuses. As they are a profit-sharing company, this bonus increase would make up for the loss of incentive money. Also, over time, as the teams became more efficient, less time was taken up each meeting. According to a worker, however, a major factor for accepting a reduction in incentive pay was the reward of involvement (see also Chapter 8). For so long, he says, management would never listen to anyone 'out here on the floor':

> but now management *is* listening, and it's giving the people a little bit different idea saying, you know, maybe this few extra dollars out of my pocket is worth it because now somebody's beginning to listen.

From this worker's perception of the matter, therefore, money was not the central and deciding issue. Collaborative involvement, being listened to, was a more important reward than monetary reward (see Chapter 8), and it supports the view that disputes over pay are very often a front for grievances and dissatisfaction over not being involved (see also Chapters 12 and 13).

In general employees *do* want to be involved, they do want to start thinking, take responsibility, and be helpful. They are often not responsible and not helpful because they are not involved. The resistance of the Belling factory workers to change is an example (Example 1, Chapter 5). A factor in their resistance to the introduction of the Just in Time system was a concern over pay and how piecework would fit in to the new system, which rewarded group performance not individual performance. The concern of the workers was over the possible situation where someone in their group was not pulling their weight – they did not even have the worry about losing pay attending regular team meetings as at Steelcase. But this was the very reason why the workers' concern was not sorted out even two months later. There was no forum in place, no structure of team meetings, which would allow workers to air their concerns, be listened to by management, and be involved in the decision-making process. In short, there was no 'involvement' reward to counter (and deal with) the concern over pay. Pay remained a central concern, and management would not talk about it, they would not listen to the workers, and there was no related debate or dialogue.

Middle management opposition – lack of self-confidence, loss of power, etc

Managers and supervisors, unlike the majority of employees, will previously have had a certain amount of autonomy and control over people, and because of their background and training they are likely to have more entrenched hierarchical attitudes, and authoritarian, autocratic skills. Experience shows that they feel more threatened than the majority of employees by collaborative/participatory working practices. For example, it has been said concerning the organisational change at British Petroleum that: 'the majority of people will accept the benefits of changing', but 'a major task [will be] winning American managers over to the new culture' (*The Money Programme*, 20.5.90). This is because, as Gini Rogers, head of BP training points out:

> We are talking about individuals, men and women, that have been raised and rewarded for behaving in a certain way, and we are suddenly . . . saying 'throw that out, now you are supposed to do things differently' . . . So you don't immediately cast people as villains when they don't do it right the first time around (*The Money Programme*, 20.5.90).

Those people in middle management, supervisory and teaching positions have in fact been trained in the 'non-learning' hierarchical attitudes and skills referred to above. Teachers who might object to this should remember that, in the main, teacher training is more about how to *talk* rather than how to *listen*, and how to judge and assess others rather than how to judge and assess oneself – self-appraisal – despite all the rhetoric about listening, self-evaluation and caring. In general, however, most teachers are likely to have less deeply embedded hierarchical attitudes than certain middle managers and supervisors, as they strongly feel a lack of autonomy and reward. Nevertheless, teachers, as middle managers and supervisors, are going to need to be given time – and to give themselves time – to develop a collaborative approach. The need for time for people in these positions cannot be over stressed. For example, Gray, in the educational sector, estimates that:

> To build a fully functioning team of half a dozen people would take a good trainer working full time over a year to make significant impact with good will on the part of the members. With a history of competition, anarchy, suspicion, rivalry and simply not knowing one another it would take much longer (1989, p130).

People in positions of management, therefore, are likely to need more time and training than others to adapt to the new culture. People will not change over night, or even after training. Steelcase found this. The top manager there, aware that other organisations had experienced resistance from middle management and supervisors to a team approach, instigated training for them before their team programme started. Even then they found a number of managers still felt threatened, and needed to be given more time and help (*Business Matters*, 8.8.91).

Similarly, Geoffrey Murray, who has researched into the impact Japan has had on Britain, observes that problems with adopting Japanese working styles seem to occur more often at management level, and he reports:

> Dr Max Munday at the Cardiff Business School has found that most shop-floor personnel are perfectly happy to work for a Japanese company, but there have been problems at management level (1990, pp40, 41).

Murray maintains that the root of the unhappiness is the changed demands of the Japanese 'open style' of management (op cit p14). And it is not that the Japanese are being insensitive and high-handed about *imposing* their methods. On the contrary, as considered in Chapter 5, it is their general custom to avoid imposing on people. It has been considered generally above that the collaborative attitudes and skills of good leadership are also the skills of effective learning, which is why the Japanese are both good leaders and good learners. They are also the attitudes and skills of good teaching, and the Japanese's teaching approach – which does not involve putting people down but treating them as equals, both socially and intellectually (see also Chapter 13) – has been appreciated by Western employees. For example, a group of car-workers at a Japanese transplant in America, joined together to make this statement of appreciation to their Japanese managers and supervisors – in Japanese! – 'You Toyota people are wonderful . . . Thank you teacher.' (*Nippon*, 18.11.90). And the workers' strength of feeling and comradeship towards the Japanese managers was plain to see. Some Western managers also appreciate the Japanese approach, but many do not. For example, John Gragg, manager of the small family firm Qwik-Tool, Kentucky, has found the Japanese helpful in producing ideas to help his firm reduce costs. He says 'they didn't really tell you how to run the business, they came in and made suggestions.' Despite their politeness and sensitivity, however, some Western managers respond negatively, as John Gragg notes:

> . . . some people feel like they're offended by someone stepping in – we're very receptive to that (*The Midlands Report*, 25.10.90).

There are two related factors in the negative reaction of managers and supervisors to more open, collaborative approaches to employees and supplier–customer organisations. There is the fear of losing power and control, and the fear of being shown up. Trained as they are in hierarchical attitudes, such as distrust and disrespect for other people and their abilities, and arrogance about their own abilities, they see it as their right and responsibility to have autocratic control over others they believe to be less capable than themselves. For example, Chaney and Teel in their project attempting implementation of participatory management in a manufacturing company, referred to in Chapter 6 above, found that some supervisors were ineffective in their use of a participatory approach. They concluded after discussion with these supervisors that one of the major reasons was: 'They were convinced that they had sole responsibility for making decisions affecting the group' (1977, p229).

Managers' and supervisors' distrust in others also makes them fear that any 'loosening of the reins', by having a more open approach to subordinates, will bring about insolence, rebelliousness, subversion and general disorder. Part of this fear of losing power and control is the fear of having their own superiority challenged if their weaknesses are revealed. Concerning the fear of being shown up McGregor writes: '[Some managers] are fearful of having subordinates who are too competent – they worry about having their own weaknesses shown up' (1987, p201). Similarly, Chaney and Teel conclude that some 'ineffective' supervisors: '. . . felt insecure and were reluctant to reveal their own weaknesses by asking their employees for help in solving work-group problems' (1977, p229).

This is part of a non-collaborative, judgemental culture – just as people lack respect for, and trust in, others and their abilities causing them to be judgemental of others' weaknesses, so they fear being judged. This contrasts with Japanese managers, for example, who not only have the humility to ask someone for help, but also, linked with that, trust others will act with fairness and tolerance and so are not fearful of being adversely judged by admitting they do not know something (see also Chapters 6 and 8). It just is not seen as an inbuilt personal weakness – just part of the learning process – and respect is maintained for the individual. This is part of a collaborative, non-judgemental culture – just as people have respect for, and trust in, others and their abilities making them tolerant and non-judgemental of their 'weaknesses', so they do not fear being judged.

The contrast between the outcome of underlying hierarchical attitudes – ie the power-fear factor and related hierarchical skills – and the outcome of underlying collaborative attitudes – ie no power-fear factor and related collaborative skills, is well summed up in the observations of Chaney and Teel. They found that the 'successful' supervisors showed a *genuine* interest in employee ideas and feelings, they encouraged an *open*, supportive atmosphere, they *listened* attentively to employees without making snap judgements. The outcome of these collaborative skills was that they openly acted to implement employees' suggestions giving feedback, and brought about significant performance and productivity gains in the employee group. In contrast, most of the 'unsuccessful' supervisors showed *insincerity* and an *inability to listen* to employees: they 'went through the motions of asking for employee comments and suggestions but actually did not pay much attention to them'. The outcome of these hierarchical skills was a cynicism and lack of cooperativeness on the part of the employees, who quickly saw that they were part of an artificial exercise and 'typically offered only superficial or negative comments' (1977, p229; see below).

Managers and supervisors should realise that developing a collaborative approach with employees will not so much bring about a loss of power and control, but a gain in motivation, loyalty and commitment from people. The 'power' they have under a more authoritarian approach is limited in that people under them are unlikely to be working to their full potential. They are, in fact, more likely to be working against the manager or supervisor in certain ways (see Chapter 2). As McGregor points out: 'Antagonism between line and staff will prevent the kind of collaboration that is essential for achieving organizational objectives' (1987, p150).

As considered above, many middle managers and supervisors are not going to realise this quickly, as it will need a change in their underlying interpersonal attitudes – attitudes about themselves and others – which are often deeply embedded. To aid the process, there are three main things a top manager needs to do.

1. Ensure he or she has regular informal team meetings with senior and middle management. This will serve two purposes. Firstly it will set an example. Genuinely respecting and listening to middle managers' and supervisors' ideas would begin to encourage them, in turn, to respect and listen to each other's and employees' ideas, as well as generating enthusiasm and motivation. Secondly, it would enable middle managers and supervisors openly to discuss their concerns and air anxieties, and to tackle them constructively without fear of judgement or reprisal. This would begin to lessen and remove such fears. An important part of this would be for top managers to reassure middle managers and supervisors directly that a team approach does not make them redundant – it just requires their role to change to one of employee coach and mentor, and for them to have a greater concern with overall planning than they had previously.
2. Provide a training programme for middle managers and supervisors which centres on developing collaborative interpersonal attitudes and skills. This goes hand in hand with (1) (see Part III).
3. Give definite recognition/reward to those middle managers and supervisors who move away from an autocratic approach to employees and concern only for their own rewards and promotion, and instead begin to involve collaboratively, listen to and cultivate employees (see also Part III, Chapter 15).

Summary – Collaborative top management and the caring culture

Despite the inevitable resistances that a top manager will meet in developing a caring organisational culture, he or she has the means to surmount any problems. In particular, he or she can give people time, be flexible, allow mistakes, reward collaborative behaviour, and instigate a collaborative team structure that involves *all* employees in the decision-making process; and he or she can invest in collaborative leadership-team training, particularly for managers and supervisors. These moves are *necessary* for the well-being and survival of all organisations in these times of increasing competition and decreasing skills and resources, and they will pay off. A plant manager at Steelcase, where they are making similar moves to a team approach, realises what all top managers should: 'it's the *only* way we're going to survive in the future'. A member of the BP 'Andrew' team makes a point that is true for most organisations in the West at the beginning of the 1990s, namely, if they want to be the most successful oil company in the nineties, '. . . it is unlikely that the previous organisation, the previous structure, the previous culture, would actually achieve that' (*The Money Programme*, 20.5.90).

8

The collaborative culture – caring for the employee

Employee involvement, recognition and reward

The first two points in Chapter 7, p116, are in fact linked. Being respected, and therefore listened to and encouraged by management to participate in decisions is probably the most effective way to recognise and reward, and therefore motivate, employees, eg as at the Nissan car plant in Sunderland:

> Anyone coming up with an idea is given the opportunity and the facilities to work that idea through from conception to maturity and for larger projects, Kaizen teams are set up to work together on finding solutions (Nissan, 1985, 'Quality', p4).

An explanation for this is provided by writers such as Blumberg and McGregor, who say respectively:

> Participation . . . [gratifies] basic human needs for respect, appreciation, responsibility, and autonomy. (1968, p130)

> Commitment to objectives is a function of the rewards associated with their achievement. The most significant of such rewards [is] the satisfaction of ego and self-actualization needs . . . [The worker] achieves recognition and other important social and ego satisfactions from utilization of his . . . know-how and ingenuity. (1987, pp47–48, p114)

Participation, responsibility and autonomy are their own reward. The testimony of a worker at Steelcase (referred to p118) that, at a certain level, being listened to and involved by management is a greater reward than monetary reward, is an instance of this. Another example is provided by a young design worker at Nissan in Japan. She designed a small vehicle suitable for small businesses, and although management did not 'quite grasp' why she had produced such a design, they said 'Go ahead, give it a try.' This way of working occurred because, as the president of Nissan explained with humility, he felt that the younger designers would know best what type of car is in demand from their generation. The fact that management respected and trusted her abilities in this way and her car went into production, greatly rewarded and motivated the young designer. She says she received:

> Nothing at all. Nothing, no *money*. But I get a second chance, and a third chance, to make very creative vehicle. This is very important for me to make car. This is very happy for me to make new car (sic) *(The Money Programme,* 6.1.91).

Similarly, in the same company, production workers are willing to sacrifice half their lunch break to get together to sort out problems, indicating the extent to which they are motivated by being consulted and involved by management (see also pp138, 261).

Recognition and reward in the form of perks and benefits for employee performance have a limited effect on motivation, and Iain Arthur, (then) a director of the KLP Group rightly points out: 'Offering extra cash is probably the worst possible form of motivation . . . if regularly achieved [it will] not be perceived as an award for extra effort' *(Money Box,* 19.5.90). More effective recognition in this area, which was found in a number of successful organisations in the USA, is given by:

> . . . hidden benefits such as helping people to share with colleagues, or giving appropriate publicity for unusual efforts . . . [or] giving people an opportunity to talk about what they were doing to a wider audience (conference, informal network of peers from profession or other companies ['networking'], etc) (Beck, 1989, pp24, 27).

Or the benefits might be overt, such as the incentive scheme operated by the Victoria Wine Company *(Money Box* 19.5.91), which awards points to employees that can be saved up in exchange for items from a catalogue, such as televisions or garden chairs. But it is important to take heed of the view voiced by Iain Arthur, that any incentive scheme should have no losers – '*everybody* must win' (op cit). Concerning this point, certain oil rig workers at British Petroleum, which in 1990 began a programme of freeing people's decision making throughout the organisation, have voted against having rewards for *individual* performance, as they believe this 'conflicts with the idea of having a good team' (*The Money Programme*, 20.5.90). Their wish for the *team* to be recognised for performance represents the eminent good sense of the BP work people, and it is being taken account of by management.

Although the first three points in the previous chapter (p116) serve to indicate to employees that the employer cares for them – and therefore will lead to increased motivation – they do not necessarily do so to the same extent. Only those managers with the collaborative interpersonal attitudes and skills referred to, will be willing and able to commit themselves fully to caring for the employee by collaboratively involving the employee, investing in employee training and R&D (see Chapters 11 and 12), and endeavouring to provide job security – which together are the most effective ways for recognising and rewarding, and therefore increasing employee motivation, commitment and loyalty. Reward in the form of money and perks only, is not so effective, and is just the icing on the cake when the above factors are in operation.

Caring for the employee – performance appraisal and quality

Self-team appraisal vs traditional performance appraisal

The collaborative skill of self-appraisal, and its concomitant team-appraisal, is an essential characteristic of collaboratively run organisations (see Figure 4.1, and Part III, Chapter 15). It is an integral part of the motivating *participatory* process, whereby employees are able to take responsibility for appraising their own contribution to organisational objectives, and to planning their future goals. And it is through this process that personal growth and organisational objectives become welded together.

Self-team appraisal is incompatible with the traditional semi-annual or annual performance appraisal, as the latter has been used *judgementally* as a way of enforcing management control and discipline. In order to direct people to work towards organisational objectives, it has been thought necessary for management to 'tell [people] what to do, judge how well they have done, and reward or punish them accordingly' (McGregor, 1987, p77). Punishment, for example, might be in the form of affecting pay and conditions of service, or even sacking; reward may be in the form of improving pay and conditions of service, or promotion.

The evidence shows, however, that performance appraisal has been counter-productive in bringing about personal and organisational growth (eg McGregor, 1987, p77ff; Deming, 1986, p101ff). This is not surprising given the strong judgemental element within such appraisal, which evokes responses of defensiveness, secretiveness, dejection, and fear of reprisal in the employee. A factor within the judgemental nature of appraisal is the tendency to allocate *personal* blame to individual employees without a rational consideration of other relevant factors within the work environment that might be affecting their performance (Deming, 1986, p109). Quite understandably, therefore, the response of an employee to a negative appraisal will be one of cynicism as well as fear, believing that the assessment if *unfair*.

With the increasing rhetoric on 'people-centred' approaches, some managements may try to get around the negative response employees have to appraisal by including a 'self-evaluative', 'self-appraisal' element. But using this as a gimmick to try to appease employees' defensiveness, etc is likely to be counter-productive (cf McGregor, 1987, p88; see also Chapter 4 above). Employees within a hierarchical organisation will know full well that it is not meant genuinely, but merely as a ploy to manipulate them. It is an obvious example of the danger of making piecemeal additions of aspects of a collaborative structure to a mainly hierarchical organisation, as referred to in Chapter 6.

As long as employees can be penalised for 'failings', it is unrealistic to expect them to undergo effective self-team appraisal, which would require them *openly* and *honestly* to 'bare their souls' and admit to their concerns, failings and mistakes. Within most organisations employees, quite legitimately, cannot *trust* management to respond positively, with non-judgemental, non-punitive tolerance and constructive rationality. Erskine also questions the legitimacy of the Department of Education and Science's proposal for self-evaluation applied collectively in a 'whole-school' approach. Her reason is: 'Such arrangements may in human terms foster an atmosphere of serious competition between colleagues, which will conflict with openly stated aims for cooperation among them' (1990, p20). However, she expects and seems to accept, without any concern for competition and conflict, the coming of a performance appraisal procedure for teachers that will include 'the holding of interviews between appraisers and teachers' and 'the need for written reports to serve *inter alia* as information for promotion purposes' (op cit, p22). Also, at the top of her list of important themes to be established in staff appraisal systems is 'support for teachers' (op cit, p22). It is highly doubtful, however, whether an appraisal procedure that is used as a basis for evaluation judgements for promotion (and possibly for evaluation of accountability and discipline), could ever be seen as truly 'supportive' by the employee. In this context Doug McAvoy, General Secretary of the National Union of Teachers, warns: 'What we're totally opposed to is merit pay, or performance related pay, where appraisal becomes the trigger to a teacher getting more money. That would be divisive.' (*BBC News*, 10.12.90). Similarly, Deming talks about the 'devastating' effect of reward based on annual performance appraisal or merit rating: 'It nourishes short-term performance, annihilates long-term planning, builds fear, demolishes teamwork, nourishes rivalry and politics' (1986, p102).

Nothing could be worse for the employee and the organisation. However, concerning the government's proposal to bring in a system of teacher appraisal – which the majority of teachers are said to welcome – the Education Secretary, Kenneth Clarke, has made the following reassuring statement:

> The aim is not to lead to disciplinary procedures or anything of that kind . . . The aim is to comment favourably or unfavourably on aspects of a teacher's performance, and help that teacher to bring his or her performance up. (*Channel 4 News*, 10.12.90)

If the system were used *purely* to identify problem areas, and then to follow these up constructively to remedy them in the form of development/training provision and support for teachers, then it would have value for motivating and improving quality of performance. However, given the generally hierarchical nature of educational organisations, where the prevailing attitudes of management and the organisational structure incline towards a judgemental system of competitive reward and punishment, it is unlikely to be used purely for remedial/development purposes. In this context the links made in the following statement by Kenneth Clarke are ominous:

> Disciplinary procedures will remain separate but may draw on appraisal records. In advising governing bodies on the exercise of their responsibilities for remuneration head teachers will be able to

draw on relevant information from appraisal, along with other factors. (DES, 389, 1990)

Individual rivalry vs collaborative growth

The truth is that within hierarchical organisational structures, *any* system of performance appraisal (apart from self-appraisal) – and not just those advocating 'self-colleague' appraisal as Erskine maintains – is going to produce conflict, distrust, and competition between colleagues, and distrust, cynicism and fear between employee and manager. A truly open, honest, objective and rational appraisal of concerns, 'failings' and 'weaknesses' – required on the part of employees and managers for *effective* staff development – is unlikely as long as the culture remains judgemental, the main reward achievable by employees is individual and financial, rather than through creative collaborative involvement (see earlier in this chapter), and there is a possibility of the employee 'losing out' financially and in the promotion stakes. The fear that employees have about revealing shortcomings, will only be removed by removing the fear or reprisal, and an essential requirement in achieving this would be for organisational structures to become more 'horizontal', with very few tiers of the hierarchy (Chapter 6, p79, point 1), where people work in 'equal' teams throughout an organisation (point 2). This would enable employees to concentrate on work issues, where: 'The focus is not on competing for awards but on improving the effectiveness of the enterprise' (McGregor, 1987, p115).

This positive effect of a genuine team approach was appreciated by a member of a group of middle and senior managers seconded from their firms to work as advisors for work-experience placements for school children under the Education and Enterprise Initiative in Scotland (featured in *Walk the Talk*, 18.5.91). Charles Handy points out how this particular person found the team spirit enhanced because the team members were not competing with each other, and the person himself comments:

It's strong because we're not part of a corporation where there's competition . . . whereas in normal circumstances your peers would normally be in competition for promotion, etc., that pressure is off you . . . we're not looking at each other's job as being a potential next promotion, and that's probably the greatest strong point of secondment, the pressures of competition have been lifted.

A team structure, where there is non-judgemental, mutual support, is essential for genuine and effective open self-team appraisal, which, in turn, is essential for effective personal and organisational development, and improvement in quality. There is need, therefore, to replace the present system where individuals mainly work for their own personal advancement, not for the development of others and the organisation as a whole. And, as considered in Chapters 6 and 7, in order to achieve a genuine team culture the very top manager will need to develop collaborative attitudes and skills. The fact that in most organisations each individual is primarily concerned with their own advancement, reflects hierarchical organisational cultures that are the outcome of hierarchical attitudes and skills in top managers, who are primarily concerned with their own short-term advancement, at the expense of developing their employees' and organisation's potential (see Chapter 11, p180). The goals of non-collaborative top management, therefore, directly conflict with employee and organisational development; a true *common* purpose – arrived at collaboratively, incorporating the needs and views of employees – where everyone can gain, is impossible; conflict, rivalry and employee resistance to management is inbuilt; and everyone is the loser (including top management) in the long term (see also Chapter 12, p228).

Therefore, in order to achieve effective self-team appraisal, learning and development, staff development needs to be separated from staff promotion, and this requires the kind of collaborative organisational structure outlined in Chapter 6. However, the call by a local education authority inspector for improving 'policies for promotion and the concomitant issue of staff development and training' (Jones, 1990, p35), is generally representative of how closely linked the two are in the minds of people in both education and industry, and indicates the extent to which attitudes will need to change in future.

Open, less fearful, learning cultures

The link between fear and personal-organisational performance and development can be further illustrated. According to Deming, fear governs almost everybody in the workplace (1986, p59ff). In fact, fear begins early in the 'learning' workplace, ie school. Most of us will remember how we would regularly sit and keep quiet rather than admit to the teacher a misunderstanding we had or a mistake we had made. Because of the judgemental culture in schools, as in society generally, we there learn to be *ashamed* of not understanding something or making a mistake. It is judgementally perceived as a fault or a weakness *inbuilt within the person*. So we learn to be less open and more dishonest about it than if it were perceived less personally.

For the same reason people fear new knowledge, as they believe it might reveal them as being personally inadequate (cf Deming, 1986, p60). And this, in turn inhibits their ability to question their existing beliefs and practices, and to search honestly for new and better ways of doing things. Again, because of the fear of reprisal, there is a fear of questioning existing organisational beliefs and practices, and expressing an opinion to management that does not fit in with existing views. So, generally, in most organisations people are afraid to question, to be open to new ideas, to express an opposing opinion, and to admit their shortcomings, mistakes, etc – the basis for genuine self-appraisal – in turn the basis for effective *learning* and *development* (see also Chapters 6 and 7).

Removing this fear would require a shift in the underlying attitudes of management to more collaborative ones of respect, trust, humility and honesty, etc, which would enable them to respond more openly, more tolerantly, more rationally, and less judgementally, to employees. It would also mean that management itself would be capable of self-appraisal and be able to admit openly to their mistakes and take critical feedback from employees (see also Chapter 15). There would, therefore, be no fear on either side – matters would not be personalised. Instead mistakes, shortcomings, different viewpoints, etc would be perceived objectively and rationally as learning opportunities. It is obvious to see, therefore, how more open, less fearful, collaborative cultures facilitate personal learning and growth, which in turn is the basis for improved quality of performance and general organisational development and well-being. In this context, Stenning, referring to the low trust that has become a feature of the education system in recent years, maintains: 'In the absence of high trust, improved performance is unlikely to be attained and certainly not sustained' (1989, p230). Deming makes essentially the same point: 'A common denominator of fear in any form, anywhere, is loss from impaired performance and padded figures' (1986, p59).

Quality through people not departments, traditional appraisal, quality control circles, BS 5750, external consultants etc

Unlike the impaired performance and quality of non-collaborative 'non-learning' cultures, employee performance and quality is continuously enhanced in more collaborative cultures, such as exists in the UK Nissan motor manufacturing company. Here there is no in-process quality control, no special quality controllers, but instead quality is the responsibility of 'every single person at the plant, from the telephone receptionists to the employees working on the line and the administrative staff, including the managing director' (Nissan, 1985, 'Quality').

Deming is one who advocates the removal of quality control departments on the basis that they remove the job of quality from the people who are able to contribute most to quality, namely, all employees including management (1986, p133). So often, he says, Western management see the use of such things as quality-control circles as 'a lazy way out' of the quality issue, and 'get rid of the job' by appointing quality facilitators. But without the *active* involvement and support of management for decisions taken, quality control circles will be ineffective and disintegrate. The same applies to the use of such techniques as the JIT inventory system (Chapter 5) and the British Standard for quality in management systems (BS 5750). In themselves, they will not improve quality and customer care unless there is a culture shift where management and employees become *equally* involved. Similarly, the use of external consultants will be a costly, relatively ineffective exercise in the long-term, unless it helps to initiate employee involvement. For instance, the plant manager at the Honda factory in Swindon says that they never bring in external management consultants. And the radical re-structuring which has taken place at the Engineering and Heating Systems Division of Lucas Aerospace without the use of consultants, illustrates the same philosophy (see also Example, Chapter 9, p152). This philosophy is simply expressed by the 'culture change' manager at Lucas, Allan Brown:

> It's quite traditional in many companies for consultants to be brought
> in to re-design the manufacturing and lay-out of the factory. But of

course the best people to do that are the people involved in the day to day running of the business (*State of Training*, 29.9.91).

The move over recent years to employ consultants in both the educational and health sectors, based on traditional industrial practices, is therefore misguided, and fails to recognise the message of more progressive practices, namely, quality and efficiency rests first and foremost on every employee. In the words of Deming, to achieve successful improvement in quality and productivity it 'must be a learning process, year by year, top management leading the whole company' (op cit, p137).

And of course the main theme of this book is that such a learning process should centre on the development of collaborative interpersonal attitudes and skills. Management need to act collaboratively – *genuinely* involving all employees, giving them *real* responsibility, acting on their decisions, thereby making sure 'everybody is fully aware that they have a valuable and significant contribution to make' (Nissan, op cit). It is the consequent motivation produced in employees that is the necessary ingredient for achieving efficiency, innovation and high quality. These are the people on whom quality depends; these are the people on whom effective and innovative ideas depend. Successful organisations, and in particular many Japanese organisations, have realised this key ingredient for success. If people are given real responsibility, they will be (self-) motivated to feel and act responsibly. For example, a Nissan car worker at the Sunderland plant is reported to arrive 45 minutes early for his shift every morning, and he talks about how he likes his work, how he closely identifies with the company, how, by everybody being involved, 'we are always seeking to improve things that we do, and the way we do it' (*Newsnight*, 29.10.91; see also p258). Similarly, a line worker at the successful Japanese Sony plant in South Wales, comments:

> You are responsible for your work, you know. If you do it wrong you've let your team down . . . when we're down on the board or whatever . . . we all feel sort of . . . *we shame ourselves more or less.* That's the way they make you feel, you're *part* of them aren't you [turning to a colleague] really, basically (*Business Matters*, 6.6.91).

And of course the way 'they make you feel' responsible, is not through a *judgemental* performance appraisal process and reprisal, as with non-collaborative cultures, but through a process of *non-*

judgemental involvement that respects and trusts people, gives responsibility, and develops self-esteem, self-motivation and self-appraisal. In short, by being part of a community and being empowered and recognised by that community, not by being alienated, imposed on, judged and sometimes ostracised by it.

One way the Nissan UK plant achieves quality through people is by the use of Help Lamps.

> A wire running the length of the production line can be pulled at any time by an operator who has a 'Quality Concern'. This activates a siren and a flashing light and draws the attention of a supervisor who can investigate the area of concern . . . The use of the lamps is positively encouraged . . . (Nissan, 1985, 'Quality', p1).

Who, in most organisations, would draw attention to themselves with a siren and a flashing light when something is amiss? It works at Nissan because people are not fearful of receiving a judgemental and censorious response from the supervisors. As considered in Chapter 6, the openness the Japanese showed in not knowing or understanding something when they were trying to learn from the West after the Second World War, indicates both their humility and lack of fear of being *personally* judged over such matters. Saying you don't understand something and admitting you have made a mistake is quite obviously seen by them as part of the learning process. In fact, the shame for them would be to be dishonest and not open about it, an attitude that has rubbed off on a British inspection supervisor in the Japanese company Komatsu, in Newcastle: 'Mistakes will always happen, the mistake is to hide the mistake' (*Business Matters*, 27.9.90).

Some example material from industry and education

The following material from education and industry exemplifies some of the above points, and also further illustrates the difference between hierarchical and collaborative cultures.

Hellawell interviewed a group of 24 primary school headteachers concerning their perceptions of who should appraise them (Hellawell, 1990). A significant finding for the theme of this book is that two or three of the headteachers gave 'much praise' to pilot 'collaborative ventures' relating to their appraisal, which involved a team of appraisers and headteacher self-appraisal (op cit, p9). In general, however, the relationship between headteachers and advisors/inspectors was reported to be 'problematic'. There was general opposition by the headteachers to appraisal by a single person or category, such as an LEA officer, particularly when the notion of that person being a 'boss' or 'line manager' was introduced into the interview. Hellawell speculates that this is because the word 'boss' made the headteachers aware of the underlying issues: 'In our culture the word "boss" is not a neutral one as it carries with it overtones of hierarchy with which many "professionals" are uncomfortable' (op cit, p10).

Are the headteachers similarly aware of these issues in the case of teacher appraisal, one wonders, where – in the case of primary schools – it is 'taken for granted by all concerned that the headteacher will normally appraise the staff' (op cit, p3)? It seems that some heads do at least draw a parallel in the related area of control over decision making, where they acknowledge that their relationship with LEAs and their officers resembles the teachers' relationship with them. Hellawell summarises that perhaps all '. . . professionals would quite like those in authority over them to have responsibility without power' (op cit, p12) where by 'responsibility' he means 'authoritative support and protection'. It is beyond the scope of this book to consider in detail aspects of power, but some general comments might be useful. For example, Sara Parkin of the Green Party has remarked that one cannot be free of power relations as they will occur in any social group, even in the family, but it should be realised that: 'Power in itself is not bad – it depends on how it is used. Some people would not abuse it' (Schumacher, 1990). Ian Wetherburn, the inspection supervisor at the Japanese-owned Komatsu factory in Newcastle makes the same point: 'There is a sense of power, there, obviously – it's how you treat that sense of power' (*Business Matters*, 27.9.90). His colleague, Alan Scott, production welding supervisor, goes further:

> I suppose you could actually misinterpret the job that you've got, and I suppose in a way you could go out and do things that you wouldn't normally be able to do. I tend not to think of it that way, I don't tend to think of it as power. I tend to think of it as a job, and you know, I try to do it to the best of my ability. (*Business Matters*, 27.9.90)

Quite clearly for him power is not linked with being a dominating and judgemental taskmaster. It is not surprising, therefore, that a worker in his team comments: 'Well, he looks after his men, he's always got time for you.' Mostly, however, the general unequal distribution of power within hierarchical institutions is manifested in judgemental control, with the fear of reprisal, etc, referred to above.

Concerning the distribution of power, White refers to a *participatory* democracy, where there is 'equality in the exercise, or control, of power' (1983, p13) – an equal *sharing* of power – that is based on the underlying moral principle of the equality of all normal human beings as choosers (p14). In a collaborative organisational culture 'power' can be said to be shared in that people are equally involved in the decision-making processes that affect them. It is in this equal involvement in what goes on that people will have autonomy – a control over what they are doing as a basis for motivation and quality.

Returning to the opposition of headteachers to having a 'boss' observed by Hellawell, he noted that two of the heads saw their own conscience as their 'boss'. He compared this with the following statement by Etzioni, which, indirectly, points to the need for collaborative organisational cultures:

> Students of the professions have pointed out that the autonomy granted to professionals who are basically responsible to their consciences ... is necessary for effective professional work. Only if immune from ordinary social pressures and free to innovate, to experiment, to take risks without the usual social repercussions of failure, can a professional carry out his work effectively. (in Hellawell, 1990, p12)

'The usual social repercussions of failure' no doubt refers to the judgemental/reprisal aspect of hierarchical cultures, and to the extent that this interferes with a person's ability to experiment, to take risks and to innovate, which directly corresponds to the view represented in this book. But there are two aspects which do not appear to correspond* but rather oppose this view.

Firstly, if it applies only to 'professionals', the question arises: how are people who are not classed as 'professionals' – schoolchildren, shop-floor employees, schoolteachers – supposed to experiment, take risks and innovate? The view represented in this

---

* To be definite about this would require an analysis of Etzioni's book. That is beyond the scope of this book, and unnecessary for the general point being made.

work is that it is inconsistent to draw a line between people – *every-one*, from schoolchild to chief executive needs a climate of rational tolerance in order to grow. Secondly, if by 'immune from ordinary social pressures' is meant operating independently of negative social feedback, then again, the statement opposes the view being put forward here. Certainly, people should not be punished for failure – they need to be able to learn from failure – but they need social feedback, at least customer feedback, in order to completely identify 'failure' or problems. Manufacturers need feedback from their customers; doctors need feedback from their patients; teachers need feedback from pupils and parents. Interpersonal attitudes will need to change before this occurs as a matter of course, and customers' views are seen as other than irrelevant interference, or a pretext for punishment and reprisal. The medical profession, for example, is notorious for its inability to listen to the patient (see eg Jones, 1988; *Medicine Now*, 13.3.91); and this prompts a possible definition of a professional':

> Someone who can operate with complete autonomy from their customers and (except in extreme circumstances) from their fellow professionals.

This is only meant as a half-serious response to the difficulties people have had in defining the term 'professional' (Hellawell, 1990, p12ff). The concern over finding valid criteria to identify a 'professional' from a 'non-professional', reflects the general preoccupation with hierarchy and differentials between people. However, as Hellawell points out, the situation is changing, even for doctors, as increasingly 'the professional is becoming more open to public scrutiny' (op cit, p14). But the situation concerning the medical audit for general practitioners – assessment of their quality of performance – contrasts with the situation concerning teacher assessment, and underlines the cause for concern. *Medicine Now* (13.3.91) refers to research undertaken in Holland that used fake patients to assess doctors' performance, described by Dr Robin Hull of Birmingham University as 'audit by consumer'. He believes that this is a good thing, assessing both the medical ability and, very importantly, the caring qualities of the doctor. He acknowledges, however, that it would probably not be acceptable to make such audit mandatory, as it could be 'very threatening indeed' to some doctors. Dr John Chisholm, a practising GP, would like all doctors in the future to be involved in a process of audit, but he is very definite about what this audit should entail:

> We very much see the audit of a doctor's performance as something that's helpful to the doctor in an educational way, rather than being something that is involved with *managing* the doctor, or even *punishing* the doctor. It's a way of helping the doctor to improve care.

I am sure all teachers would echo his belief in the area of education, that audit should be an integral part of 'how any caring professional should be working'. Chisholm points out that it is very important that doctors *trust* the confidentiality of the process, and *trust* the validity of the process. This, he considers, will be achieved by audit being voluntary, so that initially it 'might be adopted by the more pioneering and *willing* GPs' and, if they 'felt happy, then more and more GPs would be willing to participate'. Happiness, trust, absence of management, absence of punishment, etc – important ingredients for constructive 'educational' appraisal for doctors, teachers and industrial workers alike. But this manner of introducing appraisal is a far cry from the proposed mandatory approach in the educational system, and the management driven performance appraisal prevalent in industry.

Summary – Caring for the employee, appraisal and quality

People should not be afraid to express ideas, to ask questions, to admit mistakes, etc – the basis for effective self-appraisal, motivation, and therefore learning – in turn the basis for quality and innovation. They are afraid because of the organisational cultures they are part of. There is legitimate concern over scrutiny in the kind of judgemental, hierarchical cultures that prevail, but the general lack of constructive 'scrutiny', accountability and customer and employee input at the 'professional' level is of equal concern. The dilemma will only be resolved by developing more collaborative organisational cultures. In such cultures, performance appraisal would not be a process of judgement and punishment by 'superiors', colleagues and customers, but one where all these people work together cooperatively and constructively, through self-team appraisal, towards personal and organisational empowerment and growth. In Deming's words, there is need to abolish the annual performance review and substitute leadership, where:

A leader, instead of being a judge, will be a *colleague*, counselling and leading his people on a day-to-day basis, *learning from them and with them* (1986, p117; my emphasis).

Caring for the employee and the non-traditional employee

With demographic changes resulting in the reduction in the number of school leavers, both industry and education will in the 1990s have to turn to, and cater for, the non-traditional worker and student. These will include women returners, older people and the long-term unemployed (eg CBI, 1989, p29ff; White Paper, 1988, pp5–9). Therefore, the need for organisations to adopt a more flexible, supportive and caring collaborative approach, which has always been necessary to improve people's performance in school, college and work, becomes even more pressing if the needs of the non-traditional worker and student are to be met. Consequently, the issues relating to women in the workplace, for example, are bringing to light the changes that are generally needed to improve work practices.

The particular issue of women in the workplace came to the fore-front in 1990 because of the general skills shortage and the fact that over the next three years it was predicted there would be 20 per cent fewer school leavers available; and it was reported that British industry already 'desperately' needed mothers back at work*. Concerning the situation, the CBI refer to the prediction that women will provide 90 per cent of the work-force increase over the next decade (CBI, 1989, p30). Rod Thomas of the CBI maintains that the main things employers can do is to provide flexible, part-time working hours, but he acknowledges that adequate childcare facilities will also need to be available. However, it has been reported that there are only 160 workplace nurseries available nationally, and only 30,000 council nursery places nationally for full-time day care. This contrasts badly with, for example, France, where affordable day care is provided for more than 80 per cent of children between the ages of three and six years. But the lack of care in Britain does not stem

---

* The quotations and factual information for the ensuing paragraph are taken from *Check Out*, 6.11.90, unless otherwise stated. The interpretations are this author's.

from top managers only, but also government. In contrast, childcare facilities in France are jointly funded by employers, government and parents. Peter Moss, coordinator of the European Childcare Network believes:

> The future lies in partnership, I think, with a contribution from employers, parents contributing something according to their income and their ability to pay, and also a substantial, very substantial, growth of public spending . . .

The importance of a collaborative partnership between organisations and government is considered in Chapters 11, 12 and 13 below. It is rightly feared from the fact that Britain lags far behind most of Europe in childcare facilities and providing company (and government) support for working mothers, that the situation:

> . . . is not only frustrating many young mothers who want to lead a productive working life, but, as the competitive new Europe of the 90s draws on, it may also be handicapping British children and British industry in the bargain.

A collaborative culture would do more than just provide childcare support. Flexibility in work hours and work practices is inherent in such a culture, and, as Kanter points out, it would mean that women with families could operate without:

> the bosses looking over their shoulders every minute. They could come in a little later, or leave a little earlier, as long as they are getting the work done, as long as they're taking it home with them, as long as they are working longer hours sometimes (*Business Matters*, 21.6.90).

As is generally being considered in this book, such a flexible, collaborative team environment is needed for improved efficiency and effectiveness for *all* employees, and not just women employees (Chapter 6, p79); and Kanter also points to the broader need to create organisational flexibility for attracting 'the best and most qualified workers', which she maintains organisations will be competing for in the 1990s. The link between the needs of non-traditional workers and all workers comes out of a consideration of the following two examples, which were featured in *Public Eye* (25.1.91). The second example also illustrates the point made in Chapter 6, that attempts to make piecemeal changes to hierarchical organisations by introducing certain aspects of a collaborative structure in isolation, are likely to have limited value and might even back-fire.

Caring for the traditional and non-traditional employee – Example 1

British Airways are beginning to adopt working patterns and provide nursery facilities to make it possible for women to work in traditionally male-dominated areas. Deputy Chairman Sir Colin Marshall hopes to broaden the process to *all* departments, making available: nursery facilities, contracts for flexible working time, job sharing, job combinations and 'career breaks'. But the value of these kinds of 'caring' facilities is now being increasingly recognised for the effectiveness of the traditional employee. For example, career breaks can provide an opportunity to exercise creativity, self-reflection, and general personal development, as a basis for increasing initiative back in the workplace. The National Westminster Bank, for instance, are trying to encourage more men to think more broadly on this issue (see, eg, *In Business*, 18.9.91). And flexibility in working hours, combined with a greater responsibility and autonomy of employees – an integral part of a team approach leading to increased motivation, quality and innovation (Chapter 6) – is increasingly being recognised as a way of improving customer care (see Chapter 9).

In this context of the greater effectiveness of a caring culture, Anita Roddick recalls how all the early Body Shop franchisees were women, which pleased her: 'I could see . . . that women were better at dealing with people, caring and being passionate about what they were doing' (Roddick, 1991). Men, she saw were good at 'the science' of business, 'at talking about economic theory and profit and loss figures'. She acknowledges that, of course, some women are good at that too. It might also be acknowledged that some women are poor at 'dealing with people', etc, and some men are good at it. But generally 'caring' is socially and culturally a feminine characteristic. In the same vein, Rhiannon Chapman, director of the Industrial Society, points out that there are already examples of organisations led by women which 'feel and behave structurally and organisationally different' from organisations led by men; and in line with the point being made here, she maintains that these organisations will not only benefit women, but also 'It will give men a better deal – there's no question about that at all' (*In Business*, 18.9.91).

Caring organisational cultures, therefore, give both the traditional and non-traditional employee 'a better deal', and they thereby achieve the best in human potential in the ways considered above.

And it is the reason why top men, as well as top women, need to develop the core collaborative attitudes and skills.

The following comment by Maralyn Fulker, a Planning Control Superintendent, shows that British Airways have some way further to go along the road to a collaborative culture and the kind of autonomy referred to by Kanter above:

> I'd like to see them looking more at the prospects of working from home . . . I'd like them to look at more flexible working hours . . . I think maybe if I wanted to rise higher up within the company, you might have to put more hours in . . . you might find that . . . a meeting is called and you've got to go to it – what do you do if you've got a child to pick up from the nursery?

Caring for the traditional and non-traditional employee – Example 2

An organisation that has gone further than just providing more flexible working patterns and crèches, is Gloucestershire County Council. They believe that such measures will not redress the imbalance in numbers of women in the workplace quickly enough. Consequently, they have introduced a system of targeting – setting targets of numbers of women to be recruited over a certain time period, and financially rewarding individual personnel officers/ heads of departments if their departments achieve the set targets (cf Chapter 6, p79, point 5). Their view is that this public commitment to equal opportunities will bring about a quicker change in attitudes and behaviour in the workplace.

Targeting, however, is generally seen to be controversial, and the *Public Eye* survey of a hundred major companies produced a response which, in the main, varied from unawareness to opposition. The reasons given against targeting are revealing. Firstly, there is the reason that people might not be fairly recruited to a job on the basis of merit and ability. Always a possibility in *all* appointments, the fact that it causes concern in this context suggests that there is an underlying belief that the pool of able women is smaller than the pool of able men. But it seems that the concern over recruitment is not as great as when targeting is used in the area of promotion, as reporter Jenny Cuffe points out, 'It's the fear that targeting would lead to promotions for reasons other than merit that makes it such a controversial measure.' Some firms, such as British Airways, have

CARING FOR THE EMPLOYEE • 145

so far rejected the use of targeting because top managers there are concerned that there might be a possible 'backlash' from men. When one reads between the lines of the reasons given, however, it seems that they believe that a male backlash might occur not so much because of their concerns relating to merit (although that is a factor), but because of an underlying irrational personal rivalry. This, for example, is recognised by Mohan Yogendran, the then Equal Opportunities Officer at Gloucester, 'There's always a likelihood of a backlash, because the issues we are talking about are ones that hit at the heart, not just at the head.' All that they are trying to achieve through targeting, he maintains, is to avoid unfair recruitment and promotion and 'to make sure that people are promoted, selected, recruited, and maybe even sacked, on merit'. He and others believe that the present situation, where women are under-represented at the top, indicates that there is an invisible 'glass ceiling' that unfairly prevents women with merit and ability from being promoted. But presenter Peter Taylor in his summing up makes the pertinent point that attempts at targeting are 'Controversial because they not only imply a change of *attitude* on the part of men, but a readiness to *step aside*' (my emphasis).

Summary – Caring for the employee and the non-traditional employee

As long as there are many levels in an organisation, hierarchical attitudes will prevail. As long as the structure requires one person to lose while another gains, whether man or woman, there will be competition rather than collaboration in the workplace. It is the inbuilt rivalry between people in organisations, and inbuilt hierarchical attitudes such as arrogance and distrust in others' abilities, that largely underlies the opposition to targeting. *Public Eye* reported that later in 1991 there would be a major initiative by the Women's Economic Development Group – which includes organisations such as Sainsbury's, NatWest, BBC, SOGAT, ICI, etc – to promote a flexible package of measures to enable women to break through the 'glass ceiling' and climb further up organisation hierarchies. But top managers should not be so much concerned with removing this glass ceiling to promotion, as with removing the preoccupation with promotion itself. As was considered earlier in this chapter, this will only be achieved by greatly reducing the levels of the hierarchy as part of the process of tying reward to factors other than pay and promotion. A policy of rewarding personnel officers for 'equal-opportunities' targeting, therefore, would be less opposed if tied to a policy of removing levels of the hierarchy and replacing 'equal' teams of people throughout an organisation.

The changing attitudes of top managers towards women in organisations such as British Airways and Gloucestershire County Council are laudable. But attitudes will need to shift further to realise that the goal of effectively integrating women into the workplace *is one and the same goal* as effectively integrating *all* employees into more flexible, supportive, collaborative team cultures; and it will only be fully achieved through a comprehensive and genuine implementation of the kind of collaborative structure indicated in Chapter 6 above.

9

The collaborative culture – caring for the customer, supplier and other organisations

Caring for the individual customer in industry and education

The value of a collaborative approach is not restricted to people within an organisation. A flexible and open-minded management will be responsive to feedback from the customer, as well as from the work-force, as a means of improving product/service quality. The fact that this 'customer care' is pivotal to an organisation's success is expressed clearly by Deming when he points out that without the customer an organisation 'might as well shut down' (1986, p174). Unfortunately, this simple and what should be obvious truth, is often forgotten. Hierarchically run organisations lose sight of employees 'lower down' the organisation, let alone the individual customer who comes at the end of the chain. But it is an irrational and costly mistake to show such contempt; and there is evidence to show that organisations that focus on the customer and quality of service grow sometimes twice as fast as their competitors, and they increase market share three or four times faster (*Business Matters*, 19.8.91).

In the context of customer care, Beck noted the following characteristics of some successful organisations in the US:

> . . . concepts such as 'customising', listening to what the market is saying or market orientation, getting every aspect right, after-sales care, and encouraging customers to participate in product specification and development, are commonly heard themes (1989, p27).

Seeking and listening to the views, suggestions and needs of the customer provide a valuable source of ideas for improvement and innovation. Peters and Austin, for example, go as far as to maintain that 'forward-looking customers . . . are the best source of leading-edge innovation' (1985, p120). And of course the link between the customer and organisational efficiency goes without saying – efficient organisations do not produce shoddy goods and services, do not keep people waiting around for delivery of goods or services, etc, etc.

Increasingly in the area of management, therefore, a major message is: *working collaboratively with employees* and *with customers are the cornerstones of successful organisations*. And indeed, they are inextricably linked. This link is perhaps most obvious in the service industries:

'If you want your people to treat your customers with courtesy, doesn't it follow that you must first treat your people with courtesy?' True. Obvious. And rare. In factory or school it seems. (Peters and Austin, 1985, p395)

In particular, only if there is a culture of respect, listening, and responding to the ideas and needs of the employee, will the employee – the main organisation-customer interface – be empowered and enabled to respect, listen to and fully respond to the ideas and needs of the customer. It is these linked relationships that are the bedrock of high motivation, efficiency and innovation necessary to achieve a high quality of product and service (see Figure 1.1). This, for example, is recognised by the chairman of the highly successful Federal Express transport company in the USA who says, 'Our people-service-profit philosophy came from the recognition that any service business was only as good as the customer contact element . . .' He also says that they spend as much time managing their employee relations as they do their other business relations. They achieve a high quality of service by showing a collaborative care to their mainly part-time employees, by investing heavily in staff training; by providing medical care, and reimbursing college tuition costs; and by enabling self-motivation through a team approach that 'give[s] people lots of authority' (*Business Matters*, 29.8.91).

Unfortunately, in education, one of the largest service 'industries', there seems to have been a general blindness to the importance of employee relations and quality of service. Lightfoot observes that: '. . . teachers are typically cast in low positions in the school's hierarchy, and not treated with respectful regard' (1983, p334). She is referring to American schools, but the same is generally true for teachers in Britain. Consequently, as she points out, 'If teachers are infantilized . . . then it will be difficult for them to establish consistent and . . . mature and giving relationships . . . with students' (p342).

However, it is of vital importance that the customers of education, ie the pupils or students (and parents), are treated respectfully and maturely as *equals*, as this is central to the learning process. In Chapter 1 evidence was cited for saying that *the more people participate in dialogue and the decision-making process, the more they are motivated to work and learn*. In line with this there is an increasing amount of talk today about the need for collaborative group work in the learning and training environments, where the teacher or trainer acts as a coach, an enabler, a facilitator, not as a talker or lecturer. Some attempts at this have been made (eg Jones, 1989a; Meighan, 1988; Prideaux and Ford, 1988; Ruddock and Cowie, 1988). And in fact, only if 'the teacher' or 'the trainer' has the collaborative skills to facilitate an effective team approach, will he or she thereby inculcate the same skills – ie listening, openness, tolerance, consistency, rationality, self-appraisal, etc (Figure 4.1) – in 'the learner' – skills that as already stated, are the basis for empowering 'the learner's ability to effectively relate to others, their decision-making skills, self-development and self-directed learning, increasingly called for in both the learning and work environments (see also Chapter 14).

However, all the rhetoric about the need for a team/group approach in the learning or training environment, is unlikely to be effectively translated into practice if teachers, lecturers and trainers generally work in hierarchical institutions. In particular, unless 'the teacher' or 'the trainer' is enabled to participate in a team approach with colleagues and management, it is unlikely that he or she will develop the collaborative skills necessary for effecting the participatory approach needed with 'the learner'. In other words, if he or she is not shown respect, listened to, and enabled in the decision-making process, etc by management, then he or she in turn will not respect, listen to, and enable 'the learner' in the decision-making process. Or, if by any chance they have been able to develop their collaborative skills, their work with pupils/students will be against a general tide of opposition (see also Chapter 6). The situation is aptly summed up by McGregor's statement: 'Classroom learning is

effective only within an organisational climate conducive to growth'
(1987, p225; see also Chapters 11 and 15 below).

In general, educational and training establishments are hierarchical
and authoritarian (see eg White, 1983, p93; Comer, 1989, p9), and
this is reflected in the following statement by the Confederation of
British Industry Task Force on Training:

> Yet skill needs can only be met by the creation of effective training
> markets in which the customers – individuals and their employers –
> exercise more influence over education and training provision (CBI,
> 1989, p9).

Educational and training organisations will need to develop less
hierarchical, more collaborative cultures in order to develop a partnership with their customers in which they are open to 'influence'
from them (see also Chapter 13). The need to become more flexible
and 'customer friendly' becomes even more urgent as education,
just as industry, increasingly needs to attract and cater for the non-
traditional student in the 1990s. As has been considered generally
above, the key to this change, in education as in industry, lies with
top management.

Individual customer care – Example

The success of the restaurant chain TGI Friday, while other restaurants
were closing down daily as a result of the recession, has been put
down to staff training and the company's commitment to keeping
the customer satisfied. The company, featured in *In Business* (3.4.91),
aims to go from the customers needs *first*, instead of imposing their
menus, time constraints, etc on to the customer. And they are able
to achieve this by having good staff relations with everyone, including
the kitchen staff – they all get a percentage of the profits and there
are twice-daily staff meetings to foster team spirit. As one employee
puts it, '. . . if we're having a good time it means the customers at the
other side of the bar are also having a good time.'

Because of the success of the company other restaurant chains
have copied the TGI decor, such as the tiffany lamps and the pol-
ished wood floors. But of course their success rests on nothing so
tangible as that. As the *In Business* reporter observed concerning the
copiers: 'What they rarely manage to reproduce is the company culture which the general manager . . . instils into all newcomers.'

Cost of customer dissatisfaction

Losing customers is costly. Some research has found that it costs at least five times more to gain a new customer as to keep existing customers; and long-term customers spend two to three times as much per year with an organisation than do newly-gained ones (*Business Matters*, 29.8.91). It has been claimed by Deming that the cost of customer dissatisfaction 'defies measure' (1986, p175). Dissatisfied customers often do not complain, they just switch. For example, an indignant building society customer, annoyed by the way customers such as herself were being treated – in particular, the way the society did not make any attempt to tell their customers of changes in rates and new products available – intended to move despite the fact that they have given her 'marvellous service' for many years, 'I'm moving my account out as fast as I can. I'm going to leave' (*Money Box Live*, 4.2.91). The *Money Box Live* presenter pointed out that they had received nearly 50 letters that had made the same complaint, and asked her whether she had complained to the society. In fact she had, and typically, they had taken no notice of her. What's one customer, or even several? But, as Peters and Austin point out, there is no such thing as a *small* customer. They relate the view of a car salesman who maintained that 'each angry person has 250 friends, 100 will hear from him about the rotten experience he had . . . 50 per cent of them, in turn, will tell their 150 friends' (1985, p83). No organisation can afford to neglect and be contemptuous of even just one individual customer. It has been reported, for example, that 2 per cent of the TSB Bank's customers leave every year because they are unhappy with the service. It does not sound a great deal but it costs millions in lost income, and consequently they are now aiming to improve quality and customer service (*The Money Programme*, 3.3.91).

The cost of customer dissatisfaction in education will increasingly figure as schools, further education colleges and colleges of higher education, compete to attract customers – increasingly the basis of their funding. Those that do not provide an effective, flexible, customer-orientated service will become less popular, and ultimately go out of business.

Cost of customer dissatisfaction – Example

In 1986 Rover launched its Rover 800 saloon car too early, before its flaws had been sorted out. It has been reported that five years on, the mistake has proved to be extremely expensive (Lorenze, 1991). One reason for the cost was the write-offs that arose from Rover's decision to pull the car out of the American car market. But the price paid by Rover was higher than that because the retreat damaged its marketing strategy:

> ... the company struggled for four years to restore the image that was tarnished so badly after its premature launch. (Lorenze, 1991)

Rover planned to launch a revamped saloon in November 1991 as a last effort to establish itself in America, but lack of resources forced it to scrap those plans. The company is reportedly being 'hit hard' by the recession in Britain, with car sales heading for the worst since 1976; and even when car sales recover, competition from Nissan, Toyota and Honda is expected to hinder Rover's recovery. The company, therefore, was in no position to stab itself in the foot by incurring customer dissatisfaction and therefore lost markets and huge financial losses, as it did in the case of the Rover 800.

Caring partnerships with the customer–supplier organisation

As well as caring for employees and the individual private customer, a collaborative management will also work more cooperatively and productively with other organisations with which it has dealings. In this context, Deming, for example, refers to the way a supplier organisation can get help and suggestions from the customer organisation on how to reduce mistakes and increase efficiency, which benefits both (1986, p196ff). Similarly, the sales and marketing director at Richardson Sheffield, the highly successful cutlery firm, maintains that it is essential for a supplier organisation to understand the business of its customers and their needs, in order to develop business with them 'to any serious degree' (*Business Matters*, 29.8.91).

Collaborative flexibility and customer care – Example*

In the early 1980s, Lucas Aerospace realised that they would need to learn from the world's best organisational practice in order to be able to compete effectively in the future, and they went first to the Japanese. They learned that a key factor in success was being able to respond effectively and quickly to the market and the customer with a quality product (in their case customer organisations); and they realised that the traditional rigidity in the skills of the work-force worked against this. For example, the general manager at the Engineering and Heating Division in Luton, describes how previously 289 of their 515 employees were single-skilled, which meant that if any of them were away for any reason, then the customer was not satisfied. Even on this 'simple' level of delivery, therefore, and leaving aside the need for general improvement in skills for achieving improvement in quality, they realised that they would need to evolve, through training, a more multi-skilled, 'flexible' work-force. But they also learned that 'flexibility in skills' was not enough. These skills would need to be *enabled* through a corresponding flexibility in structure, where people work in small 'equal' teams, being given responsibility for such things as quality, and being able to move between teams, departments and customers – in order to respond better to customers' overall needs relating to delivery (including fluctuations in order book levels), quality and innovation (see points 2, 3 and 6, p79; and the following section; and Chapters 7 and 11 on organisational culture and effective skills training).

The respect, responsibility and empowerment given to the employees will have increased their motivation to learn and improve their knowledge and skills as a basis for improving their product and service; and therefore they will be more eager to get feedback and have dialogue with the customer concerning their view of the product and their general needs.

---

* The quotations and factual information for this example are taken from *State of Training*, 29.9.91. The interpretations are this author's.

Long-term collaborative customer–supplier partnerships – its value*

Long-term collaborative partnerships are a characteristic of many Japanese organisations – partnerships between employees, where people work in 'equal' teams, between teams and between departments, as a basis for partnerships with supplier and customer organisations. Although the Japanese have been working this way for decades, in the late 1980s and early 1990s in Britain it is being heralded as a 'new' revolutionary way of increasing responsiveness to customer demand by radically reducing the time it takes to go from product or service conception to customer delivery. And it is contrasted with the more rigid traditional working practices where departments work separately and in sequence – for example, in manufacturing industry the sequence might be: first there are the people who have the concept, which then goes to engineering who make the design, then design goes to product engineering, then finally manufacturing will make it and arrange for sub-contract suppliers to come in. The whole process takes a considerable amount of time. Also, as Alex Clarke of Hewlett-Packard in Bristol points out, time is lost in traditional rigid structures by the way information needs to be passed up and down the hierarchy and people have to wait for decisions and directives from the top – which has less knowledge about jobs than the people actually doing them – before being able to go ahead with work. By departments working together simultaneously and having a less hierarchical, more team approach, the time needed for the various work processes is considerably reduced.

But this 'Time Compression' or 'Accelerated Product Development' or 'Time to Market' as it has been called, is more than just a way of improving time efficiency. A flexible team approach, which fully informs and involves people, giving them real responsibility, and which enables the interchange of ideas between departments and with supplier and customer organisations, empowers and motivates people to learn and come up with better ideas as a basis for further improvement in time and other efficiencies, quality and innovation. This is the key to customer responsiveness. Generally in Japanese

---

* The quotations and factual information for the ensuing section are taken from *In Business*, 2.10.91. The interpretations are this author's.

companies, for example, all departments, from original conception and design to final marketing, are involved together right from the outset, as are the supplier organisations. This, together with the 'equal' team approach they embrace, greatly enables the interchange of ideas, and explains their highly creative (despite the myth that the Japanese are uncreative) and innovative organisational cultures.

George Stalker, referred to as one of the American gurus of Time Compression, maintains that most companies in the West operate to minimise costs at the expense of time, and they should take a perspective that includes time in order to stop wasting time. He refers, for example, to Federal Express, which achieved success by reducing their service time not just marginally over the general postal service, but drastically, delivering packages overnight compared to around five days. But merely looking for time reductions within a given structure is just as much a case of putting the cart before the horse as concentrating on cost reduction. This is recognised, for example, by Alex Clarke who points out that first you should 'change the ground rules', by which she means changing to a less hierarchical structure, where power is devolved down through an organisation, empowering people and enabling their skills. If this is done, time and cost savings follow while maintaining and improving quality. And indeed, as considered above, Federal Express, the example used by George Stalker, achieves a high time efficiency and quality of service through collaboratively caring for, enabling and empowering their staff by implementing a team structure.

While the Japanese have led the way in effective, flexible team approaches, and some big American companies have been catching up with the Japanese, together with one or two organisations in Europe that are approaching Japanese standards, the bulk of British manufacturing business is far behind, according to Professor Colin New at Cranfield. Why is this? The reason is that it requires a radical shift in underlying attitudes to more collaborative ones by top managers in order to enable the less hierarchical, more 'equal' and flexible team structures that are needed. In the words of the *In Business* presenter, it will require, 'Managers [to wake] up to the fact that the people they employ have heads as well as hands.'

Significantly, the deputy chief executive of Stewart Broughton, a clothing factory in Derby, who recognises that *'everybody* needs to change' to implement a flexible team approach effectively, points out that they have lost quite a few people through the change – but not, she says, because they have had to lay people off, 'No. I'm talking about management. They haven't been able to change, so through perhaps us or them we've lost them on the way – they have actually left us.' This illustrates the point made in Chapter 7, that where top management is committed to bringing in a more collaborative team approach, most people in an organisation will welcome it, although it will mean them changing – the employees in Stewart Broughton had to change from piecework to flexible teamwork and a different form of payment (cf Steelcase and Belling examples, Chapter 7 pp118–19). But resistance is more likely to come from middle management and supervisors who have more deeply embedded hierarchical attitudes and behaviour.

Improving customer responsiveness, therefore, rests ultimately on developing a collaborative organisational culture; without the latter, improved efficiency, quality and constant innovation will be blocked, making the level of customer responsiveness that will be needed in the increasingly competitive 1990s unattainable.

Long-term collaborative customer–supplier partnerships – their use

A constructive collaborative partnership between its supplier and customer organisations, is a central characteristic of the Nissan UK plant in Sunderland. For example, their information sheet on 'Quality' states:

> ... Nissan's philosophy is to involve [suppliers] at the earliest possible stage of design. This way components and processes can be *jointly* developed ... The company has a small dedicated team whose job it is to work with suppliers not only to help them improve their quality but also to help them improve their productivity ... the Supplier Development team will continue to work with many suppliers to achieve better quality, better delivery and lower costs for all concerned, not least for the end customer (Nissan, 1985, p4).

The company, other organisations, and the end customer, are *all* better off – a truly collaborative approach. Such a close and constructive partnership between a collaborative organisation and its supplier organisations, will require corresponding collaborative attitudes and skills in the supplier organisation (cf previous example). As already pointed out in Chapter 7, the supplier organisation will need *humility* to be able to admit 'weaknesses' and the fact that they might need help from the customer organisation to improve their quality and efficiency. And they will need a corresponding *respect* for the ability of the customer and *trust* that they will be acting with *honesty, fairness* and *justice* in coming up with the most rational and effective ideas for improving the supplier's efficiency and quality – and trust that they will not be judged, ridiculed, or taken advantage of in any way, for needing to improve. This for example, is revealed by the managing director of a Nissan supplier. He relates how Nissan were prepared to go along and talk through jobs with them, taking their skills and their engineers into his organisation to see if they could help them produce things more economically, and he admits how initially he was fearful and untrusting of the openness it required on his part:

> My first reaction [was] I would *not* open my books to *anybody*, because . . . I certainly didn't want anybody knowing what my profitability was, and then perhaps squeezing me on the profits (*In Business*, 11.9.91).

His usual secrecy in these matters, as no doubt that of most others in his position, was based on his distrust that the customer would be operating with fairness, honesty, justice, and so rationally to achieve effectiveness on his organisation's behalf. Once he realised that the Japanese company had no intention of 'squeezing' his profits, but on the contrary, they were anxious to work *with* him to reduce his costs and improve his profitability, he says, 'I changed my attitudes', and he became more trusting and open. For him it was 'an entirely different *concept* of how to work', which had not happened before with his British or European customers – although he believes now that more and more are beginning to follow that trend, changing their 'old confrontational attitudes', and going along with his Nissan-gained attitudes of close supplier involvement from the very early stages of product design and development.

Therefore, the fact that an organisation such as Nissan operates collaboratively, involving and helping their suppliers and thereby showing respect and trust, etc, should develop in most suppliers' top managers, reciprocal attitudes of respect, trust and openness towards the customer organisations and also to their own employees – the latter as a basis for developing a more efficient team structure. It is the same with most relationships, whether between organis-ation and suppliers, managers and employees, management and unions (see Chapters 12 and 13), teachers and pupils (see above), etc. Generally, if people are treated collaboratively – fully involved, informed and listened to – they are being shown respect and trust, which creates a reciprocal respect, trust and openness in them towards others, producing an eagerness to cooperate and commit themselves to learning and finding better and mutually beneficial outcomes. However, some top managers (and middle managers/supervisors) will have hierarchical attitudes and authoritarian ways so deeply embedded, that they may not respond so positively, and will remain arrogant, lacking in humility, secretive and fearful, rendering them unable to develop a constructive working partnership with their customer organisation and their own employees (see Chapter 7). Collaborative organisational cultures, therefore, will be unable to 'do business' with companies with such top managers; and it is a key factor when Japanese organisations select their supplier organisations.

Toyota in America operate in a similar manner to Nissan. John Gragg of Qwik-Tool is one of their suppliers:

> Every year about this time we have a price reduction get together with Toyota, and they're very helpful in the fact that they'll produce some engineering ideas to help reduce costs – they want us to make a profit . . . Toyota tries to extend its teamwork concept even down to its suppliers and it's worked out real well for us (*The Midlands Report*, 25.10.90).

The collaborative spirit of the Japanese is perhaps illustrated best by a comment by Takashi Hayashi, managing director of the Sony plant in South Wales. Sony, like Nissan, Toyota and other Japanese companies, develops the same close partnership with their suppliers. As considered above, this is part of a general wish to work collaboratively with people, with employees and individual customers as well as other organisations. This general wish is revealed in Takashi Hayashi's comment that, ' "Welanese" is a kind of new word which I created – Welsh-Japanese. So that means a new *national* company' (*In Business*, 11.9.91). His viewpoint reveals no wish to impose on, dominate, or take over others – more a wish to help and share as a true partner, on an equal footing with all employees, customers and suppliers – a relationship where *everybody* gains. Geoff Woods, managing director of Toray Textiles (Europe), formerly part of Courtaulds, is one who has recognised this wish by Japanese organisations to work in partnership with *everyone* they have dealings with; and indeed, as pointed out above, the various interactions are inextricably linked:

> ... there's much more of a long-term commitment in everything that's done, in terms of the partnerships both with the banking world, the suppliers, the employees and the customers, such that there's a better morale (*The Thatcher Audit*, 4.9.90).

The practice in successful organisations of developing long-term collaborative partnerships with their supplier and customer organisations, based on respect, trust, loyalty and commitment, is essential for quality and it contrasts with the short-term, adversarial, non-collaborative relationship that generally exists between supplier and customer organisation in Britain today. The prevailing British non-collaborative relationship between supplier and customer is revealed in a comment by Lord Rayner, the then out-going chairman of Marks and Spencer that '. . . this business . . . seeks for quality . . . and it seeks to establish good relations with staff, suppliers and customers – an unusual combination don't you think?' (*In Business*, 3.4.91). The generally non-collaborative relationship between organisation and customer and supplier organisations that generally exists in Britain is further exemplified in Chapter 12.

The need for customer–supplier care – Example 1

A collaborative respect for, and commitment to, the employee, and a corresponding system of collaborative, long-term partnership with their suppliers, from raw materials to finished product, has been a distinctive feature of Marks and Spencer. It is through such long-term partnerships that they have been able to achieve the high quality of product and service that has been the basis of their success.

Despite a good history of staff, supplier and customer relationships at Marks and Spencer, because of increasing international competition, Lord Rayner recognised; 'I would hope we're going to give the customer a better deal in the 1990s, and if we don't we will not succeed' (*In Business*, 3.4.91). To achieve an increase in care for the customer, however, will require a further building of the collaborative partnership with employees and suppliers. In the spring of 1991, however, the long-term relationship with employees took a knock when over 500 jobs were cut. A director at Marks and

Spencer denied this had any significance. 'We will *never* change the basic approach of this business and its culture towards our staff, our customers, and our suppliers' (*Business Matters*, 29.8.91). He goes on to say that the latter have been with them for over a hundred years and will be with them for the next hundred and many more. Suppliers maybe, but evidently not employees. However, the relationship with one cannot be separated from the relationship with the other. Deny it as he might, shedding jobs will have had an inevitable effect on remaining employees. Amongst other things it will have begun to erode trust; yet achieving high trust – right through from the supplier organisations to the end customers' trust that they will receive a quality product and service – has been the hallmark of the organisation's success. Undermining that trust at any link in the chain will ultimately undermine the strength of the whole organisation. Essentially the same point is made by David Clutterbuck, chairman of The Item Group, who maintains that a truly customer-orientated company has to do good business with *everyone* who is involved – with the customers, the employees who have to deal with those customers, and the suppliers.

> If it doesn't do that, if it leaves out any of those bits of the chain, then the chances are that it's not going to be able to satisfy all of the needs of the customer (*Business Matters*, 29.8.91).

The job cuts made by Marks and Spencer indicate that improvement is called for in that link in the chain; and a greater loyalty and commitment between top management and employees will need to be developed to achieve the further improvement in quality that Lord Rayner says will be needed to succeed in the 1990s.

The need for customer–supplier care – Example 2*

The giant computer company IBM has been heralded by Peters and Austin as a company that excels in customer care (1985); and its great success in the 1960s and 70s was, no doubt, in large part due to this factor. However, in the second half of the 1980s the company experienced a collapse in profits by nearly a half, and in early 1991 it was reported to be undergoing restructuring in an attempt to

---

*The quotations and factual information for the ensuing example are taken from *The Money Programme*, 3.2.91, unless otherwise stated. The interpretations are this author's.

sharpen its competitive edge and become more entrepreneurial.

The poor situation IBM found itself in, however, was not an indication that the kind of collaborative customer service it operated was ineffective. On the contrary, in early 1991 the top management acknowledged:

> Increasingly it was clear that our customers were needing more help . . . they wanted answers to their problems, solutions; they wanted us to understand their business . . . And when we looked at the structure that we developed over the years, it wasn't geared specifically to that (Tony Cleaver, Chairman, IBM UK).

> . . . perhaps the industry changed more rapidly than we had anticipated, we've had to go back and say 'well, let's re-focus on that service to the customer'. And we've looked at how does it mean we should communicate with the customer – we've found that we weren't as open as we should have been (David McKinney, Senior Vice President, IBM).

So the company's problems have not been a case of 'caring for the customer' not working, but of the organisation not keeping up with its original policy of focusing on the customer. Consequently, the restructuring of the company centred on 'a return to its roots' and a change back to 're-orientate itself around the customer'. Among other things, this involved, within the UK division, moving hundreds of employees from backroom administrative jobs into high-profile sales work.

Why did IBM move away from the customer? One aspect, according to a former IBM salesman, was that although in the 1950s and 60s customers knew less than the salespeople and so were happy to see them, somewhere in the late 60s or early 70s the customers became more knowledgeable and specialist themselves, and therefore, '. . . the IBM people weren't quite as necessary in there. And IBM recognised this and they started to think – gee, we could sell as much without as many people in the field.'

A determining factor in the change of culture will have been the change in top management that inevitably occurred in the organisation's 30-year history. The imprudent nature of that change is revealed by the phrase 'the IBM people weren't *quite* as necessary' in the above quotation. However knowledgeable and specialist the customers become, it could never of course be a basis for saying contact between the manufacturer and the customer is totally unnecessary, or even secondary. It appears that the IBM management had allowed profit considerations to come before consideration of the customer and his or her needs. Such non-collaborative thinking is counter-productive, and always backfires in the long term (see also Chapter 12).

For example, an aspect of IBM's 'moving away' from the customer relates to the growing trend towards flexibility in computer systems. Customers are increasingly demanding that both hardware and software become more easily interchangeable. IBM's critics have accused it of 'dragging its feet' on these developments. Why? It seems a situation where immediate 'short-term' profit consider-ations dominated, because with the traditional 'non-interchangeable' proprietary systems, customers get locked into the equipment of a particular manufacturer. In the past this made selling a new system more profitable for that manufacturer. The fact that IBM have lost customers on the basis that they are not able to supply a flexible enough system, clearly indicates that putting profit before people is counter-productive. The difficulties encountered by IBM, therefore, exemplify the claim made in Chapter 2, that the skills of collaborative leadership – centring on respect for people's ideas and needs – form the bedrock of successful financial and technical decisions.

At the beginning of this chapter the point was made that working collaboratively with customers is inextricably linked with working collaboratively with employees. The question therefore arises as to whether the respect for the employee by management, necessary for a collaborative relationship, had been lacking at IBM. *The Money Programme* presenter referred to the 'powerful company culture' that includes basic beliefs such as '. . . the code of ethics which guide IBM's corporate life. Amongst those beliefs: respect for the individual and a philosophy of life-time employment.' As considered in Chapter 6, a *written* code of ethics tells us nothing about an organisation's culture – it all depends on action. From the fact that it was reported that about 10,000 jobs had gone in IBM's US operations over the two years up to 1991, and there were plans to axe 1200 jobs over 1991–2, it seemed that the lifetime employment policy, which had indeed been acted on in the past, had been abandoned. However, the *manner* in which the company intended to reduce the work-force indicated that they had not abandoned the basic ethic of respect for the individual. The chairman of IBM UK reassures:

There are some approaches that some organisations might take. The straightforward one of saying 'well, we're going to lay off 10% of the people', – that's something that we don't contemplate. You don't take the easy way out.

He continues to say how that means the process will take longer, and will require better planning ahead by management. But their policy of respect for the individual does not seem to have gone as far as equal respect for their ideas, and involving them in the decision-making process. Thus, a key aspect of the restructuring process was reported to be 'decentralisation. Increasingly, decision making is being moved out from the corridors of power'. Even Peters and Austin, while championing IBM in the mid-1980s, acknowledged how bureaucratic the organisation was, and 'on many dimensions it's quite centralized' (1985, p92). They maintain, however, that IBM's 'customer responsiveness' was possible because of 'the autonomy of the (sales) branch manager', who is 'responsible for customer satisfaction, [and who] is indisputably at the top' of the bureaucracy.

But in a hierarchical, bureaucratic, culture, no branch manager can truly be 'at the top of the bureaucracy', and can truly have complete autonomy. Always ideas from the true top will affect the extent and quality of the manager–customer relationship. While product competition posed no great threat to IBM, the 'humanness' in its customer relations referred to by Peters and Austin (1985, p73), was undoubtedly a key factor in its past success. But, as its more recent troubles testify, 'humanness' without a culture of *genuinely listening* to the needs and ideas of the customer, and a corresponding culture of genuinely listening to the needs and ideas of employees, will be insufficient for the organisation to be able to respond and produce the level of efficiency, product innovation, flexibility and quality needed to compete in the rapidly changing market place. Although there had been moves towards less bureaucratic structures and practices, with the creation of independent business units (Peters and Austin, op cit, pp137-8), the main culture had remained largely bureaucratic.

The UK chairman, Tony Cleaver, acknowledges that the company went through a long period 'in the same mould', and he hopes that having been through the restructuring changes they will not repeat the same mistakes by sitting back and saying 'Now we've done it.' Similarly, IBM's senior vice president, David McKinney says: 'We believe we've got the right strategy for the future, and if we don't we must be flexible enough to change.' And, of course, they are never likely to sit back and be inflexible to change if they are open to the ideas of the employees and the customers. The flexibility to learn from past mistakes and to change existing practices is a necessary ingredient of collaborative cultures (Chapter 6). The changes that have already begun to take place at IBM show that they do indeed have such flexibility, and it augurs well for those changes to lead to a more innovative, market-led organisational culture, collaboratively involving both employees and customers.

10

The collaborative culture – caring for the environment*

The collaborative–'green' link

There is growing pressure on all organisations to become more environmentally responsible, and alarm bells are being rung. For example, Peter Costain of the Costain Group, and Professor John Stopford of the London Business School, respectively warn:

> Business will be ignoring this issue at its peril, and therefore it's critical that business address the subject now and address it in a business-like manner.

> The consequences for Britain if we don't really get up to speed very fast, I think are going to be quite severe.

The pressure on organisations come from four directions: the consumer, the employee, the investor and the government. You might think that the effect of consumer pressure is restricted mainly to manufacturing organisations, but it also affects the service industries quite markedly. For example, by embracing a green strategy, Tesco's technical director claims that: 'Our business in the last five years doubled in turnover, and we trebled in our profitability and net margin level.' And it is possible that it could become a selling point for educational establishments, as consumer choice is increased in that sector. This might be so not only because of the increasing environmental concerns of parents, children and students,

---

*The quotations and factual information for the ensuing chapter are taken from *Nature*, 5.11.91, unless otherwise stated. The interpretations are this author's.

but also because a 'green' school or college policy would be seen to be indicative of a broader caring and responsible value system deemed to be of importance for the customer in education.

The strategy adopted by Tesco is not merely to stock environmentally-friendly products, but also, for example, to improve energy efficiency in their stores, to use more environmentally-friendly equipment, to put pressure on their suppliers to reduce packaging and use recycled materials, to recycle all their waste, etc. This is in line with the general pressures being put on organisations now to: reduce the consumption of raw materials; use, as much as possible, materials that are environmentally friendly and/or recycled; cut waste; cut consumption of energy; produce a less wasteful and more environmentally-friendly product. From what has been said above, it would be expected that an organisation with a collaborative culture would be fitter and better able to meet the increasing environmental challenge. After all, inbuilt into such a culture is the better use of people's ideas – through listening, training and research and development – to achieve better and less wasteful processes, and to produce better quality, greater efficiency and more innovative products.

This inbuilt innovativeness of organisations with a collaborative culture, means that they will be better able to control and reduce their waste pollution to meet increasing customer concern and government and EC restrictions. For example, in the 1970s people in Japan's car industry were able to make breakthroughs in cleaner engines to meet anti-pollution requirements (*Nippon*, 18.11.90). And in Norway their biggest and most successful industrial organisation, Norsk Hydro, listened and responded constructively to public outrage over pollution, thanks to the underlying 'caring' attitudes of the company's executive president, and his commitment to collaboratively involving and developing the work-force. With humility he accepts that it is legitimate that the company should be subject to pressure from their surroundings, and their operations be subject to careful government monitoring. With corresponding openness the company publishes a great deal of information about its emissions in an annual green audit (*Business Matters*, 18.7.91). At the time of writing the European Commission are reported to be 'pushing hard' for companies to make a 'cradle to grave' audit and publish it (*Tomorrow's World*, 30.5.91), and they are drafting proposals to make environmental audits compulsory. Collaborative organisational cultures will be best suited to meet the challenge of this pressure.

Profit and the collaborative–'green' link

Many of the leading 'innovative' organisations realise that 'green' practice pays. For example, talking about the company's 3P programme (pollution prevention pays), the Chief Engineer of the UK division of the American Company 3M, one of the world's biggest manufacturing companies, says:

> . . . this is a quality issue. Pollution is waste, and good businesses strive to reduce their waste, so it's a cost-effective way of improving performance (*Where on Earth are We Going?*, 23.7.90).

The company, while reducing its waste pollution considerably, has made savings of more than $420 million through not having to buy pollution control equipment, and by reducing consumption of materials and energy. Likewise, the British family firm Johnson Wax, has said:

> In the area of waste management we've reduced waste and scrap on the line from around 3 per cent to just over 1 per cent, and this is saving us hundreds of thousands of pounds a year.

Similarly, it has been said of the German and Swiss chemical industries, who are 'setting a brisk pace in going green', that 'their hard-headed businessmen aren't doing it for anything other than hard-headed reasons'. In the same context, it has been said of Anita Roddick, managing director of The Body Shop, that in the early days of her now highly-successful business, she started 'a refill service as an ecological way to reduce the need for new containers, which she couldn't afford' (Burlingham, 1990, p44). The point simply but forcefully makes the link between 'greenness' and efficiency/profit – between ethics and good business.

Perhaps one of the most original 'green' examples of dealing with what otherwise would be a polluting waste, is provided by the Japanese solution to the sewage sludge problem. Because of the difficulties encountered in dealing with the problem, it has been pointed out that 'imaginative thinking', and not just politics and technology, is needed to solve the problem. No one would maintain that imaginative thinking has been lacking in the Japanese in this context – they remove the problem by creatively and profitably converting the treated sludge into products such as paving stones, jewellery, flower-pots and garden tables (*Nature*, 10.12.90). As government and EC restrictions on water pollution tighten, a more collaborative approach, releasing creative and innovative ideas, will also be needed if Britain is going to deal with the problem efficiently and profitably.

'Green' organisations in Britain are rare and we lag behind our competitors in Europe. Significantly, we lag behind in collaborative practices also. The collaborative-green link is illustrated by the 'greening' of one particular product in the Johnson Wax company that involved suggestions from the employees in the factory: 'they came up with a package which is made from 100 per cent recycled materials'. It is obviously a collaborative culture where employees are listened to and involved in the decision-making process. Similarly, it was by involving their employees that Japanese organisations were able to make considerable savings in energy and raw materials consumption following the oil crisis in the early 1970s, as Taizo Katsura, manager of Sharp in 1974 relates:

> We received over 3000 suggestions from our workers. We sifted through them, and selected what we could use. We managed to reduce our electrical consumption by 44 per cent over a ten-month period. Our target was to cut energy consumption by half, cut manhours by another half, and cut the raw materials we use by two thirds (*Nippon*, 25.11.90).

Again, the director of policy at AEG, the German manufacturer of washing-machines and dishwashers, has commented, 'We ask them [the employees] to give us their ideas of improving the green aspects to make the whole plant green.' They have found that 'the whole behaviour of our employees has changed'. They now, for example, pressure management to recycle paper, glass, PVC and everything that can be recycled, and pollution from the factory has diminished. As a reporter comments, this implementation of a green policy at AEG springs from more than just good intentions. 'It's real source seems to be a drive for managerial excellence . . . quality management.' As considered generally in this book, this, in turn, requires underlying collaborative attitudes and skills in management, which enable them to respect, listen to and involve the work-force in the decision-making processes.

The move by Pilkington Glass, Lancashire, to set up environmental committees with a cross-section of managers and shop-floor operatives – in order, amongst other things, to audit the raw material, processes within their plant and the working environment – has been reported to have 'revealed previously untapped skills in their work-force'. It is the workers on the shop-floor and not the management who have come up with ideas to save the company money and save them wastage (*Business Matters*, 18.7.91). A collaborative culture enables the ideas of the work-force, the best ideas for efficiency, innovation and success.

Significantly, the profitable move by the Japanese (through the Ministry of Trade and Industry, MITI), to develop an electronics industry was strongly promoted because of a concern to reduce energy and raw material consumption, combined with their respect for the value of people. Nahiro Amaya, head of planning at MITI in 1970, recalls their thinking at the time, which was before the oil crisis:

> We have to change our industrial structure to those industries which consume less energy ... We thought that the most abundant resource in Japan is our human brains. So we have to develop our resources in this small box instead of the resources underground. (*Nippon*, 25.11.90)

Richard North, of the *Sunday Times*, makes an interesting observation on the link between environmental concerns and profit, which encorporates the 'collaborative' factor:

> What's weird and exciting and unexpected ... is the way that running safer, cleaner leaner plant, being conscious of the waste stream, seems to fit *so* well with making a *higher* quality product with a more interested work-force. (*Business Matters*, 18.7.91)

And he proceeds to 'guess' that it will be those organisations that do this that will also be the ones able to meet the environmental challenge of developing a 'real relationship with the society around it', producing environmentally responsible products, as a basis to 'go on to manage profit'. 'Exciting' yes – but 'weird' and 'unexpected' no, when the collaborative-green link being made here is recognised and understood.

Ethics and the collaborative–'green' link

The link being made here between collaborative and 'green' or environmental practice is echoed in the view of the environmental consultant, John Elkington:

> . . . I think what you will see is that companies that are properly managed and embrace the total quality message, will also tend to be the ones that are the high achievers, the top achievers in the environmental area too.

Similarly, Professor John Stopford of the London Business School has commented: 'Those [companies] in my view on environmental questions who don't pay attention to it, tend to be rather sloppy in other things too.'

The link is again made by the chairman of the Social Investment Forum, Alan Miller, who also indicates the underlying ethical dimension involved. According to Alan Miller, investors are not just going to be concerned about issues such as the environment, South Africa, nuclear power, armaments, alcohol, animal experimentation and community involvement, but also – over the coming 10 or 20 years – 'the issue of employee involvement':

> In other words, the word 'environment' doesn't just mean environment in terms of air, but 'environment' means *people* environment, *working* environment, the attitude of a company to communities in which it does its business (*Money Box*, 27.4.91).

In this same context, the authors of *Changing Corporate Values* (Adams et al 1991), assessed British, American and Japanese companies under various headings, including employment conditions, environmental action, animal testing, political and military involvement, and disclosure of information. Joint author Jane Carruthers reported how American companies are further down the road of social corporate responsibility, and added: '. . . surprisingly, the Japanese companies were also certainly very open and responsive to the issues, if not in the lead.' But not really surprising – rather *predictable* openness and responsiveness, given the mainly collaborative cultures of Japanese organisations. She concluded:

> Generally, companies that have a good ethical responsibility record tend also to be good employers, because they have a whole corporate structure that is geared to maximising their social responsibility (*Money Box*, 27.4.91).

Significantly, they found UK organisations provided 'far less corporate social information . . . though this is changing'.

The Body Shop is a clear exception to the predominant non-collaborative nature of organisational cultures in Britain. Genuine collaborative attitudes from the top in that company mean that there are inbuilt ethical values that do not distinguish between respect and caring for the employee and for the broader environment and other species.

'The broader environment' includes the community in which an organisation is situated. Showing a responsibility to, and involvement in, the local community, is going to figure increasingly in the well-being of organisations. Organisations show social responsibility when, for example, they:

1. provide, as far as possible, jobs and training for people in the local community, rather than mainly for people brought in from outside;

2. provide welfare benefits, such as housing, education and recreation facilities to employees;

3. provide financial and technical support to help develop the local community,
    a) through supporting employees who wish to be involved in social schemes;
    b) through developing direct partnerships with (non-employee) community people, to develop their own projects.

To be effective, support for the community must not be viewed in terms of a charitable hand-out. When 'support' is provided in this way, often for publicity and the personal kudos of top management, there is little long-term benefit for an organisation or the community. And of course such 'support' is the outcome of hierarchical attitudes and skills such as arrogance, disrespect, dishonesty, insincerity – quite the opposite from the collaborative attitudes and skills that guide, for example, Anita Roddick, who believes that:

> . . . it is immoral for a shop to trade in the middle of a community, to take money and make profits and then ignore the existence of that community, its needs and problems. (1991; see also example below)

What is needed, therefore, and what actions 1 to 3 above represent, is an approach that develops collaborative relationships or partnerships between the organisation, the employee and the wider community, to the long-term mutual benefit of the organisation and the community. The mutual benefit gained from action 1 is obvious.

Action 2, as part of a broader collaborative caring relationship between organisation and employee, helps enhance motivation, commitment and loyalty, so benefiting the organisation as well as the employee. It is an aspect of many Japanese organisations; and looking after employees' welfare in this way has historically been part of certain firms in Britain, such as ICI, Pilkington, and Lever Brothers.

Action 3a also increases employee empowerment, motivation, commitment and loyalty, thereby mutually benefiting organisation and local community. For example, one employee at IMB, where they run such a programme of community involvement, refers to the way it has 'actually grown me, and I think at the end of the day that actually benefits IBM'. And another says he has a more positive attitude to the company, not just because it allows him to do community work, but because he sees 'them as being a good citizen, and therefore someone it's worth working for and being loyal to' (*Business Matters*, 22.8.91). The mutual benefit gained from IBM's philosophy of community involvement and the 'caring capitalism' it represents, is recognised by IBM UK's director of personnel and corporate affairs, Sir Leonard Peach:

> We also get the benefits of a motivated employee, because many of our employees want to contribute to social work, and at the same time they want to belong to a caring company. (*Business Matters*, op cit)

Action 3b also has mutual benefits. For example, John Ward, nothern regional director at Barclays Bank, who are involved in such community partnerships, believes that if 'the region is prospering, my business is prospering'. Similarly, Sir Leonard Peach comments, 'we believe we benefit by belonging to a healthy and prosperous community' (*Business Matters*, op cit). Of course, action 1 is also instrumental in creating a prosperous local area benefiting the organisation in the long term. And for 3b, again the organisation benefits from the increased motivation and loyalty of employees that result from the organisation showing care to the community in this way.

Collaborative ethics and organisation-community health – Example 1

The Body Shop undertakes all the 'community' environment actions above. For example, their factory and headquarters are based in a small town and, unlike most other organisations, managing director Anita Roddick says that they encourage husband and wife teams: 'we have the family unit very strongly – it's a small town so that's exactly what happens' (*In Business*, 18.9.91). As part of this they have built a day-care centre for children. They set up a soap-making plant in an area of high unemployment in Easterhouse, Glasgow, where 25 per cent of the profits are ploughed back into a trust fund for the benefit of the local community. And they have a Community Projects Department encouraging employees to be active in the community by giving talks to local schools, helping hospitals, charities, the elderly and handicapped, and in providing work experience for young people (NatWest, 1991, p5). Every three or four months they also send groups of staff (about 30 people), to Romania to work in the orphanage project – all done in their pay time. According to Anita Roddick, this community work '. . . is probably the most motivating force for our staff . . . you've got a team of people who are just so empowered!' (*In Business*, 18.9.91). With the range of community involvement by The Body Shop, employees are both cared for and empowered. Little wonder, therefore, there is high morale, motivation, loyalty, and commitment to personal and organisational growth – obviously of benefit to employee, organisation and community alike (see also 'adding value', Chapter 12, p227).

Collaborative ethics and organisation-community health – Example 2*

The work of the Urban Development Councils (UDCs), reveals the importance of the above community actions, particularly action 1. UDCs were set up to tackle the problem of inner city decay, but it has been said of them that, although they have achieved much, it has often not been to the benefit of the local community and local

*The quotations and factual information for the ensuing example are taken from *Public Eye*, 26.4.91. The interpretations are this author's.

174 • THE HUMAN FACTOR

employment. Developers involved in urban renewal schemes such as those at Teesside and London Docklands, were the first to voice concern over the social divide that is being created by not involving and benefiting local communities. This is not just for reasons of altruism, however, but from a growing realisation that development that does not benefit a local community ultimately undermines its own efficiency and well-being.

In contrast to the UDC approach to date, a large part of east Birmingham is being developed by a new private company, Heartlands, a partnership between the city council and five large developers, that uses a more 'people-based strategy'. Board member councillor Albert Bore explains:

> We identify *with* the employer what his or her employment needs are going to be in the future – what sort of skills will be associated with those jobs, and *with* the employer we put together a training package specifically related to those jobs that will be created by that employer.

That means much of the work that is going on, he continues, in terms of design, planning, etc is undertaken cooperatively between the council and the five developers, and 'it's got to be cost-effective'. Given the pressure on government expenditure, a *Public Eye* reporter summised: 'the Heartlands model appears to offer an approach to inner city problems that is both cost-effective and targets the benefits of urban regeneration at those who need it most.' But of course, as pointed out by the above councillor, they both go together. Significantly, the reporter adds concerning the Heartlands development: 'It's also in accord with what seems to be the new spirit of the age, which is one of cooperation rather than confrontation.'

Organisational survival and the collaborative–'green' link

The fact that we lag behind in this area is causing the inevitable concern about the effect on organisational performance and competitiveness. Performance will suffer from the decreased consumer demand for lower quality products. This is happening, for example, with washing-machines. AEG produce machines that use less water and less electricity than British washing-machines. They are made out of fewer types of material, and increasingly use fully recyclable plastic. Although they are generally more expensive, the UK imports twice as many machines as it exports to Germany. Add to this EC regulations, which will have more force after 1992, and British companies not producing to the required standards will be unable to export into other parts of the market. 'In fact we may not be able to sell in our own backyard without compliance to the new regulations', says Professor Stopford. And even if the products are comparable in terms of the impact they have on the environment, consumer and EC pressure is such as to favour those products/services achieved through less polluting processes. It's AEG's and other organisations' adoption of the 'cradle to the grave' concept, which pledges to enforce environmental standards 'from the very first mining of the raw materials right through to recycling the product at the end of its life', that is going to attract the increasingly environmentally aware customer (see also 'adding value', Chapter 12, p228).

Performance of organisations will suffer directly if they produce costly waste and pollution. They may suffer doubly by having then to pay fines for overstepping government and EC effluent standards.

And finally, environmentally unsound organisations will increasingly lose out as investors, employees and customers become increasingly concerned about ethical issues generally, relating not just to areas such as nuclear power, South Africa, vivisection, and environmental pollution, but also to the need for social responsibility in the working and community environments.

It is not surprising, therefore, that the warning bells are ringing. HRH The Prince of Wales, who has set up the organisation 'Business in the Environment', commented in his address to business leaders in July, 1990, '. . . I feel a sharp sense of urgency about the need to move from talk to action in so many aspects of environmental practice.' This corresponds to the urgent need referred to above, to move from talk to action in collaborative working practices generally. Later that year, Prince Charles told a meeting of top executives that the companies that care about the environment are more competitive (reported in *News at Ten*, 8.11.90). As a BBC commentator noted: 'Prince Charles' Business in the Environment initiative may turn out to be as much about saving British industry as saving the environment.'

11

The collaborative culture – education, training and development

Collaborative leadership and support for education and training

A theme that has run through many of the previous chapters is that collaborative cultures are learning cultures. Top managers with the core attitudes and skills of collaborative leadership (Figure 4.1) – also the attitudes and skills of effective learning and teaching – will lead through a process of learning and teaching, enabling others to develop the same core collaborative attitudes and skills as a basis for empowering their learning. This ideal situation is succinctly described by Deming:

> A leader, instead of being a judge, will be a colleague, counselling and leading his people on a day-to-day basis, learning from them and with them (1986, p117).

Similarly, McGregor talks about a manager's task being one of helping employees and: 'to act as teacher, consultant, colleague' (1987, p152). This goal is equally relevant for the industrial, business, and educational manager and employee.

It follows from this centrality of the learning process that *the encouragement of, and support for, education, training and development, is an integral part of effective collaborative leadership.*

In line with this, Beck reports how certain successful organisations in the US see the leadership role to be shifting 'to that of coaching, or helping people to perform better and be more creative' (1989, p26). And he observed: 'One loop in the "business = people" equation was completed by a recognition of the business contribution of training and development' (p27). In particular he found that the managers of the successful companies became involved in their *corporate training centre*, which was a base for facilitating a coherent development of cooperative ways of working and organisational research and development needs. The Nissan Company at Sunderland encompasses this same philosophy:

> Only by developing the human resource – our staff – can we improve and develop the company. Training is concerned with practical skills development, staff development – to improve their general abilities – and leadership, which we pay particular attention to . . . As well as traditional training courses, *a new Flexible Learning Centre has been opened at the plant* . . . (Nissan, 1985, 'Employment', pp5, 6; my emphasis).

And of course it is through the learning process, and the educational and training programmes that support and enhance it, that organisations achieve the continuous improvement and development in quality and innovation necessary for long-term survival and success.

The CBI, for example, maintain that 'Employers who invest in people achieve enhanced competitive performance' (1989, p29); and they list organisations that have benefited from investment in education and training, achieving major improvements in all of the following areas (1989, p30):

- higher productivity;
- higher profitability;
- lower staff turnover;
- lower absenteeism;
- short innovation cycles;
- lower unit labour costs;
- improved customer service;
- quality.

And the same benefits of training apply in the educational sector. Staff training and development are the basis for quality in teaching performance, which means an improved service to their customers, encompassing individual pupils, students and parents; student teachers; in-service teachers; and individuals and employers from the business and industrial sector. Just as in industry, it will be those educational establishments that are willing to invest more in their people and their skills through staff training that will be able to improve efficiency and quality of service, so greatly increasing their chances of surviving and thriving in the 1990s.

When an employer invests in education and training it is a sign that they put a certain value on the work-force, and it also serves to give some boost to employee morale and motivation, but it does not indicate that an organisation is necessarily generally run collaboratively. It is important to realise that the more collaboratively run an organisation, the greater the benefits of training. The point was made in Chapter 7 concerning the training of managers, that there needs to be genuine action from the top to instigate a collaborative team structure throughout an organisation, in order for training to be fully effective. The same applies to all training. This is because ideas, knowledge and skills gained in courses, will only be fully utilised and further extended and developed in the workplace if the trainee is fully involved in the decision-making process, fully empowered to produce quality goods or services, and fully recognised for doing so (see also Part III, Chapter 15). Relating to this point McGregor, for example, says:

> Classroom learning is effective only within an organisational climate conducive to growth. A negative environment will wipe out the gains from classroom education in a relatively short time. (1987, p225).

Similarly, Geoffrey Whalen, chairman and managing director of Peugot Talbot, believes that training will not achieve much if people, especially senior managers, do not change their attitude to the work-force:

> . . . it's all about involving people in the business, asking their advice, telling them what's going on . . . taking note of the customers' needs and so on, and as a *very* important part of all that, training and developing people (*State of Training*, 7.4.91).

Deming does not mince words over the matter and warns: 'Money and time spent for training will be ineffective unless inhibitors to good work are removed' (1986, p53).

Significantly, the CBI have reported that 'smaller firms can be the ones seeing the most spectacular gains' from training (op cit, p30); and indeed one would expect smaller organisations generally to have less rigid hierarchical structures, a greater collaborative involvement and autonomy of employees, and so fewer factors inhibiting the possible gains of training, than larger organisations. The importance of the organisation culture to effective training, and the central role top management plays in that culture, is strongly voiced, for example, by Jean Irvine, director of information technology at the Post Office, when she says:

> I think it's an employee culture, not a training culture. I mean, many companies in the UK to-day tend to think the people on the shop-floor don't really know how to do their job – their supervisor knows better than them. But most of us I think now would recognise that it's often the management in a company which is disabling moving ahead, not the people on the shop-floor.

She further drives home the point when, in reply to the question what is the future for training, she says: 'Getting to changing the culture or you're dead' (*State of Training*, 29.9.91).

Collaborative cultures for effective training – Example*

The Engineering and Heating Systems division of Lucas Aerospace at Luton consider their training budget to be an *'essential* ingredient' of their business plan. According to the general manager, Philip Barrington, they spend 2.4 per cent of their sales on training, which is about £1100 per person per year – more than most other industries. After three years of initiating the training programme, their sales per employee were doubled. As considered in Chapter 9 (p152), the introduction of their training programme was an integral part of a radical culture change at the factory; and it is unlikely that the training would have produced such a good result, and be continuing to improve efficiency, quality and innovation, without the accompanying increase in employee involvement and responsibility through developing a team structure.

---

*The factual information for this example is taken from *State of Training* 29.9.91. The interpretations are this author's.

Management short termism and inaction on education and training

The record of investment in training by British managers is generally a poor one. In January 1990 it was reported that the average British organisation spends one-sixth on training of that which its French and German counterparts do (*The Money Programme*, 22.10.89). In December 1990, Dr Andrew Sentance of the CBI saw the falling investment that was taking place during the recession as a matter of 'serious concern for our competitiveness' when already 'companies in France and Germany invest on average about a thousand pounds more per employee than we do in the UK' (*BBC News*, 19.12.90). And figures from bodies such as the National Institute of Economic and Social Research indicate that considerably more employees are trained each year in France and West Germany than in the UK. The concern is voiced by the government in its white paper *Employment for the 1990s*, which states:

> . . . the breadth and depth of our training, its quantity and its standards, still show up badly by comparison with our competitors on the Continent, in North America and in the Far East. (White Paper, 1988, p29).

Consequently, only 26 per cent of the work-force in the UK are qualified, compared with 45 per cent in France and 70 per cent in Germany (Golzen, 1991, p9).

The record of staff training and development in education is probably even worse than in industry. For example, Her Majesty's Inspectorate report that in a typical polytechnic, only 12 per cent of the so-called staff development resources were devoted to the improvement of teaching skills, and 'this distribution is not unusual' (HMI, 1989, p11). And it is claimed that: 'Managerial weakness within institutions is failing to give sufficient weight to the promotion of quality in teaching and learning' (Bocock, 1989, p10).

The Confederation of British Industry taskforce on Education and Training has strongly voiced its concern over the fact that skills levels in Britain are lower than those in most competitor countries, 'and the gap is widening'. It claims: '. . . a quantum leap is needed in Britain's education and training performance' (CBI, 1989, pp29, 9). In turn, this will require 'a quantum leap' in the underlying attitudes of top management. For example, it is recognised by Gregory Hyland of the Thames Valley Training and Enterprise Council (TEC), that 'it is going to be quite difficult' to persuade chief executives of the value of training (1990, p9). Similarly, in the area of education, some headteachers believe that 'it's going to take something rather draconian to make staff development an urgent and respectable issue' (Jones, 1990, p28).

Peter Wickens, the director of the Nissan Plant in Sunderland, makes a comment that is very revealing of the situation that generally held in Britain in the late 1980s and early 1990s. 'The important thing is that we actually do a lot of training *as opposed to talking about it*' (Nissan, 1985, 'Employment', pp5, 7; my emphasis). As tends to be the case in other areas relating to the human resource, rhetoric abounds. However, although there is increasing *talk* about the importance of training, the *inaction* of many British managers, both in industry and education, indicates that they are yet to be convinced of the benefits of investing in people in this way. It is remarkable, given the benefits of investing in education and training provided by the German and Japanese models over many years, that pleas such as the following are still having to be made in the early 1990s in the West:

> We're a long, long way behind. Employers have never really esteemed education and training, and employers have got to learn that they've got to become investors in people (*The Thatcher Audit*, 4.9.90).

It has been the underlying non-collaborative attitudes in top management that have made such pleas necessary. It is these attitudes that have kept top managers blind to the value of the human resource, and made them unable to learn from best practice. A lack of collaborative attitudes, such as respect and trust in people, their abilities and their value, has prevented top managers perceiving their organisations, their products and services, as a means of creating opportunities for people to improve their quality of life. It makes them more interested in short-term, personal gain (through salaries and dividends), than in directing funds to people and their training; which they correspondingly perceive as a short-term *cost* rather than a long-term *investment* (see later in this chapter and Chapter 12). This contrasts with the German and Japanese models, and also certain successful organisations in Britain, where top managers have more collaborative attitudes towards people and their value, and who correspondingly are more interested in the long-term building of their organisations – through investment in people, their training and equipment – than in short-term financial gains.

Chris Hayes, of the Prospect Centre training consultancy in London, reveals the non-collaborative lack of respect by top managers for employees and their abilities, when he talks of 'a poor top management' that has 'low expectations' that are passed down the managerial line (cf a corresponding low expectation of people in education, Chapter 13). These low expectations, he says, mean 'the workers they employ can get by', realisation of which gives them no incentive to get qualifications (*The Money Programme*, 6.5.90). Poor top management, therefore, puts little value on the human resource, and sees spending money on their training as an unnecessary *cost*.

Government inaction – a non-interventionist strategy

Despite government rhetoric on the importance of training, such as that contained in the White Paper referred to in the previous section, the *actions* of government indicate that not all the fault for inadequate training lies with management. John Lloyd of the *Financial Times* put the situation into a nutshell when he wrote, 'The British State has been among advanced nations inefficient in developing the intelligence of its citizens and it remains so' (*The State in Question*, 17.1.91). In 1990, government funding for training was cut in some areas by as much as 20 to 25 per cent, and many people have expressed concern that this will reduce the quantity and quality of training (eg *The Money Programme*, 6.5.90; *Money Box*, 26.5.90). In the Autumn Statement of 1990 the government's overall training budget was cut again for the following year. In July 1991, as the latest British recession continued to bite, the European Commission's annual report strongly criticised Britain's poor education, training and skills programme, and maintained this as a major factor in her economic problems. The government dismissed the report as out of date, but many people within Britain involved in education and business, as well as the opposition political parties, echoed the EC's concern over Britain's education and training performance, and the long-term effect it would have on the country's economic and social well-being. Fears over possible further cuts in government support for training and a further attack by opposition parties on the short-term attitudes of government, were aroused in September 1991 by a leaked government letter relating to the negotiations between the Treasury and various government departments on spending budgets. In the letter to the Department of Employment, the chief secretary at the Treasury proposed various cuts in government training programmes, which the Labour opposition claimed would amount to £1 billion over three years. It was claimed that within the letter, the chief secretary wrote: 'I see no automatic link between higher unemployment and the need for further government provision for training' (*Channel 4 News*, 23.9.91).

The TECs, which are run by people from local business, trade unions and education, were set up by the government to 'revolutionise' training and tackle the country's skills deficit. A commendable aim is to forge a better match between training programmes and industries' skills needs; and the hope is that local business leaders will be more successful than government in persuading employers to invest more in training their work-force. At the same time as expecting employers to contribute more financially towards training through the TECs, however, the government has seen no need to intervene and help remove factors that discourage employers from investing in training – as is the practice of those countries that are internationally most competitive. In West Germany, for example, 16-year-olds can only start work if it is part time; part-time education and training must also continue until they are at least 18 years old; wages of higher craft trainees are fixed by national and regional agreements; and trainees have to remain with their training employer for a minimum of four to five years. This means that employers are not competing with full-time wages when setting wages for trainees, and they are not losing trainees – by poaching from other organisations where the trained employee sells to the highest bidder – before they get a return for their investment, unfortunately the case in Britain. The German trainees also benefit:

> . . . in return for lower wages, they get a broader education giving them more choice in later life . . . young engineering apprentices are being trained . . . far more than would be required simply to operate one of the machines . . . On the production-line, over-training benefits the company. It means qualified workers are flexible, able to switch machines as production demands and they're better prepared for new technology when it arrives. . . . Despite high German wages, these skills keep their company competitive. (*The Money Programme*, 6.5.90)

The German situation is interesting in that it shows that high wages do not necessarily lead to decreased efficiency/productivity (increased cost per unit output), as is mainly believed to be the case by government and managers in this country. Directing more funds towards employees, their training and equipment, within an environment that collaboratively involves them in the work process, motivates the work-force, resulting in better ideas, less wastage of time, materials, and energy, reducing costs, and increasing sales with lower priced, higher quality, innovative, products and services (see Figure 1.1). An organisation is then in a better position to give high wages without it increasing costs and decreasing productivity overall (see also Chapter 12, p238).

For completion perhaps it should be noted that the government not only generally did not intervene to remove factors discouraging employer investment in training (or to provide incentives to them for investing in training), but also, in 1991, were accused of intervening to hinder training and development. EC funding had been awarded to regions in Britain such as South Wales and Yorkshire, because they were suffering from the decline of coal-mining. They therefore badly needed funds for the building of new enterprises. However, because of the British government's policy that regions that received the funds would have to cut back in other areas, the EC had no guarantee that the money would be spent where they intended it to be spent, namely, for jobs and training in areas that had lost coal-mining. As a result the EC froze the funds and said they would not pay them out until the British government gave a categorical assurance that the money would do what it was intended for. Both EC officials and public and private representatives in the regions that had been awarded the funds, criticised the government's attitude – and there were suggestions that it would jeopardise Britain's chances of receiving other types of EC regional aid worth millions of pounds. The attitude, in fact, seemed one of blatant non-collaborative disconcern for the people of the rundown areas, their suffering, and their desperate need for jobs, training and development.

In contrast to the German model, where government intervenes to support training, what exists in Britain is a case of one set of non-collaborative attitudes – in managers – being reinforced by another – in government.

Investor short termism and inaction on education and training*

As well as a non-interventionist government strategy, it is claimed by some that top management has the cards stacked against it from another quarter concerning training, and research and development (R&D). They maintain that the 'short-termism' of City institutional fund managers – their interest in short-term profits and dividends – ties company managers' hands concerning the amount they can safely channel into long-term activities such as training and research, before risking the possibility of too great a drop in share prices and the threat of takeover.

This, for example, is precisely what has been happening to ICI, according to Professor Colin Mayer, who has undertaken a major study of takeovers in Britain. Because of increasing pressure over several years, he says, ICI has 'moved away from emphasising its training, research and development activities' to more short-term concerns 'about how to prop up its share price, how to reduce costs, how to dispose of businesses that are not fully profitable' (*Newsnight*, 23.5.91). These restructuring activities to increase profit and share price, have heightened with the fear of a hostile bid from the Hanson Trust following Lord Hanson's acquirement of 2.8 per cent of the shares in the company in May 1991; and the announcement of higher than expected profits for the first half of 1991 fall in line with the view that top managers have been directing their energies and resources to that end. Similarly, Brian Oakley, chairman of Logica, claims there are countless examples where R&D and training programmes have had to be cut back, and he goes as far as saying 'anything that might affect the share price, like an investment, we daren't make'.

David Hopkinson, chairman of Harrison and Crosfield, believes that people in the City now 'work on behalf of themselves' not their clients, and the new breed of investment managers and analysts are 'arrogant and driven by self-interest'. These negative views of City investors are echoed by successful private companies that are not on the stock market. The chairman of the private company JCB, for example, sees the lack of shareholder pressure as 'a very big plus' for the long-term success of his company (*The Thatcher Audit*, 4.9.90). Similarly, Pat Grant, managing director of Norfrost, a highly successful and rapidly expanding private company, is concerned

---

*The quotations and factual information for the first part of the ensuing section are taken from *The Money Programme*, 24.6.90, unless otherwise stated. The interpretations are the author's.

with directing profit back into growing her business, rather than handing it out in the form of dividends to investors. She comments:

> I think that Britain really has lost out in manufacturing because we don't take a long-term view of manufacturing, neither the government nor the stock exchange (*In Business*, 17.10.90).

David Murray, managing director of Murray International, also a highly successful and rapidly expanding private company, has the same view, based on an underlying collaborative commitment to his employees:

> I have no ambitions to be in any industry, it's the people I'm backing . . . I'm backing a team of people who I think will pay dividends. I'm delighted I'm not a public animal because I would not then be controlling my own destiny (*In Business*, 17.10.90).

This attack on the City by company managers is endorsed by the Department of Trade and Industry's Innovation Advisory Board. In 1990 the DTI produced figures to show that since 1975 investment by British industry in research and development has fallen behind countries such as France, America, Germany and Japan – German and Japanese annual increases being nearly twice and three times as much as Britain's. The Innovation Advisory Board blames Britain's poor record on pension fund managers (although it should be noted the latter are not completely free agents as they run the risk of being ditched for underperforming by the institution's trustees).

There is no doubt that the 'takeover' culture has had a detrimental effect on the level of investment in research and training, but some believe that it does not stem primarily from City fund managers but from the company managers themselves. It has already been considered earlier in this chapter that in general managers do not see the importance of education and training, so the takeover culture cannot be solely blamed for that. Also, as Professor John Kay of the London Business School points out:

> . . . management has a preoccupation with deal-making – on the one hand there are expansive or sometimes megalomaniac managers whose main concern is to do the next deal rather than to develop their operating business.

The deal-making chief executive has been a characteristic of the 1980s, and examples include John Ashcroft of Coloroll, John Gunn of British and Commonwealth Financial Group, Asil Nadir of Polly

Peck, and Sir Ralph Halpern of the Burton Group (see also Chapter 2; p28). This, according to Professor Kay, is believed to have caused a culture in the City that is concerned with where the next bid is going to come from rather than with a fundamental analysis of the quality of the business. Further, in defence of themselves, investment managers say that the stock market demonstrably prefers companies with a well-defined long-term strategy; that short termism is a charge mainly from badly performing companies – an alibi for poor management. This seems to be borne out by the fact that The Body Shop and the B Elliott Group, which are run on the philosophy of involving and empowering people, and investing long term in the building of their organisations through training and equipment, rather than being run primarily on the basis of strict financial control and short-term profit, are both approved of and liked by the stock market.

However, the long-term attitude of City fund managers will be put to the test, if the speculated bid by the Hanson Trust for ICI takes place. The possibility has caused much concern among ICI employees, managers and many politicians, who believe the Hanson approach to business, which centres on dealings and financial-cost control rather than internally 'growing' a business, would not continue with the more long-term commitment and support ICI has traditionally shown to its employees, their training and research and development. It is speculated by a City analyst, however, that if Hanson makes an offer that is significantly above the current share price, fund managers will find it hard to resist the prospect of making an instant big profit, 'even though they themselves may feel that it's the wrong move in terms of industrial development of this country (The Money Programme, 16.6.91). The larger than expected profits announced for the first half of 1991, which would make ICI more expensive for the Hanson Trust, was hoped to help stave off a takeover bid by Lord Hanson. But if such a bid were ever to occur and succeed in the future, then the City's claim not to be short termist would be severely undermined.

Summing up the situation generally, there seems, in fact, to have been fault on both sides, the company managers and the investment fund managers. Professor Keith Bradley has noted that there has been a coincidence of interests between the City and chief executives – or it might be better to say a coincidence of self-interests. Both company managers and City fund managers benefit from short termism. Top managers' pay is usually tied to annual profit and share dividends, and money is channelled in that direction at the expense of investments in training and R&D. Significantly, British firms pay out in dividends more than double the average for the rest of the world. Also, because a manager's success is measured and rewarded in terms of the number of deals that he or she makes, top managers have directed funds towards the acquisition of other businesses, rather than towards the *building* of the existing business through training, equipment and R&D (see also below). In the 1980s, directors' pay rose by 40 per cent more than average earnings (see also Chapter 12, p226). Short termism has meant that increasingly neither company managers nor fund managers have been working together 'collaboratively' for the long-term benefit of the company, its employees and customers. There is a general lack of long-term commitment by top managers, as much as there is with fund managers. And their private gain makes the work-force very cynical, which in turn reduces their commitment. The result has been an increasing number of firms getting into financial difficulties, many collapsing entirely.

The general short-term attitudes that prevail in managers and investors seem to have been compounded by a questionable honesty and lack of openness in accountants, who have been accused of colluding with top managers to produce misleading audit reports on company accounts that overstate profits. In the short term this benefits a top manager's salary, and the accountants who thereby stand to receive extra business from the management – including work when a company makes an acquisition. The tendency for there to be a lack of collaborative commitment to the long-term well-being of an organisation on the part of accountants, is borne out by the collapse of organisations such as Sock Shop, British and Commonwealth, Coloroll and Polly Peck, all of which overextended in the 1980s, and all of which received their auditor's seal of approval a relatively short time before they went under (*The Money Programme*, 17.2.91). The BCCI auditors, Price Waterhouse, were criticised by a BCCI depositors' lawyer, among others, for not insisting much earlier to be shown files proving fraud, but instead giving their seal of approval, when they had found major irregularities in the company's accounts (*Channel 4 News*, 2.8.91).

As in the case of the relationship between government and employers referred to in the previous section, therefore, here again we have one set of non-collaborative attitudes – in City investors (and accountants) – reinforcing another set – in top managers.

Non-collaborative short termism of banks

The short-term outlook of the other investors in organisations – the banks – also reinforces non-collaborative short termism within organisations. Even with well-managed organisations, banks seem to show a general distrust and reticence for supporting long-term investment in training people, new ideas (R&D) and equipment. For example, a managing director of a small manufacturing company recounts his bank's response to his request to lend him further funds for new plant and equipment for the company he had turned around in two years – despite oput-of-date equipment and buildings:

> Hey, wait a minute, we've already made an investment in the business, and we need to see a return on the first investment before we plough significantly more funds into the business (*The Thatcher Audit*, 28.8.90).

Contrast this with a comment made by a German small business manager about the relationship he has with his bank:

> . . . they come in my factory, and they look and then we speak together, and then they say for example, 'OK, do you need money, you must buy a new machine', and so on, yes, and we try to have always the best one, for example, so that we have a chance to survive on the market (*In Business*, 28.8.91).

The British manager said the financial return would come: 'but it's a question of timescale – if we were a Japanese company maybe we would be working to different timescales'. The Japanese, and Germans, in fact, generally work to a longer timescale. Their top managers and investors (mainly banks but also shareholders), are not looking for a quick return as a basis for their own personal advancement, referred to earlier in this chapter as the case for many Western managers and investors. Rather, they are more willing to risk more funds for a longer time in order to *build* businesses. The reason for this is that they have more collaborative attitudes and therefore commitment towards people; and organisations and their products and services are seen to be there *primarily* for the benefit of people – employees, customers, and the community generally – and not just to make profit (see also Chapter 12, p196). It is their underlying respect and trust in people, their value and abilities, which leads them to support investment in them, and their training and equipment – all necessary ingredients in the building process. Within the close partnership between investor (bank or stock market) and organisation, the collaborative attitudes of the investor reinforce the collaborative attitudes in top managers. This, for example, is recognised by Geoff Woods, managing director of Toray Textiles in Nottingham, formerly part of Courtaulds, who found the Japanese approach contrasted sharply with the British, and 'opened [their] eyes to some different attitudes':

> The environment which senior Japanese management is operating is one where the stock market allows relatively small improvements in short-term results to be completely overshadowed by what that company is doing in investment terms – whether it be in capital expenditure or in research and development . . . or in terms of education and training.

And he also points out there is 'much more of a long-term commitment . . . in terms of partnership . . . with the banking world' (*The Thatcher Audit*, 4.9.90).

The general relationship between banks and their business customers in Britain is a far cry from the close partnership that exists in the German and Japanese models. In addition to a general reticence of banks to support long-term investments, small business people complain, for example, about a lack of flexibility in the rates of interest, secretive bank charges, and the changing terms of loans and overdrafts, which they believe to be unfair, especially within times of recession. On the other side, banks maintain that it is difficult to come by management information, especially when a business gets into difficulties. The generally poor relationship that exists is well summed up by Stan Mendham, chief executive of the Forum of Private Business, as a 'fear-based, adversarial relationship', and he calls for: '. . . more of a collaborative basis between the two so they work together more as a partnership' (*Money Box*, 10.11.90).

A survey undertaken by the Institute of Directors (IOD), indicated that small business organisations did not in fact want 'easy money', but rather they wanted banks to take an interest in their business in the long term (*Channel 4 News*, 2.8.91). Of course they would prefer a 'collaborative' partnership, where banks give long-term support, particularly through bad times, as do German and Japanese banks with their business customers. Similarly, a survey done in Germany showed that organisations said that their idea of good banking relations was 'a reliable relation in difficult times' (*In Business*, 28.8.91). The difference between Germany and Britain is that their organisations generally get this support, whereas British organisations do not (see also Chapter 12). A long-term, collaborative partnership will only become the norm if top managers, in business as well as banks, develop more collaborative attitudes towards people, moving away from adversarial, non-collaborative ones that centre on short-term profit and personal gain at the expense of investing in people, their training and equipment – essential for long-term success.

Collaborative long-term restructuring and education and training*

The general situation between company managers and fund managers in Britain has been summed up by *Analysis* presenter, David Walker, as follows: 'In the British model, loyalty and long term get short shrift. In Germany they do things differently.' The following indicates just how differently. Professor Julian Franks of the London Business School found that the common denominator in a small group of restructurings in German companies was: 'The *increase* in capital spending, or the very small reduction that took place in capital spending. The *increase* in training. The *increase* in research and development.' He compares this with the British restructurings that took place in the early 1980s, where the common denominator there was: '. . . closures, reduction in capital spending, reduction of R&D, anything to save cash flow – to improve the profit and loss account.'

The same has generally been the case in the latest recession. Professor Franks found it 'striking' that the German restructurings had a much longer-term horizon, focusing on *new* products and *product development*, involving significant increases in investment, even when companies were performing very poorly. Professor Colin

*The quotations and factual information for the ensuing section are taken from *Analysis*, 29.11.90. The interpretations are this author's.

Mayer puts this down to the fact that, 'the main investors [the banks] in the firms are *consulted*. There is a strategy that is agreed'. As a result, he says, because the banks are involved in forming the strategy, they are strongly behind its implementation and so there is no possibility of one of the investors deciding to allow a take-over of the company. David Walker summarised: 'In trouble in Germany you don't sell up but invest, in order to recover in the long run. Germans, having agreed a corporate plan, tend to stick to it come boom or bust.'

The Japanese, as already considered, have the same attitude. Even within the latest British recession, while British organisations generally cut back, Japanese transplants took the long-term view and continued to invest in people, their training and equipment. Their top managers are backed up in this collaborative commitment to the organisation and its people by a corresponding collaborative commitment of investors. A closer partnership between organisation and investor, whether bank or shareholder, where each partner is collaboratively committed to building a business, means that investors do not so easily withdraw funds or sell out to the nearest bidder, and hostile takeovers do not occur.

Because of the success of the German and Japanese approaches, there is increasing agreement that British managers and investors 'need to spend a bit more time in bed together'. Charles Nunelly, chairman of the Institutional Fund Managers Association, is just one of an increasing number of people calling for improved 'communication' and more involvement between investors and companies. One would indeed expect more long-term loyalty and commitment from investors if they were communicated with more, and especially if they became more involved in company strategy through consultation, though, not necessarily to the point where they would stick to a company 'come boom or bust'. Further, there would be problems in bringing about closer communication and involvement between company managers and investors, as is pointed out by Professor John Kay. The present situation is one where company managers feel the need to be *secretive* rather than *open*, and this (and the related legal aspects), reflects their lack of *trust* in the investors to be loyal and committed to acting in the best interests of companies when provided with 'inside' information. It would, therefore, take more than just increased communication, or even consultation, concerning strategy, for investors not only to stick with a company when it starts performing badly, but also to provide increased investment for training and R&D, etc at those times, or even in good times. It would in fact require a fundamental shift in attitudes to more long-term, collaborative ones on the part of the investors. It would also, as considered above, require a similar shift in the company managers' attitudes themselves. Collaborative attitudes of mutual respect, trust, loyalty and commitment are the vital ingredient that distinguishes the German and Japanese long-term approaches from the British short-term one.

A general lack of collaborative attitudes in the British way of doing things, therefore, has led to poor investment in people's education and training; and this has been accentuated within the latest British recession as the following example, and further examples in Chapter 12, illustrate.

Collaborative attitudes and survival – Example*

An example of just how important underlying collaborative attitudes are for long-term success, and how business and employees can suffer when they are absent, is provided by the venture capital industry. The industry was set up to finance young companies in return for a stake in the business. It also enabled managers to buy the companies they worked for 'and to invest in their own success'. On the surface, therefore, this would seem a recipe for more long-term loyalty and commitment to the business by both managers and investors. But this has not always been the case, and now some companies have got into crisis as a result. The main reasons have been as follows:

1. Some venture capitalists have encouraged managers to expand and make big deals, rather than collaboratively focusing and directing funds to the existing business and employees – ie more education and training, more R&D, more equipment.

2. They have subsequently pulled out when the firm has got into difficulties.

3. Top managers have pulled out when the firm has got into difficulties, rather than acting collaboratively to save the business and employees' jobs.

---

*The quotations and factual information for the ensuing example are taken from *The Money Programme*, 2.12.90. The interpretations are this author's.

These events occurred, for example, in the case of the electronics component company General Hybrid, about which the following comments have been made:

> The immediate plight of General Hybrid stems from a management buy out three years ago ... Its problems are typical of many companies which over-reached themselves in the late 80s and are now hard hit by the recession ... The senior executives involved in the buy out have now left. They were backed by venture capitalists ... ECI Ventures [which] have since pulled out (*The Money Programme*).

> We put more money up, we assisted in management changes, we put a *lot of effort* in to trying to resolve the problems that the company had. But it does take time, and at some stage one has to ask the question whether one should put more money in or leave the business to its own fortunes. (Venture capitalist).

In contrast, three years would be considered short term for German and Japanese investors, and organisations have access to long-term 'patient' money. And as far as the successful Japanese companies are concerned, it would be unthinkable for top managers to be moving around as they do in the West. Loyalty and commitment are very strong, employees are taken on by an organisation for life, and the top managers have worked their way up.

The then acting chief executive at General Hybrid, Martin Tarr, however, showed more collaborative commitment to the business and the work-force than the previous senior executives, when he said:

> What is at stake is the continuation of the business and just over 200 jobs ... There have been redundancies – what we want to do as part of this financial re-structuring is to have an *end* to redundancies.

So too do the present venture capitalist investors (Northern Venture Managers), who have put together a rescue package to save the firm. Admittedly, venture capitalists are under pressure for short-term gains from the City fund managers who supply them with their capital. But they need to put their own house in order relating to their underlying 'short-term' non-collaborative attitudes and concern for expansion and deal making. As *The Money Programme* reporter concluded:

> Venture capitalists want to learn from their experiences in the 80s,

but they need to save and re-build companies like General Hybrid to show that where they venture, *everyone* gains.

Summary – the collaborative culture, education and training

With prevailing non-collaborative attitudes that have led to a generally 'poor top management', a non-interventionist government strategy, and a general short-term outlook in investors, it is little wonder that far less of the work-force in Britain are qualified than for our major competitors abroad. The situation is serious for individual, organisational and national well-being. Chris Hayes of the Prospect Centre, for example, says unless we greatly increase education and training, 'we haven't got a dog's chance in the competitive game' (*The Money Programme*, 6.5.90). And Hilary Steedman of the National Institute of Economic and Social Research warned in 1990:

> If we don't get our training right *immediately*, if we don't change
> things this year or next, then in five years' time and more especially
> in ten years' time, the situation will be quite catastrophic, and we
> shall be totally uncompetitive. (*The Thatcher Audit*, 4.9.90)

It is urgent, therefore, that closer partnerships are formed between organisations, government and investors, where there is a greater collaborative commitment to building organisations through commitment to employees, their training and equipment. But it is important to realise that it is not just more education and training that is needed. Just putting more money in for more training could be a costly waste of time. Relevant 'work-based' training which incorporates on-going self-team development in the workplace is essential if training is going to be effective, and this will require enabling collaborative organisational cultures (see Part III). It is urgent, therefore, for top managers to begin to develop their collaborative attitudes and skills, both as a basis for increasing the quantity of training, and for developing *enabling* collaborative organisational cultures necessary for that training to be fully effective.

12

The national culture – education, training and UK incorporated

Although the previous chapter set out specifically to consider the link between a collaborative organisational culture and effective education, training and development, it brought to light the importance of factors outside an organisation that are determined by the broader national culture.

The non-collaborative, 'not-care', national culture

The nature of that national culture is pinpointed in a statement by a leading investment manager:

> I think there is a real problem of an unclear relationship, a *'not-care'* relationship, if I can put it that way, between investment managers and company managements. There needs to be much more understanding of the motives of each by the other (*The Money Programme*, 24.6.90 private communication; my emphasis).

A non-collaborative, 'not-care' attitude is in fact part of the general culture of Britain. It exists within organisations, between organisations and suppliers, organisations and customers, organisations and investors, industrial and educational organisations, and organisations and government. It puts immediate, short-term profits and financial costs before people and product-service quality, although the latter are essential for long-term performance and success. It is in direct contrast with the more collaborative approaches used, for example, by, and between, Japanese organisations, which put people and quality *before* profits and financial costs (see also Chapter 11; cf

Deming, 1986, pp99, 100). For instance, Sir Peter Parker is one who has pointed out how Japanese organisations are not run in the interests of profits and shareholders alone, and he refers to the 'extraordinary meshing of interests, of banks, of MITI, of capital and labour', where shareholders 'are never going to accept a bid from somebody else' (*Open Mind*, 22.6.91). A similar longer-term commitment and loyalty is shown by German investors (banks and shareholders) towards organisations (Chapter 11), and they are described as having 'a great distaste for hostile bids' (*In Business*, 28.8.91).

Prevailing non-collaborative British attitudes also contrast with the philosophy and practice of top managers in certain successful collaborative organisations in Britain and America, who remain committed to the work-force, their education, training and equipment, despite short-term, non-collaborative external pressures. For example, Anita Roddick of The Body Shop says, 'My responsibility is not primarily to shareholders and speculators – it is to keep the employees employed . . .' (Schumacher, 1990). The NatWest Investment Bank Group refer to the different, non-traditional approach of The Body Shop to business, its values which create staff morale, and its holistic view that, 'It is not simply a creator of profit for shareholders but a force for the welfare of its employees, the community and ultimately the planet itself' (NatWest, 1991, p5).

This investment group believes that '*the Body Shop difference is good management*' (see also 'adding value' p228). Similarly, Maura Stannon of the successful Rainbow General Store in San Francisco, has basically the same philosophy as The Body Shop:

Making a profit is not what's important – what's important is keeping our workers happy, and also to keep the store going and to keep it going collectively. (*Where on Earth are We Going?*, 23.7.90)

The generally non-collaborative national culture also permeates the educational sector, and prevailing attitudes contrast with those exceptional schools which collaboratively involve teachers, pupils and parents (eg Gibbons, 1989; ILEA, 1986) This will be further considered later in this chapter.

Interestingly, the non-collaborative national culture, with its preoccupation with short-term cost, profit and personal gain, is reflected in the contents of national newspapers – particularly the business sections. This, for example, is pointed out by economic consultant Graham Bannock, who, on the basis of research carried out at the London Business School, refers to a 'short-term and remote attitude to industrial management', and contrasts it with Japanese attitudes:

> If you pick up a Japanese newspaper . . . [it] is concerned with new products, with people building research centres or with new materials, you know – with practical things. Our business press is pre-occupied with takeovers, mergers, financial results (*Analysis*, 29.11.90).

The non-collaborative national culture of blame and buck passing

The judgemental nature of a non-collaborative culture means that when problems and difficulties arise, there is a general tendency for people and organisations to blame others rather than to consider their part in the problem constructively. It will often be the case, for example, that government blames global forces, or reduced demand of the market place, or companies and the work-force, or the educational system and teachers, or the weather, etc; company managers often blame government, or employees, or banks, or the stock market, or the other creditors, or the educational system, etc; creditors (banks and the stock market) often blame company management, etc; teachers often blame government, or pupils, or parents, etc.

For example, anyone who followed media items relating to the latest British recession, might have become a little confused about how it had come about. Here are just a handful of comments made at the time.

> The government blamed the bad [unemployment] figures in part, on the cold weather in March (*Channel 4 News*, 18.4.91).

> Undoubtedly, the rise in interest rates . . . was the main factor which made our business go under (managing director on *The Money Programme*, 17.3.91).

> This *awful* recession, which is causing so much grief, is a *failure of government economic management*. It is government failure, *not* a market failure (director general Peter Morgan, IOD Conference 23.4.91).

> Everyone regrets the rise in unemployment that there has been . . . I've been warning for some months that if wage rises stay high, that will have a necessary effect on jobs (Prime Minister John Major on *Channel 4 News*, 13.12.90).

We [British managers] don't have the cash, we don't have the low cost capital the Germans have got . . . we haven't got a ready supply of highly trained employees which is what the Germans have got, and the French have got, and the Italians have got (managing director on *Panorama*, 18.3.91).

. . . the return of two million unemployed after only two years below that level is stirring memories of the deep recession at the start of the 1980s. As then, ministers blame global forces (*BBC News*, 14.3.91).

In all my forty-odd years in manufacturing, I've never known two key markets simultaneously to have serious economic difficulties, namely the US and the UK, and have that compounded by the very serious situation in the Gulf (Vickers chairman justifying job cuts on *Channel 4 News*, 25.2.91).

There is usually some truth in most of the 'blamings' that are made. In fact, in the case of the organisational collapses and unemployment within the latest British recession, for example, the truth is that most of the major players had some part to play in the outcome – most operated with a non-collaborative, short-term lack of commitment:

- the government for encouraging an 'enterprise' culture of borrowing, creating conditions for easy credit, and setting interest rates too low in the 1980s; which consequently led to them setting high interest rates to counter the inflationary effects of the resultant boom;

- banks for cavalier over-lending, and some for over-extending in terms of acquisitions, in the boom time; and for reducing and making lending more difficult within the recession;

- organisations for over-borrowing, and some for over-extending in terms of acquisitions, in the boom time;

- the stock market for short termism in boom or recession.

However, the British disease of approaching problems by judgementally allocating blame to others is one way in which individuals and organisations avoid admitting their own faults and mistakes, and evade recognising their own responsibility in bringing a situation about. There are exceptions. One manager of a steel erector firm, for example, did not immediately jump in to put all the blame on others for the fact that his company had to call in the receiver; he seemed to show more honesty and humility than is usual within the British culture, and thereby came to a closer understanding of the situation:

> Is it my fault, or do I blame anybody else, or do I blame the recession? I just think it's the whole situation of the country – it's in such a poor state (*BBC News*, 18.4.91).

And it is the view of this author that those managers who do not judgementally blame others, but who instead show more humility and self-appraisal concerning their own actions and a generally more collaborative approach with other people within their organisations, who are more likely to lead their organisation to efficiency and quality. In turn, therefore, they are more likely to be able to meet and survive adverse external factors and recession. After all, not all organisations collapse or get into difficulties within recession (see The Body Shop, the B Elliott Group, etc). And, for example, at a time when car dealers were being particularly badly hit due to large falls in car sales, and three car makers were cutting their prices, a Honda dealer was reported to be confident of holding on to customers without joining in the price war:

> We've maintained our sales figures so far through the recession; we consider we will be able to maintain them as well through the competitive stance that we've already taken with the business sector, and the way we are conducting our business at the moment; and thankfully the specification of the car we are selling (*News at Ten*, 4.7.91).

A quality product and service, therefore, is of paramount importance to survival and success, and overrides adverse factors such as high interest rates (see Example 2 p203). (That is not to deny, of course, that all organisations would be better off if they received more general collaborative support from government and creditors.) Further, there is the chance that not only will collaborative top managers gain the commitment of their employees and private customers, but also by collaboratively involving outside organisations – customers, suppliers, bankers, etc – they have a better chance of bringing these along with them and gaining their commitment and support.

A generally non-collaborative national culture means that as well as there being a tendency for individuals and organisations to 'pass the buck' in terms of who is responsible for difficulties arising, there is also the tendency to pass the buck in terms of financial burden. For example, when organisations get into difficulty through over-borrowing, inefficiency, and general bad management, it is of course a form of financially passing the buck when employees are put out of work. The latest British recession furnishes two other examples of non-collaborative financial buck passing.

Non-collaborative buck passing – Example 1

The relationship between customer organisation and supplier organisation that generally exists in Britain is in marked contrast to that which exists in more collaborative national cultures. Deming, for example, says of the Japanese organisation–supplier relationship:

> More important than price in the Japanese way of doing business is continual improvement of quality, which can be achieved only on a long-term relationship of loyalty and trust . . . (1986, p43; see also Chapter 9)

The more non-collaborative nature of the British organisation–supplier relationship was highlighted within the latest recession by the fact that as the economy began to slow, bigger organisations began delaying paying their bills to their smaller suppliers. In this way, bigger organisations were using their suppliers as a source of cheap credit in order to cut their costs to deal with the difficulties of a lower market demand. The economic damage caused by growing numbers of late-paying customers meant that some firms went bust and others needed to borrow more. This was the case, for example, for the plastics component manufacturer, Bluemay Ltd:

> Really, they [the larger customer organisation] are using us to finance their operations, they're saving themselves the hassle of going to their bank or their shareholders asking for increased lines of credit or more money, and instead using their influence, their buying power, to exert pressure on suppliers to finance their operations (company secretary, on The Money Programme, 3.3.91).

The situation indicates how non-collaborative, disloyal, short-term pressure gets passed down the line to the weakest. If the relationship between investors (banks, shareholders) and organisations was more collaborative, and the former were more involved and more committed to seeing organisations through in times of difficulties – as is the case with many European and Japanese investors – then the larger organisation would, in turn, be less likely to put pressure on smaller ones in the form of late payments. But, of course, organisations cannot totally hide behind the general non-collaborative national culture to justify passing the buck in this way – after all, not all larger organisations used their suppliers to help shoulder their financial burdens within the latest recession.

The company secretary at Bluemay has first-hand experience of the different relationships that exist in Europe. They have an agent in Holland who pays them on 20 days, and he says they never have to chase that particular customer for the money (compare this with UK settlement periods very often up to 120 days during the recession – *Money Box*, 28.9.91). Similarly, a Briton who now manages a bank in Germany says that late payment is not a problem for her small business clients, and she observes: 'the British generally have a bad reputation for that', and certain German companies in Britain 'were always amazed that the bills were never paid on time' (*In Business*, 28.8.91). In Germany, she says, the matter is taken far more seriously, and firms are offered a discount if they pay on time, so that many are paying ahead of time so improving the cashflow of smaller companies. Consequently, as the company secretary of Bluemay recognises, European competitors do not have the sort of overhead costs of financing credit and credit control operations chasing money – they get their payments on time and make their payments on time.

Dr Roger Baxter, chief executive of Electrolux UK, which had a policy of paying bills more slowly to its suppliers during the recession, admits that he does not understand 'concepts of European views on how business should be operated'. He believes, 'Our survival is not dictated by general statements of policy. Our survival, our progress, is dictated by the marketplace' (*The Money Programme*, 3.3.91).

It is significant that he sees survival and progress to be at the mercy of a remote 'marketplace', rather than in terms of his own management – his relationship with employees, suppliers and customers. He must certainly have been aware that his way of operating business, passing debts on to his smaller suppliers, would reduce their chances of survival and progress. The Federation of Small Businesses, for example, claim that the late repayment of bills was responsible for the failure of many of the 23,000 businesses that went under in the first six months of 1991. Also, for those businesses that survive the recession, not only will this burden on them undermine their growth when the economy picks up, it will also undermine their competitiveness with European organisations who have not been similarly burdened.

There was also a more deep-seated dimension to this non-collaborative buck passing that would back-fire on the larger customer organisation. It would damage the relationship between customer and supplier organisation, undermining trust and loyalty and endangering their health and competitiveness in the long term. For example, David Jennings of Corn Pepper says,

> . . . we just cannot afford to finance other people's businesses . . . The lesson that we're learning, unfortunately, is not to be so trusting of other companies. (*The Midlands Report*, 21.3.91).

But, as considered at the beginning of this example and in Chapter 9, a long-term relationship of trust and loyalty is necessary to achieve continual improvement of quality; in turn necessary for progress, competitiveness and survival in the long term.

Non-collaborative buck passing – Example 2

The contrast between the collaborative way Japanese and German banks operate when organisations are in difficulties compared with British banks (see Chapter 11), was highlighted during the latest British recession. British banks were accused of operating a 'credit strike', where funds were either reduced and levels of interest above base rate increased; or even withdrawn, causing many company collapses. The banks generally have been criticised for 'cavalier over-lending' in the boom years of the 1980s, and 'pulling the rug' from organisations during the recession. This non-collaborative treatment by banks fell more harshly on smaller organisations. Larger organisations also found it more difficult to borrow, although they often had a good credit rating and so were able to borrow from foreign banks. During the recession, however, American banks began lending much less in London because of their own banking problems, as did German and other European banks because of lending to East German industry, which gave the big four British banks more power, even with the larger organisations. But it was the weaker, smaller organisations that complained the most about the 'unfair' way they were being treated by the banks. Although there will no doubt have been small businesses that felt they had been fairly treated by their bank during the recession, the following comment was representative of the growing feeling at the time:

I think the worst thing is when I asked him for advice he had no advice to give me. Now when you go to a bank at the start up of a business, they've got plenty of advice. But when you have a problem, it's just, 'I'm sorry, but we're pulling the rug from under your feet. That's it. You go and find your own way out.' I asked him simple questions about suppliers, what do I do? And he said, 'Don't know.' (*In Business*, 6.3.91).

A major part of the complaint by small businesses was that banks were not passing on interest rate reductions to them, but instead unfairly keeping overdraft rates and other charges high. The cry was taken up enthusiastically by the media in June 1991, and banks were accused of being, for example: 'greedy', 'money-grabbing', 'bullying', 'deceitful', of 'profiteering', and of making small business people boost fallen profits and 'carry the can' for the banks' past mistakes – such as cavalier lending in the 1980s, offering too low an interest rate in the late 1980s to match the rate offered by foreign competitors without matching efficiency, and Third World debt. Feelings were running high, and the concern was also taken up by politicians, including the Prime Minister, John Major, who appointed the Chancellor of the Exchequer to enquire into the facts. One fact, however, was already established – in an increasing number of cases there was something amiss with the relationship between banks and their small business customers.

In their defence, the banks said they needed to charge more for small businesses than larger ones, because they were a greater risk during an economic recession, and because additional work was involved in lending to them. But to believe it is justifiable to charge an organisation more for borrowing during a recession knowing they are more likely to have problems in that recession, only seems to underline a 'not-care', non-collaborative attitude on the part of banks.

John Watts, a conservative member of the cross-party Treasury Select Committee, is one who believes it is 'inappropriate' for banks to up the rate of interest when a customer gets into difficulties; and it cannot be justified on the basis that such customers represent a greater risk, because '. . . the time for the bank to assess the risk is when it makes the loan in the first place' (*The World at One*, 24.10.91). He decries the overlending by banks that took place in the 1980s, and the subsequent removal of their money from the resulting over-extended businesses when the market turned against the latter. He sums up the lack of collaborative partnership between the banks and small businesses when he says of the former: 'they're not prepared to share in any part of the risk-taking part of enterprise' (op cit).

As Stan Mendham, chief executive of the Forum of Private Business points out, recession '. . . is the time when small businesses need help, not hindrance' (*In Business*, 6.3.91). He acknowledges that the banks feel the recession like any other organisation, but claims they are being 'incredibly unfair' in dealing with it by keeping interest rates high and cutting down on their overdraft facilities and loans to their existing small business customers.

Rather than the banks dealing with their difficulties by passing the buck to their customers (and to their employees and private customers with branch closures and lay-offs), they could operate more collaboratively to reduce costs and operate more efficiently (see also p226). Significantly, part of the Chancellor of the Exchequer's enquiries were to include, he said, looking into whether 'the banks themselves are doing everything to control their own costs and to operate efficiently' (*Frost on Sunday*, 2.6.91).

Within the controversy, Andrew Buxton, deputy chairman of Barclays Bank, made the claim that interest rate costs are not a significant cost for business compared with material costs and labour costs (*Newsnight*, 3.6.91). Leaving aside whether this is necessarily so in each and every case, it is a valid point that if an organisation is run collaboratively to achieve high efficiency, quality and innovation, then it will be fitter and better able to deal with and survive high interest rates (and the short termism of its creditors/debtors). High interest rates need not in themselves put an organisation under. But they do not, of course, help an organisation during difficult times, and Andrew Buxton admits that 'in a recession the relationship between banker and customer gets strained', and high interest rates may 'exacerbate' that strained relationship. By admitting, with seeming impunity, that banks may be operating to exacerbate their relationship with small businesses, however, this again indicates that there is no broad collaborative, caring, bank culture.

Pen Kent, associate director of the Bank of England, believes that:

> . . . bankers who lend in good times have some responsibility when the going gets tough, to find a constructive way forward, and that can mean helping their customer to survive. They shouldn't take foolish decisions, but they can take sympathetic and constructive ones (*The Money Programme*, 16.12.90).

The reality, unfortunately, does not live up to this call for more collaborative responsibility on behalf of the banks. According to Sir Kenneth Cork, up to half of the businesses that had collapsed in the recession might have been saved if the banks had tried to support them rather than 'pulling up the carpet far too quickly' (*Check Out*, 19.6.91). The banks' preference for using the same accountants to assess a business as they eventually use to put it into receivership, endorses the criticisms and the feeling of unfairness among many business people. The latter feel that since accountants stand to earn so much more from a receivership than an investigation, then their investigation report will be biased. Understandably, they fear a conflict of interest. However, the following admission of Ian Bond, the chairman of the insolvency self-regulatory body, the Society of Practitioners of Insolvency, shows how one-sided their interest is: 'The primary job of the receiver is to get the bank its money back, it's not to save the company . . .' (*Check Out*, 19.6.91).

From the reduced lending, high charges, and what seems unnecessarily quick removal of funds in many cases, it is difficult to avoid the belief, even from the banks' own defence of their behaviour, that they are guided primarily by the goal of improving their own (short-term) profits, at the expense of collaboratively helping organisations to stay afloat and weather the recession.

For completion it should be said that the Treasury's month-long investigation into the accusations against the banks found that there was no evidence that they had colluded to keep interest rates high, but that 25 per cent of small businesses had not received the full benefit of interest rate cuts. The Chancellor wanted the banks to draw up a voluntary code of conduct on the way they treat small firms, but the Labour Party referred to the investigation as a 'whitewash' because it failed to criticise banks' profit margins. And Stan Mendham said business people would see it as a 'cop out', a 'missed opportunity' for enforcing fair contracts between banks and small businesses.

Three months later, in October 1991, a statement from the director general of the Office of Fair Trading (OFT) also cleared the banks of breaking competition rules. But he strongly criticised the banks' 'insensitive' and 'high-handed' behaviour, and expressed concern over the volume of complaints on hidden or opaque charges; the lack of warning of charges; the reduction of facilities at short notice; and the failure to act upon informal agreements or to meet customers' reasonable expectations. He called for a wider use of codes of conduct to assure the customers that they will be treated fairly and reasonably, in line with the Chancellor of the Exchequer's call for banks to be more open and publish relationship arrangements with the customer (reported on *Channel 4 News*, 24.10.91).

The deep-seated, unethical nature of the relationship between banks and their small business customers was expressed by one small businessman in response to the OFT's statement:

> It makes me angry. I do believe that technically maybe the banks haven't broken rules; but morally they're breaking rules every day (*The World at One*, 24.10.91).

Similarly, another such customer who was refused extra cash by his bank to see his company through the recession, commented:

> They don't *care*; the attitude [with which] they talk to you, the way they talk to you, as if they're doing you a big favour . . . (*News at Ten*, 24.10.91).

Because a more constructive relationship between banks and small business would require a change in underlying attitudes to more ethical, collaborative ones, it is doubtful that the government's slight criticism of banks, and the OFT's strong words, would be sufficient pressure to ensure the adherence to a mutually beneficial code of conduct between banks and small businesses.

Business leaders' concern that a voluntary code would not necessarily stop what they refer to as the banks' sharp practices, therefore, would seem to be vindicated, and legal enforcement would be a quicker way of changing practice in the short term, and underlying attitudes in the long term.

As with the case of the treatment of the small supplier by large organisations considered in the previous example, non-collaborative treatment of small business by banks is likely to back-fire on the banks themselves in the long run. Within the controversy, the Prime Minister pointed out: '. . . their [banks'] interest lies in having a sound base of small firms around for the future' (*BBC News*, 4.6.91).

By failing to give small businesses collaborative support during difficult times, more of them are likely to go under in the short term, thereby undermining business for banks in the long term. Also, more of them are likely to struggle and collapse in the medium term

when the economic upturn comes, up against the superior competition of better supported organisations, particularly in Europe and
Japan. This possibility is borne out by the events of the 1980–81
recession in Britain when, as pointed out by Guenter Steinitz, an
expert on the state of businesses '. . . more companies failed when
we were coming out of the recession than when we were in the
depths of the recession itself' (*Channel 4 News*, 28.8.91). Again, this
will undermine business for the banks. Finally, of those businesses
that do survive the recession and the upturn, more are likely to
struggle in the long term, as the non-collaborative treatment by
banks, especially in bad times, undermines the quality of the relationship between banks and their small business customers, a point
recognised by Simon Eccleston of the National Small Firms Council:

> At the moment there's a lot of *distrust* and *dislike*, and one gets the situ-
> ation I think where the bank manager who ought to be a friend, and
> an advisor in some elements, is becoming an enemy (*In Business*,
> 6.3.91).

Such deep-rooted feelings and attitudes are not easily overcome,
and they put back further the time when relationships of trust and
loyalty can be formed as a basis for long-term partnership – just as
essential between organisation and banks, as between organisations
and customer and supplier organisations, for achieving the efficiency, quality and innovation necessary to compete and survive
against the competition of the more collaboratively supported
organisations of the Japanese and Europeans. Again, this undermining
of small businesses means that the banks themselves are set to lose,
as indeed is the economy as a whole – a concern voiced by the
Small Firms Minister, Eric Forth:

> . . . we're talking about one of the *keystones* of our economy – the *relation-
> ship* between the lenders, the banks, and the borrowers, the small
> businesses (*Newsnight*, 3.6.91).

> I think the message is quite clear – to the banks anyway – your cus-
> tomers aren't happy, and you *must* sort your act out . . . (*BBC News*,
> 5.6.91).

While British banks *talk* about supporting their small business customers, foreign banks *act* to fulfil the rhetoric. For example, German
banks typically charge interest rates with a smaller margin above
the base rate than do British banks, give more years to repay an

overdraft, and rarely levy bank charges. But the difference does not just come down to financial figures. It is based on the underlying relationship that exists between banks and small businesses, a closer, more collaborative partnership, where business people know and feel that they are being genuinely helped and supported through good and bad times, and *trust* the banks to be giving them the *fairest* deal possible. No amount of talk will substitute for this relationship, as evidenced by the outcry from small business people which caused a major bank to withdraw a television advert claiming that the bank was a supporter of small business. And no amount of talk will counter the detrimental effect a non-collaborative bank-customer relationship has on the well-being of organisations, banks, and the country in the long term.

Non-collaborative buck passing – Example 3

Linked with the general financial climate in the later 1980s and early 1990s, colleges of further and higher education were finding themselves under greater constraints concerning their funding and other arrangements. Certain of the constraints legitimately required colleges to undergo restructuring. But some colleges have been accused of unnecessary reorganisation and restructuring, and there is concern by unions about management's 'ability to plan educational expansion, manage budgets and successfully perform other tasks associated with the running of higher education institutions' (Lawrence, 1990, p29).

In fact, a programme of restructuring can be one way in which top management can direct blame away from their own mismanagement and pass it down the line. Financial difficulties can be blamed on the present college structure. Senior management can be used as scapegoats by pressurising them to take 'voluntary premature retirement'. The escalation, within reorganisations, of the tendency 'for more and more work to be piled on staff without additional reward or additional support services' (Lawrence, 1990, p28), has been a case of financial buck passing by poor top management. And, of course, short-term savings can be looked for by having a programme of staff redundancies, both voluntary and enforced.

Summary – The non-collaborative culture of blame and buck passing

The national culture of judgementally allocating blame and passing the buck, rather than individuals and organisations developing the humility to self-appraise constructively their own responsibility in bringing about a difficult situation, is diametrically opposed to developing collaborative partnerships. These, however, are the only basis for achieving long-term, mutually beneficial strategies necessary to avoid the misery of poor performance, recession and job loss.

The non-collaborative way with people, education and training

The general non-collaborative approach in Britain is exemplified by the response to her entry into the European Exchange Rate Mechanism in 1990, and to the latest recession. Although the immediate problems posed by ERM entry relate mostly to the manufacturing sector, the manner in which the problems were dealt with apply also to the service sector, including education, as this chapter goes on to discuss.

In a nutshell, the problem was as follows. The percentage rise of British pay in the last part of 1990 was roughly twice as much as the rest of Europe, to match the then higher inflation rate in Britain. The concern was that this would put up unit costs (which are now determined by the more fixed value of the pound within the ERM), and make us uncompetitive in Europe and particularly Germany. The government and the Confederation of British Industry (CBI) therefore called for wage restraint by workers – although the Chancellor of the Exchequer added (and the CBI agreed), 'It is as relevant to pay in the boardroom as it is to pay on the shop-floor' (The Lord Mayor's Speech, 18 October, 1990). Without this, the Chancellor warned, there will be 'lost markets, redundancies, plant closures and ultimately company failures'. At the time the CBI believed that the recession would get worse in 1991, and predicted that 9000 jobs would be lost a month. (In fact between December 1990 and May 1991 80,000 jobs went per month, and unemployment was predicted – by, for example, the OECD and the National Institute of Economic and Social Research (NIESR) – to reach 3,000,000 by the end of 1992, and to remain high for some time after that.) Michael

Howard, the Employment Secretary, therefore called on people to 'behave sensibly' (eg *BBC News*, 18.10.90; *Panorma*, 12.11.90).

There are two concerns surrounding the stance that was taken. Firstly, as has been considered above, wage restraint in itself, without more funds for education, training, and R&D, will not make us competitive in the long term. A fact that was recognised at the time by some top managers:

> But being competitive, and being competitive in Europe, is not just a question of financial dimensions. There are many other important ones as well, like education and training, which we are very concerned with (Anthony Platt, then Chief Executive of the London Chamber of Commerce on *Newsnight*, 18.10.90).

Yet, as considered in the previous chapter, government funding for training was being increasingly cut, and it did not intervene in other ways to help employers in the training of employees. Secondly, the government saw no reason to intervene and collaborate with industry on the immediate problems of ERM entry, apart from stating the need for wage restraint.

Generalising from this particular example, it can be said that when British organisations are faced with problems due to high costs (through increased interest rates, energy costs, raw materials costs, wages, etc), and reduced demand:

- managers and government see cutting production costs and raising efficiency (to improve competitiveness) *first and foremost* in terms of the short-term measures of reducing labour costs – either by restraining wages or increasing unemployment – and cutting investment in equipment, training and R&D;

- government does not intervene to collaborate with organisations in short-term or long-term strategies;

- unions strongly resist wage restraint;

- investors tend to look for short-term gains and pull out when the going gets rough.

Non-collaborative 'leaner but not fitter'

The folly of the first point above was simply but forcefully expressed during the latest recession by the manager of the Japanese photocopying firm, Ricoh, based in Telford. He said, 'If we were to shed labour, we would not be fully prepared to take advantage of the next expansion of the economy' (*News at Ten*, 15.3.91). Generally, as has been considered earlier, Japanese and many European managers have respect and trust in people and their abilities, and consequently they value the human resource as a major resource in an organisation's success. While British organisations cut back during the recession, Japanese and German transplants in Britain continued to invest in people, their training and equipment. And, as mentioned earlier, they are supported in this collaborative, long-term attitude by a corresponding attitude in their creditors – the banks and shareholders.

However, economists again predicted a widening of the trade gap as home demand increased; despite:

- the evidence of the success of more collaborative, long-term thinking provided by, for example, the German and the Japanese approaches;

- the fact that a lack of investment and job losses in the 1980–81 recession added to a growing skills shortage, undermining fitness and competitiveness in the later 1980s;

- the warnings from individual economists and bodies such as the NIESR and OECD, that cutting back on investment will have a damaging effect on the British economy and competitiveness lasting over many years because it will lead to:

  (a) a shortage of output capacity, so that firms will not be able to meet orders when the economy recovers, leading to over-heating, inflation, and the sucking in of imports – requiring an increase in interest rates risking further recession (after the previous recession manufacturing output took eight years to climb back to pre-recession levels (*BBC News*, 7.10.91));

  (b) organisations falling behind in new technology and innovation leading to slower (and poorer quality) growth in output per head (falling further behind each year during the recovery period unless investment catches up), and uncompetitiveness, also sucking in imports;

- the confirmation of these warnings when the balance of payments deficit increased to £523 million in May 1991 and non-collaborative, short-term attitudes continued to dominate most British thinking during the recession. (The unexpected small trade surplus in June 1991 was put down to mainly increased car exports and continued depressed demand at home. Both were predicted not to last, and a return to a trade deficit the following month, and a further increase in August, supported this.*)

- the fact that European markets will be opening up after 1992 increasing the competition further against less fit British organisations handicapped by poor investment in people, their training and equipment;

The massive rise in unemployment and the sharp fall in investment during the recession was testimony to the non-collaborative attitudes that prevailed amongst managers, creditors, debtors and government. The pressure on organisations from the short-term thinking of their creditors will have been a factor in the fall in manufacturing investment of 28 per cent over the year to July 1991, and also the continued use by government of high interest rates to reduce inflation over that time. In early 1991, certain economists predicted that generally companies would continue to have layoffs and cut back sharply on their investment and training plans over the next two years, therefore adding to the past tendency of managers to under-invest for the long-term, even in good times, and greatly undermining the long-term fitness and competitiveness of organisations. A case of non-collaborative attitudes in creditors and government,

---

* The increase in deficit in July and August, 1991, was due to an increase in imports, and although exports also improved, certain economists maintained that the generally good export recovery over 1990–91 would not be sustainable in 1992. Significantly, Neil Mackinnon, chief economist at Yamaichi, for example, pointed out that the large balance of payments deficit in Britain while demand was flat within the recession, meant that Britain 'was probably the *only* economy out of the *major* industrialised economies to show a trade deficit of this magnitude' (*Business Daily*, 23.9.91). He put this down to a 'lack of competitiveness', and referred to the need for 'policies geared to improve our long-term economic performance.' Similarly, David Owen, UK economist at Kleinwort Benson, who also expected imports to grow faster and the trade deficit to get wider as Britain comes out of recession, believes that 'the government should take lessons from the OECD, and perhaps start educating and training the work-force more' in order to change that (*Business Daily*, 22.10.91).

re-inforcing the same attitudes in managers, was considered in Chapter 11.

At the time when British organisations generally operated in a way that seriously undermined their long-term competitiveness, foreign organisations continued to operate to enhance theirs, and in early 1991 the OECD forecasted that investment would rise sharply in Germany and Japan, and would increase in other OECD countries. While many developments and training programmes were being 'put on ice' or cut back by British companies, foreign transplants continued to invest. Nissan, for example, planned to double production in Sunderland, taking on 1600 people in early 1992, Sony announced plans to build another plant in South Wales, Toyota were building a manufacturing plant in Derbyshire and Honda planned to extend their factory to build cars in Swindon.

With the example of the greater success of other countries that invested more, and the continued investment made by foreign organisations under our noses in Britain, there were an increasing number of British managers voicing their concern about the harmful effects of cutting back. However, although they showed an *awareness* of the importance of investment in training and equipment for long-term fitness, this did not generally extend to *action*, and in the main they still:

- were pre-occupied with short-term 'cash-flow' considerations rather than long-term investment – in line with the general lack of collaborative support from creditors (banks, stock market, larger customers) pre-occupied with short-term financial gain;

- *failed to act* collaboratively within their organisations to ease the tight cash-flow situation rather than cutting investment in people, their training and equipment (see below).

So what you had was a situation where an increasing number of managers *reluctantly* and *frustratingly* cut back on people and investment. Here are some examples:

> I think we've been through it before. I think we now know how to cut costs. It's going to be painful – you know, we are going to have to get rid of labour that we don't want to get rid of. Training will be cut back, investment which we desperately don't want to stop, is going to be cut back (managing director, Bean Engineering on *BBC News*, 20.2.91).

The worst thing that we've done I suppose is we've postponed investment. We had a fairly important investment programme which started last year in a serious way, and that has been held up now (chief executive, Heath Springs on *News at Ten*, 6.6.91).

... one of the most frustrating things about 1990 has been that since conditions in the markets we work in have been rather difficult, we've had to spend more time than we would have liked just making sure that things were OK in the business, and maybe less time than we would have liked developing it (chief executive, Courtaulds Textiles on *In Business*, 13.3.91).

Concerning the last quotation, interestingly the chief executive goes on to say that Courtaulds plans to develop and compete on the basis of 'superior product innovation, or better service, or any factors which aren't simply concerned with cost and price', as, quite rightly, he believes that their customers (eg car manufacturers) don't buy simply on price but on performance, design and service. Yet, ironically, it is factors that *are* simply concerned with immediate 'cost and price' that are setting back and undermining that development.

But, as has been considered, these actions – cutting investments and shedding labour, which also occurred in the early 1980s recession – although they make companies *leaner*, they do not produce long-term *fitter* organisations. This, for example, was recognised by Bill Abbotts, managing director of a company that makes computer control equipment, when he strongly asserted, 'It's absolutely untrue that this country is leaner or fitter – in every measurable sense this country is in a worse mess than in 1979' (*Newsnight*, 15.8.91). And he claimed that he did not know anybody in the manufacturing industry who did not agree with him.

The following viewpoints expressed during the recession are based on underlying non-collaborative attitudes towards people, prevalent in managers and seemingly government, who see them as a dispensable resource in order to achieve financial savings to improve competitiveness. In reality, as considered above, this way provides only short-term 'improvement' in an organisation, and ultimately undermines its future fitness to compete and prosper – it has, in fact, inbuilt future uncompetitiveness and inflation.

In May 1991, Norman Lamont, Chancellor of the Exchequer, stated to Parliament:

Rising unemployment and the recession have been the price that

we've had to pay in order to get inflation down, but that is a price
well worth paying (16.5.91).

Michael Howard, Employment Secretary, said in reply to the question whether unemployment for people too old to get a job again is
a reasonable price to pay for the slimming down of industry:

> Well, you can't *ever* have an economy in which no one loses their
> jobs, and it is *absolutely* essential for the future of our economy that
> we bring inflation under control . . . if we don't do that we would lose
> many more jobs as the economy became increasingly less competitive
> (*Newsnight*, 16.5.91).

The chief executive of Rolls-Royce commenting on the 6000 job
cuts announced in May 1991 which the company said it had no
option over:

> I'm very hopeful that what we're doing now will put us in a position
> where we can survive the downturn in the business, and be very
> competitive when it up-turns. But if we continue to go down, we
> have to take appropriate action (*News at Ten*, 8.5.91).

Contrast what the chief executive of Rolls-Royce, along with many
other top managers and many in the government, considers to be
'appropriate action' – namely shedding jobs – with the quote at the
beginning of this section by the Japanese manager at Ricoh.

Non-collaborative short termism in top management – Example 1

With the news of a sharp fall in consumer spending in August 1991,
the government's hope that a consumer-led recovery out of recession
was on its way – fuelled by the rise in spending over the previous
two months – was checked. With the publication of the poor figure
for August, *Newsnight* looked at the Labour opposition's economic
policy (16.9.91). In line with more European and Japanese thinking,
the Shadow Chancellor, John Smith, claimed that the government's
wish for a consumer-led recovery was short termist, and would lead
to a further boom followed by a further recession (see above); and
in contrast they would engineer an investment-led recovery in
order to achieve sustained, long-term growth.

During the *Newsnight* programme, an executive director of a
chemical and electronics company, who had that day attended an
address by the Opposition leader, Neil Kinnock, in a CBI meeting to

businesspeople in the Midlands, listed the points that he liked in Labour's economic policy. These included:

- He (Mr Kinnock) was right when he said we must get away from boom, recession, boom, recession, that we've seen since the war.

- I did like what he said on capital allowances, particularly capital allowances for manufacturing and innovation, research and development.

- I like what he said about training the work-force – it's just what we need.

He seemed, therefore, to be in favour of Labour's investor-led programme to sustainable, long-term growth. His reply to the interviewer's question: 'You'll be voting for him?', however, was: 'I don't think so . . .' His reasons included:

- I didn't like his commitment to a minimum wage – the timing's wrong for that sort of thing, the economy is not strong enough yet.

- I didn't like his comments on credit controls on consumer spending. What this economy needs just at the moment is more spending by consumers.

- I *particularly* didn't like his taxing of higher paid executives – these are the very people who are going to lead industry out of this recession and they need motivating.

At the end of the day, therefore, despite his verbal support for a sustainable, long-term investment strategy, what tipped the balance for him against Labour's policy was a greater commitment to a short-term consumer-led strategy, and to non-collaborative, short-term measures relating to executive power and personal advancement.

Non-collaborative short termism in government – Example 2

In July 1991, the sharpest monthly rise in unemployment for that month since the Second World War, brought together the Employment Secretary, the Shadow Chancellor and business and union leaders, in a television discussion (*Channel 4 News* and *Newsnight*, 15.8.91), and it revealed the extent of underlying non-collaborative attitudes. Despite the high unemployment figure of 2,368,100 (according to government figures), the prospect of a continuing rise in unemployment throughout 1992 to 3,000,000 (according to OECD forecasts and others), and the official government figure of a drop in investment of 28 per cent over the year to July 1991, Michael Howard maintained, on the basis that inflation and interest rates were decreasing, that '. . . we are laying the foundations for sustained, long-term economic growth as we saw in the 1980s.' This contrasts markedly with the views of more collaborative cultures, such as the German and the Japanese, who would be unable to see cutting jobs and investment as a way to 'sustained, long-term growth' – indeed quite the reverse. According to the comments of Mr Howard, low inflation is seen by the government as the key factor necessary 'to create the conditions' for sustained, long-term growth, *over and above* investment in people, their training and equipment. Among other things, this seemed to be out of step with Mr Howard's support for the government's 'Investors in People' programme, which claims that investment in people needs to have top priority if organisations are going to be successful (see also next section). Further, as certain other countries well know, a low inflation rate (and interest rate) cannot *in itself* secure long-term success, if investment, the seedcorn of sustained economic well-being, has been lacking. By believing low inflation in itself is a basis for sustained, long-term growth, treating decreasing investment and rising unemployment as of secondary importance, and not intervening to counter the latter by encouraging managers to invest more in people, their training and equipment through tax incentives and giving more direct support for training programmes, the government seemed to reveal its underlying non-collaborative, short-term attitudes – reinforcing the same attitudes in managers of undervaluing the human resource (see also Chapter 11).

Summary – 'Leaner but not fitter'

It is the lack of a collaborative commitment to people, resulting in a lack of investment in their training, their ideas, and the equipment they use, that is at the root of what Peters refers to as the 'mindless cost cutting' and 'mindless leaner and fitter' that mainly goes on during times of recession in Britain and America (*In Business*, 13.3.91). Only a switch to more collaborative attitudes towards people by managers, creditors, debtors and government, will bring about truly fitter organisations and the sustained, long-term, non-inflationary and prosperous future achieved by more collaborative national cultures.

Fitter the collaborative way

The point was made in the previous section that short-term, non-collaborative attitudes in creditors and government reinforce the same attitudes in managers. For example, the large-scale defence cuts made by the government as a result of the end of the Cold War, and their refusal to intervene to help in a programme of redeveloping plants to civil markets to save related jobs and skills as is being done in other European countries, serves to reinforce the short-term views of top managers in the defence-related industries, such as that of the chairman of Rolls-Royce quoted in the previous section.

However, the non-collaborative British culture is changing slowly, and despite non-collaborative external pressures from government and creditors, some managers in British organisations not only pay lip-service to the value of the human resource and investment in them during good times, but also endeavour to act accordingly during bad times. For example, when Michael Frye became chairman of the B Elliott Group, he and his managers succeeded in turning member companies around from loss to profit by maintaining employment and increasing investment (*Walk the Talk*, 28.4.91). Similarly, as the latest recession began to bite more deeply, Tony Banks, managing director of the small firm Cameron-Price, commented:

> Some years ago with the last recession . . . we had a policy of obviously getting rid of people . . . We seem to be going through the same situation now . . . but what we are going to do is hang on to our people that we have trained, our skills, because when the up-turn comes, obviously we would require all these skills to keep us going again (*The Money Programme*, 27.1.91).

That's more like the Japanese attitude quoted in the previous section! The revolution in attitude represented by this comment is interesting – what was 'obvious' at the beginning of the decade, namely, 'getting rid of people', has changed to 'hang on to our people'

– a straight reversal. Gerald Brooks of a Midland joinery firm is an example of another manager who believes it important to hang on to his people:

> Well, we're trying to maintain the same work-force that we've got at the moment, the skills that our men have are very difficult to come by (*The Midlands Report*, 21.3.91).

A survey done by the National Westminster Bank, which showed that it cost twice as much to recruit and retrain somebody as it does to 'hang on' to people (*In Business*, 18.9.91), gives an idea, even just relating to this one aspect of cutting jobs, of the disadvantage organisations put themselves in when an upturn comes. Generally, a collaborative commitment to the work-force, which the above managers are trying to meet, will reap far-reaching dividends for them and their organisations.

Investment in people

Laying people off or holding up investment in training and equipment reduces future output, innovation and competitiveness, not only because it creates a loss of skills and out of date equipment, but also and even more fundamentally, it reduces commitment and motivation in the remaining work-force (eg p246). It is this commitment and motivation, and the collaborative leadership that is necessary to bring it about, that is essential if existing machinery is to be used efficiently, and if any subsequent training and new equipment is to be fully implemented (see also Chapter 11 and Part III).

The central importance of people in investment considerations has been recognised by a group of 17 companies, in a study undertaken for the National Training Task Force in preparation for the launch of the government's 'Investors in People' training initiative:

> There was a general recognition that investment in people is as important or more important than decisions on capital investment . . . (Drew Smith, 1991, p22).

Once managers develop *genuine* collaborative attitudes towards people and their central value as a resource, then of course it is unlikely that they will lightly cut that resource by laying people off in times of difficulties. Those that do, reveal their prior statement of 'the human resource being their most valuable asset' to be nothing but empty rhetoric (see also next section).

While some British organisations are *talking* about recognising the value of the human resource, organisations in more collaborative national cultures have actually been *operating* that way for decades. For example, it has been the Japanese's genuine collaborative respect for and commitment to people and their value that has led not only to more training and equipment, but also and more importantly, to a work-force that feels highly valued, and therefore becomes more highly motivated, more highly skilled, and more highly committed as a result. This genuine collaborative attitude towards people has been the cornerstone of the Japanese long-term outlook and the bedrock of their innovation, quality and success.

The collaborative aspect of Japanese managers' long-term investment outlook is often a major factor to be recognised and appreciated by British people working for Japanese organisations in Britain. For example, the senior production manager at the Sony (UK) plant in South Wales, when asked why the Japanese can make things in Britain when the British cannot, includes in his answer:

> . . . they are not looking for a one-year pay-back on everything that they invest, and also . . . they regard investment in people on a longer-term scale than perhaps a British company would do (*Business Matters*, 6.6.91).

And he goes on to point out that people, whether in management or not, do not have to work to a continuous profit improvement in order to retain their jobs, and they are given time to learn and develop. People's jobs, in fact, are usually for life in a Japanese organisation. The importance of this long-term commitment to people is reflected in the comments of a process engineer at the Sony plant, and an employee at the Ricoh plant in Telford, respectively.

> First and foremost I think with a Japanese company you feel more secure than especially in the [British] vehicle industry (*Business Matters*, 6.6.91).

> They're not a bad company. Pay decentish wages, like. They'll never make me rich, but hopefully they won't make me redundant (*News at Ten*, 15.3.91).

This collaborative commitment to people and their involvement, and the concomitant removal of fear in employees, has a corresponding effect on pay demands and pay becomes less of an adversarial and dominant issue (see also p238 and Chapter 13, p258). Basically people are invested in and given time to develop. With fear removed and collaborative involvement encouraged, it is little wonder that they do indeed develop, and Japanese organisations have become the success story they have. Significantly, there has never been a strike in Japanese organisations in Britain, either unionised or non-unionised.

People are, without doubt, an organisation's most valuable and competitive resource. The author acknowledges that the generally more short-term outlook of British creditors and government has meant that it is more difficult for organisations to invest collaboratively in people. But this is not the sole reason why many top managers are poor at investing in people, and not a valid excuse for them not doing so. With the right attitudes it is possible and fruitful, as previous examples of successful British organisations illustrate. If top managers put people *before* profit, and made financial and technical decisions on the basis of a collaborative commitment to people, their needs, ideas and equipment – including hanging on to them in times of external economic constraint – then their organisations will be more likely to achieve high efficiency, innovation and quality, making them more competitive and truly fitter to meet and survive increased competition and economic downturns, and to flourish during economic upturns.

Mindless short-term vs collaborative long-term cost cutting

Although through the 1980s there was increasing talk by government and top managers, both in industry and education, of the value of people as an organisation's most important resource, the latest recession revealed many of them in their true colours. The government, for example, gave verbal support to an 'Investors in People' approach, which views people and their skills as the key to an organisation's success. Yet, during the recession the Employment Secretary said that lowering inflation, even though at the expense of people's jobs and skills, was paramount for sustained, long-term success. And according to the Chancellor of the Exchequer, unemployment was 'a price well worth paying' to bring inflation down. Similarly, many top managers believed that unemployment was the price that had to be paid to increase efficiency.

Under non-collaborative attitudes, therefore, there is perceived to be a trade-off between inflation/efficiency and employment. High employment and high efficiency are generally seen as incompatible, and laying people off is perceived to be essential for increasing efficiency (see also p238). For example, Dr John Bridges of the Northern Development Company, maintained:

> Well, I think there are quite a lot of things you can do to reduce unemployment, but then you have to set that against your economic efficiency, both nationally and internationally (*Newsnight*, 13.6.91).

But how *can* it be believed that efficiency can be increased by cutting down on an organisation's 'most important resource'? The answer, of course, is by letting the human resource viewpoint fly out of the window. The recession, in fact, generally revealed it to be nothing but empty rhetoric. A true collaborative respect and trust in people and their abilities was just not there for the majority of British managers.

Admittedly, as considered in the previous sections, an increasing number of managers are developing a more collaborative concern about the effects of job losses and loss of skills on the future well-being of their organisations. But despite the view of the 17 companies referred to in the previous section, managers' concern over the long-term effect of lack of investment in machinery is often greater than their concern over the lack of investment in people and their skills. Also, although, like a growing number of top managers, the Labour Opposition and the unions generally showed a greater collaborative concern for the work-force, the following two comments by the Shadow Chancellor and a union president respectively, suggest that investment in equipment was still perceived by them to have the edge in importance on investment in people:

> . . . we're suffering . . . in terms of rising unemployment, people being flung out of their jobs, of people losing their homes . . . and worst of all perhaps for the future, the dramatic fall in investment to the manufacturing sector.
>
> . . . businesses that are still open are cutting back on jobs, and worse still, they're cutting back on investment . . . (*Newsnight*, 15.8.91).

Underlying attitudes have some way to go, therefore, before they reach a genuine collaborative commitment to people as truly an organisation's (and country's) most important resource. The contrast with the Japanese, who do have genuine collaborative attitudes, is reflected in the contrast between their economic efficiency and success and Britain's; and the contrast between their unemployment level (2.1 per cent) and Britain's (8.9 per cent, predicted to rise to 10.8 per cent). These are the OECD figures for April 1991 and they do not represent a one-off comparison. Over the previous ten years Japan's levels mainly hovered between 2 and 3 per cent according to OECD figures, whereas the British level never fell below 5.5 per cent and rose to a peak of 11.2 per cent, according to British government figures (which tend to give lower estimates than others).

The long-term effect of job losses is, however, recognised by some top managers. For example, the managing director of a joinery firm referred to earlier, who is trying to hang on to his human resource, explains, '. . . if we let them go, that's the main problem, they don't come back, they either go out of the trade or go and work for another company' (*The Midlands Report*, 21.3.91). The managing director of a machine tool manufacturing organisation further spells out the problem:

> There is bound to be a net loss of skills to the economy when this kind of thing happens because people find other work if they can, or they simply retire prematurely and don't come back into the employ-ment market. Young people do not go into training. (*Panorama*, 18.3.91).

The skills shortage brought about by job loss and poor investment in training, became a growing concern over the 1980s. In May 1991 it was reported that almost half of the firms in British industry said that they were facing short-falls so acute that it would affect their output (*Newsnight*, 20.5.91). However, although in the second half of the 1980s and the first part of 1990–91 recession, employers gen-erally valued skilled labour in short supply in the sense that they were willing to pay well for it, as the recession bit deeper, so non-collaborative attitudes permeated more deeply, and not even skilled labour was spared the drive for short-term cost-cutting. Conse-quently, there were widespread lay-offs of both skilled labour and 'professional' employees, such as solicitors, accountants and archi-tects. The skills shortage, therefore, already acute at the end of the 1980s, was poised to get worse.

Possibly the hope by employers was that the short-fall in skills would be made up by the educational sector. That, at least, seemed to be a goal of the government. To redress the under-skilling of society that had occurred, they produced a series of White Papers in

May 1991 aimed at achieving mass participation in further and higher education by, among other things, removing the academic-vocational divide and up-grading vocational qualifications (see Chapter 13, p264). At the time the Education Secretary commented:

> Now we're coming out of recession we need a better educated, better trained work-force than before. That's why we're giving them the qualifications that appeal to employers (*Newsnight*, 20.5.91).

Leaving aside the fact that two days later the CBI reported figures to indicate that the economy was still firmly in recession, borne out by the deepening recession over the subsequent months, and also leaving aside the fact that the White Papers would of course take a number of years to be implemented, certainly beyond the time when employers would need more skilled employees to cope with the economic up-turn, critics and commentators have expressed doubts that the new policies will in themselves necessarily make further education more attractive to 16-year-olds and improve the staying on rate in full-time education above only about a third (Chapter 13).

Employers within the latest recession, therefore, would have been best advised not to rely on there being a ready supply of skilled employees from the educational sector to meet their needs. With the government cutting its contribution to training and putting more onus on organisations themselves to provide training through the TECs, then, for this reason if for no other, it should have been obvious that organisations needed to hang on and continue to train their work people during the difficult times, and to look for less mindless, less short-term ways of cost-cutting and dealing with the shortage of cash within the recession.

The dawning of the need for a more thoughtful use of limited funds is expressed in a statement by the general manager of Cummins in Darlington. It was reported that if the company was going to compete, they needed more money to adapt to tougher environmental controls, but because of the recession the cash had dried up:

> Right now I feel that we've had to apply ourselves to making do with what capital is available and we've had to think from first principles about how we want to use that capital which is available (*Newsnight*, 16.5.91).

Examples of a more collaborative, more long-term approach to cost cutting and dealing with a shortage of funds, might include the following strategies before cutting jobs.

Cutting dividends to shareholders

Significantly, British firms pay more than double the average for the rest of the world on dividends. Although there has been a general short-term outlook by shareholders (see Chapter 11), they are likely to accept this measure if it is part of a long-term strategy for improving an organisation. (This is not unprecedented in British organisations, for example in March 1991 the Midland Bank halved its dividend, and although they also had a programme of branch closures, they maintained that they were dealing with this as far as possible by voluntary retirement and redeployment, etc. In May 1991 the author was informed by Midland management that there had been no compulsory redundancies so far.) Compare the Japanese approach (p238).

Cutting top managers' and middle managers' salaries

This should be done in addition to keeping employee, wage increases low (again compare the Japanese approach – p238). The former, in fact, helps make the latter possible (see p238 and next section). During the latest British recession large pay increases for top managers, while the work-force were being urged to exercise wage restraint, caused consternation among employees, MPs in all political parties, the media, and the general public; and accusations by all of 'greed' among top managers. While pay rises for the population as a whole were reported to average 8.5 per cent in 1990 – below the level of inflation of 9.5 per cent, the average increase in directors' pay was 19 per cent. Performance however – earnings per share – did not improve on average, and it actually fell in 40 per cent of companies. Only 20 per cent of top managers were reported to have taken a cut in salary. In 1991 there was wide reporting of top pay increases varying between 40 and 330 per cent (data reported in *Channel 4 News*, 23.5.91; *Newsnight*, 25.6.91).

Cutting waste

- *By avoiding or reducing head office/office expenses* such as plush office furnishings, excessive paper work, etc. A reduced need for office work and paper work is in fact brought about by a more collaborative team approach. For example, Peters refers to a small firm who went through a radical organisation change to 'little five to fifteen person teams'. Now they are able to do things that used to take months 'literally in hours', and one employee explained to Peters: '. . . we can *do* things now, we don't spend 90 per cent of our time passing papers back and forth' (*In Business*, 13.3.91).

Another example is provided by Honda in Swindon, where there is one company secretary, one office, no internal memos, and paper work is kept to a minimum.

- *By looking for ways of further reducing scrap/material waste.*

- *By looking for further ways of using people, time and energy more efficiently.* The management guru Peter Drucker for example, points out that restructuring and redesigning work operations is a far more effective way of bringing costs down than the most radical staff cutbacks (Drucker, 1991).

- *By reducing the number and size of company cars and other perks.* The cult of the company car is part of the obsession with hierarchical status differentials within British organisations. Significantly, BBC reporter William Woollard comments that there is 'nothing quite like it anywhere else in Europe' (*Top Gear*, 14.3.91).

Attracting new customers and developing new/export markets

For example, GBG Fencing in Walsall produced company literature to attract new customers by post when faced with a slump in the home market, and, with their top quality product, began marketing abroad (*How Euro Are You?*, 30.5.91).

The BM Manufacturing Group developed overseas markets for some of their products as the recession in the UK deepened. By doing this, plus other cost cutting measures that did not involve putting shop-floor workers out of work, the group was reported to be one of the most profitable and flourishing in Britain, despite the recession (*News at Ten*, 14.6.91).

Adding value to the product or service

This, for example, is what the company Countax did in a big way. In the summer of 1990 the organisation, which made parts for garden lawnmowers, was faced with disaster when their major customer reduced orders owing to two previous drought years. By everyone pulling together, even working through the night, Countax rapidly converted from making tractor parts to making a new model of tractor themselves. Through 1991, production increased to meet huge demands from home and abroad, and the managing director was able to say about the company: 'we haven't got a recession'. The company was awarded the BBC Radio 4 'In Business Survivor of the Year' award. The reason given – 'they not only showed the team effort and the marketing flair, but also had been *highly* creative' (*In Business*, 8.5.91). These, of course, go together, and high creativity is only possible through genuine team effort involving everyone.

A high quality of service, responding courteously and promptly to the customer's needs, whether in business or education, is a crucial way to add value and keep and attract more customers.

Perhaps The Body Shop is one of the best examples of how adding value to a product and service brings success. Their 'caring' community involvement and social change policy – including using ingredients in their products that do not involve harming the environment or any species within it, and employee involvement in community projects (Chapter 10) – greatly adds value to the product for an increasing number of environmentally and socially aware customers. The NatWest Investment Group refers to a 'virtuous circle':

> Body Shop presents a new definition of value retailing – promising values which customers identify with and using those ideals as the force behind the company's marketing (NatWest, 1991, p5).

Concerning the social change message, managing director Anita Roddick comments 'that is what makes the company so successful' (*In Business*, 18.9.91). The Body Shop continued to increase sales and profits during the latest recession.

All these points are aspects and outcomes of a collaborative team approach. It is important to do these things for long-term cost savings and long-term health, rather than first cutting down on people – the *only* resource capable of coming up with the ideas needed for the high efficiency, quality of product and service, and innovation, necessary to stimulate demand and survive competition in the long-term.

Of course such moves would require a culture shift, a basic shift in the underlying attitudes of top management to more collaborative ones. With such attitudes they would perceive job cuts as a short-term measure undermining long-term health, and they would instead capitalise on people, their training and equipment.

Non-collaborative cultures – the total cost

Individual, organisational and national well-being are inextricably linked. Treating people non-collaboratively, ie as a dispensable resource, laying them off in difficult times, is not a cheap option. As considered above, it produces an organisational cost by instilling fear in the remaining work-force, reducing motivation and undermining quality, innovation, and therefore organisational and national competitiveness in the long run. It creates a skills shortage, again undermining organisational and national competitiveness. It produces a direct and immediate national cost – it has been estimated that each unemployed person costs the tax-payer an average of £8095 per annum (*Newsnight*, 13.6.91). And, of course, it produces untold human cost in the form of personal suffering and misery. The situation was well summed up in a question posed by a *Newsnight* reporter during the latest recession:

> Mass unemployment can mean tragedy for the individual, for society, the waste of vast human potential, and a huge burden on the Exchequer . . . can an efficient society afford to have people out of work in the long term? (13.6.91)

The answer to this surely must be no, as it produces a situation where everyone is the loser: individuals, organisations and the nation as a whole. No country can afford not to harness its most important resource. It is a significant fact that within the group of seven most advanced industrial countries, the two most successful – Japan and (formerly) West Germany – are also the two with the lowest rate of unemployment.

The non-collaborative 'everybody loses' national culture – Example

An illustration of the generally unhelpful and inefficient national culture, is provided by the huge number of house repossessions that have taken place during the latest recession. Not only is the private individual and small business person devastated by losing their home and property in this way, and in some cases their life's savings, but also building societies, banks and insurance companies have made considerable losses. And the building societies' and banks' loss is not just a short-term one of being burdened with repossessed properties that are difficult to sell. There is a more medium- to long-term loss produced by those repossessions creating a large overhang in supply in a market depressed by high unemployment, and the fear in potential house buyers of future job loss; by the fact that repossessions, if bought by first-time buyers, mean that there are no other buyers that go on up the chain, so greatly reducing the number of overall transactions; and by the move, through insurance companies, for there to be tighter restrictions on future borrowing. All these pose a severe problem for the housing market. By lenders not being willing to have a longer-term outlook and support people through the recession, therefore, everybody involved loses.

The non-collaborative aspect is summed up by a small hotel owner, who, after building up a successful business, got into difficulties when a job on her hotel was protracted and poorly done. Lenders gradually withdrew, the hotel was repossessed, and she and her husband who moved to a small property nearby, were banned from acting as caretakers to prevent acts of vandalism on what was their precious, hard-earned property and business. She gives this perceptive, yet heart-rending comment:

> I am appalled by the stupidity of it all. The building society wanted all or nothing – what they got is nothing. The house has been on the market for a year at £250,000 – about half what it's worth. In the South East the property market is flooded, they're putting more people out of their homes, more homes on the market – building societies and banks are cutting their own throats as well as ours. It isn't just me – there were 43,000 repossessions last year; this year over 200,000 people are in arrears . . . The government must take a certain amount of blame – in their zest to create this perfect world, they have forgotten the people who feed them, and who now can hardly feed themselves. I am looking again at refinancing, but I am not looking here – I am looking in Europe (*Opinion*, 16.7.91).

Non-collaborative conflict – unemployment, skills shortage and pay

A growing number of long-term unemployed people is, of course, the other side of the coin to the growing skills shortage. Although skilled labour was valued over the 1980s, generally little value was put on the larger group of unskilled people and their education and training, even during the boom years – even though utilising this resource is essential for achieving general industrial and social well-being in the long term. Bill Daniel, the director of the Policy Studies Institute, expresses concern over the fact that the low paid, low skilled worker, who moves between short periods of unemployment and unsatisfactory jobs, represents a growing sector of the work-force. In line with this concern, in June 1991 the London School of Economics predicted that there would be a million long-term unemployed by December 1991. This growing number of long-term unemployed and the related growing skills shortage, penalises organisations, not just in the ways indicated above, but also, it is said, by creating an ever-increasing salary bill for the limited skilled labour available. Perhaps this was not so much of a factor at the height of the recession when even skilled labour was being squeezed (see previous section), but it would once again, as in the 1980s, become a factor as economic upturn came. Concerning the upward pressure on wages of the skills shortage, Paul Gregg of the National Institute, maintained that 'It is competition for jobs, it is, if you like, the fear of losing your job, that causes people to moderate wage rises' (*The Money Programme*, 27.1.91).

A skills shortage means that the competition is generally lacking in the case of skilled labour, so they are able to demand higher wages. But the situation is not quite as simple as that. The level of inflation, for example, is also a contributory factor influencing wage demands, a point recognised by some top managers. Also, some top managers, such as at Rover and Jaguar, have in the past defended their high pay awards, maintaining that they are justified by output and productivity deals. So it is not necessarily just a matter of skilled labour making unreasonable 'market' demands.

Ironically, the fear of losing a job referred to in the above quote, can work in the opposite direction to lowering pay demands. For example, within the rapidly rising unemployment during the latest recession, one worker commented, 'We'd better take the money now because we may not be here in two years time.' This distrustful and seemingly uncaring, uncooperative and uncommitted attitude among some employees was a reciprocation of the general lack of collaborative commitment being displayed by top management to the work-force. And the general lack of a collaborative, caring attitude in top management was manifested not only in a great deal of 'mindless' cost cutting in the form of layoffs, etc (see previous section), but also by the simultaneous high pay rises being awarded to them, particularly in the medium to large organisations. The generally 'uncaring' attitude of top management was recognised, for example, by Andrew Neil, editor of the *Sunday Times*:

> One of the things that has not helped the pay bargaining process is a feeling that people at the very top of this society have grown rich and *shown no concern at all about what's happening lower down* (*Question Time*, 13.6.91).

Concerning the pay issue, news items during the recession reported, for example, how employees at Rolls-Royce were 'angered' and 'saddened' by the announcement in May 1991 of 6000 job cuts, and 'seething' about the company chairman's 51 per cent pay rise the previous year (1990) despite the organisation's difficulties. Less than a week later the company imposed a freeze on annual rises and extra pay entitlements in what was generally accused of being a high-handed manner which further angered the work-force (see also p247). (Later in the year the chairman of Rolls-Royce was reported to have taken a 10 per cent wage cut.) Similarly, the sacking of 40,000 workers by British Telecom, with another 30,000 to go – although the company was not in financial difficulties – while the chairman's salary was increased 43 per cent, caused consternation among the work-force and politicians alike, including Conservative politican Anthony Beaumont-Dark:

> Now giving them £500 and a handshake, and taking another £4000 a week increase yourself, in my view, takes a lot of swallowing by people. (*News at Ten*, 7.6.91)

Another example is provided by the power industry. A 58 per cent rise in salary was announced for the chief executive of National Power, while employees had initially been offered 5 per cent in comparison, and had taken many months of negotiation to receive an offer of 8.9 per cent. This prompted the general secretary of the AEU, to respond: '. . . now the scene has been set and our people will be more determined than ever to achieve the rate that he has achieved in terms of an increase' (*Newsnight*, 25.6.91).

As it turned out, the five power unions did accept the 8.9 per cent pay offer on the basis that even though their members had voted by a narrow majority for industrial action, the strike majority was not large enough. However, the ballot was held *before* the 58 per cent pay rise announcement for the chief executive, and it is believed that if the workers had known about this, the vote for strike action would have been 'overwhelming'. The following month (July 1991), the chief executive of Powergen took a pay rise of 163 per cent, and many media reporters thought that power workers would be 'angry' at the news and the fact that they earn on average £20,000 a year and recently accepted a pay offer of 8.9 per cent. Such consternation and anger in employees as these few examples illustrate, would do nothing to help future pay bargaining.

As well as exacerbating the pay issue, this aspect of non-collaborative management, just like laying people off, has a far-reaching, long-term effect in terms of morale and motivation, and therefore quality and competitiveness. The generally large pay differential between top management and employees is a manifestation of non-collaborative, hierarchical, attitudes in managers that impose a social distance between them and employees, giving the latter lower status and lower involvement in decision making (see also Chapter 13, p258). The pay differential, in fact, is a symbol of a hierarchical structure, which, as is generally being considered in this book, leads to reduced worker morale and motivation, which in turn undermines the level of efficiency, quality and innovation needed to survive against increasing competition. It underlines the feeling in the employee that management are not committed to the work-force, and the feeling that 'we're not all in this together'. And it underlines the employee's distrust that management is working in the best interests of the employee and giving them the fairest deal possible.

The fact that the pay differential between top manager and employee was generally increased within the recession, at a time when employees (and in many cases the organisations) were facing greater hardships, only went to emphasise management's non-collaborative lack of concern for their employees (and their organisations), and a preoccupation with personal gain and power. And, in turn, this will have further undermined trust, morale and motivation in employees. The high pay rises of top managers were condemned by the Prime Minister, the Church of England Commissioners, and even the popular Tory press, which accused top people of 'greed' and reported the 'fury' caused by the contrast with the low pay rises for workers. The harmful effect of high top pay rises was also voiced by a Japanese finance minister, when he warned American executives that high pay rises weaken employees' morale and their country's competitive position.

From the above, therefore, it is difficult to be categorical about what determines pay rise demands by workers. What can be said definitely is that the fear of losing a job – or the confidence that one will not lose it – is a significant factor in the level of wage increase demands, although there are others. Fear of job loss can increase, not lower, pay demands, and it certainly makes pay a central industrial relations issue (cf p238). Significantly, deep into the latest recession, as lay-offs in skilled labour occurred, the CBI, for example, maintained that 'pay inflation' was dropping very fast, although of course other factors such as lower inflation (not just brought about by lower pay demands) and lower output had also come into play.

In contrast to the situation in Britain, a general lowering of wage rise demands below the level of inflation has been achieved in more collaborative national cultures, through a more reasoned and cooperative consideration of the situation, without management operating hierarchically using the fear factor and the threat of job loss. The latter, as considered, can only have a detrimental affect on the long-term commitment and motivation of the employee, undermining the long-term health of organisation and country.

More collaborative national cultures

The generally non-collaborative relationships that exist within and between organisations in Britain, can be contrasted with more successful countries. The manner in which Belgium dealt with the problems of ERM entry, and Japan dealt with the energy crisis of the early 1970s, are just two examples:

More collaborative national cultures – Example 1*

The Belgians managed to avoid a sharp rise in unemployment when they entered the ERM by their government insisting on a big cut in wage increases. Although there were protests, it has been reported

* The quotations and factual information for the ensuing example are taken from *Panorama*, 12.11.90; the interpretations are this author's.

that most Belgians seemed to accept the cuts, and this was helped by the fact that the country's biggest trade union decided that pay restraint was better than more unemployment. But what was the key to this being possible? Was it simply a case of them having more 'sensible' unions than we have in Britain? Consequent events show that it was probably more complex than that, relating to the attitudes of those in power. For example, a situation has developed in Belgium where pay is largely determined by a *consensus* between the government, the central bank, the employers and the trade unions. There are weekly meetings between representatives of these bodies which reporter Michael Crick observes:

> . . . prepares the ground for talks on national pay norms, and even if the government often has to impose pay policy by law, in Belgium, as in most European Community countries, the *consultation* fosters a remarkable atmosphere of *consensus*.

A Belgian central bank economist encapsulates the importance of collaborative trust, involvement and consultation:

> By the fact that the government and other directors are giving them on a weekly basis really privileged economic information, it is normal that this *dialogue* brings them together as to what is good for Belgium incorporated. Not so much for each party in itself, but for the country as a whole.

And she claims that the results for the economy of this consultation and dialogue have been 'incredible', and compares them with the performance of Germany and the Netherlands who use similar 'collaborative' procedures. A strong factor in the Belgian unions cooperating with employers and government, and calling for wage restraint in the early stages of ERM entry was, no doubt, the fact that the attitudes of management and government enabled them openly to involve and inform the unions, in turn enabling rational dialogue, making the unions feel respected, trusted and listened to, creating a reciprocal respect and *trust* in them that management and government would operate collaboratively in the best interests of everyone in the long term.

More collaborative national cultures – Example 2*

In 1973 Japan was very badly hit by the oil crisis as, having no natural resources of its own, it relied more heavily on oil imports than other industrialised countries. Organisations, therefore, were faced with greatly increased costs (for energy, raw materials, interest rates, etc), and also reduced demand. At the same time employers were faced with demands for higher wages from workers to meet the high inflation rate, which reached 32 per cent in 1974. The unions began by demanding pay rises in line with inflation, as was the case in Britain and America. But then they went along with government appeals for moderation in pay rises. Why was this so? Were the Japanese unions just more 'sensible' than British unions? The events indicate that other factors were at play that are missing in the British scene. Yoshiji Miyata, chairman of the steelworkers union in 1974, who led the way in calling for restraint in pay rises, claimed:

> I wasn't selling out to the government at all . . . I said that if we restrained ourselves now that things would get better later and the good life would be round the corner, so let's aim for that.

He did not believe he was 'selling out' to the government and the management, because he undoubtedly did not believe they were 'ripping the workers off' in any way. From his actions it seems he believed the crisis was being treated as a *joint* problem. He was able to believe this because he no doubt trusted the management and the government to treat workers fairly – that restraints now were unavoidable and shared by all, and that later improvements would also be fairly shared by all. And the unions and the employees had reason for this trust. Firstly, employees had generally received a fair deal up to that time, as one worker in 1974 realised:

> This year I will accept a rise of around 10% to 15%. Up to now we in Japan have had extraordinary growth. *Wages have risen quickly too*, but we must now moderate our claims (my emphasis).

And significantly, referring to the situation in Japan around the same time, Gensuke Okada, Manager of Kawasaki in 1967, comments: 'In Japan, unlike in America, we have no cheap labour to do

---

* The quotations and factual information for the ensuing example are taken from *Nippon*, 25.11.90, unless otherwise stated. The interpretations are this author's.

the dirty work. America still has plenty of slaves.' The same applied in Britain as America. Secondly, the government, through the Ministry of Trade and Industry (MITI), had greatly supported industry, and therefore workers, in the past. Their collaborative attitude was expressed by Yoshihiko Morozumi, MITI Vice Minister, 1971–3 when he said, 'We were working on behalf of the whole people, the whole nation, not just ourselves or a particular company' (*Nippon*, 28.10.90).

Past events, therefore, had made it possible for unions and workers to trust the government and company management to be working fairly on the employee's behalf. And the underlying collaborative attitude of management towards employees was confirmed by their commitment to the work-force through the problems of the oil crisis. Although cost cutting and raising efficiency was a major goal, shedding labour to achieve this was not seen as a major option. Whereas 'in Britain the closure of a shipyard meant mass unemployment' (*Nippon*, 25.11.90), this was not so in Japan. Takeshi Isumi, Manager of Mitsubishi Shipbuilding, explains:

> The problem was what to do with the workers . . . Japanese management has a culture, a sense of moral responsibility that we should keep people employed at all costs. And we feel this sense of responsibility quite strongly.

Instead of sacking the workers, what they did do where possible was to move workers to other factories they had. Or, in the case of car companies which faced bankruptcy, the response was to take workers off the assembly line and send them out to sell cars door to door (*Nippon*, 18.11.90). Or, with government involvement, organisations were encouraged and helped to merge and diversify, which meant that workers could be kept on and their skills not wasted but transferred, and added to, through retraining. Mitsubishi shipbuilders, for example, were retrained as Mitsubishi car workers, or in newer high tech areas.

Efficiency, productivity, and collaborative commitment to the human resource

Whereas top managers in Britain are able to receive high pay awards while laying people off, as exemplified in the latest recession (see also previous section), such a move would be unthinkable in, for example, Japanese organisations. According to Deming, when a Japanese company has to absorb sudden economic hardship the 'sacrificial pecking order' is the reverse of that which usually obtains in the West:

> First the corporate dividends are cut. Then the salaries and the bonuses of top management are reduced. Next, management salaries are trimmed from the top to the middle of the hierarchy. Lastly, the rank and file are asked to accept pay cuts or a reduction in the workforce through attrition or voluntary discharge (1986, p147).

With this kind of respect for, and loyalty and commitment to employees, fear is removed, and it is little wonder that employees are motivated and show a reciprocal loyalty and commitment to their organisations. For this reason also, pay becomes less of a dominant issue – in particular, for the following contributory reasons:

- employees trust top management to give them the fairest deal possible;

- reward comes through involvement, recognition and achievement.

This can be contrasted with the dominance of the pay issue in the British industrial and educational cultures (see also Chapter 13, p258).

Unlike in Britain, therefore, workers in Japan are not seen as a dispensable resource. Most Japanese management is collaboratively committed to, and values, employees. For example, during the oil crisis, employees' ideas were listened to, and used to bring about considerable savings in the workplace (see also Chapter 10). When faced with the need to cut costs and increase competitiveness further, management acted to increase efficiency/productivity (ie decrease cost per unit output), by increasing productivity per worker (decreasing unit labour cost) through increased automation – rather than through short-term cost cutting by cutting jobs. This might sound simple and obvious, but it directly opposes most Western thinking. As Deming writes:

> No concept has been more misunderstood by American managers, academics, and workers than productivity. For workers in America a call for increased productivity carries with it the threat of layoffs (1986, p147).

The same applies in Britain, and there were plenty of examples of this through the latest recession. For instance, in July 1991, Rover Cars announced 1300 white-collar job cuts, putting a further 12,000 workers on a four-day week for an indefinite period, and shutting down its production at Longbridge for an extra two weeks in the summer – the reason given was that the company needed to cut production because of the slump in sales, and to raise productivity to compete with Japanese cars. Increasing efficiency and productivity, therefore, is usually seen to be achievable by reducing the cost of labour – through wage restraint or redundancies – rather than through material or energy savings or other improvements in efficiency of procedures. Under this mental frame, increasing automation is seen as a way of decreasing manual labour to save costs.

An exception to this short-term mental outlook is provided by the sausage-casing company Deveraux, in Glasgow. They were reported to have increased efficiency by having a productivity deal between the manager and workers – 'a [fair] deal on pay and working practices' which increased production by 10 per cent in a year (*News at Ten*, 13.9.91). In this way, workers were able to receive a pay rise of 7 per cent, while prices went up by only 4.5 per cent; and for every 100 feet of casing produced by the company, an equivalent German factory produced 81 feet, and an American just 68 feet. The ITN reporter concluded:

> The cost battle is being won here. If more British companies and their workers follow this example, inflation would come down [below competitor countries] and stay down.

The matter, however, is not quite as simple as that. The success of an organisation is not just a question of producing more in a given time, at a given cost. In order to continue to compete effectively, there is need not only to *maintain* quality, but also continuously to *improve* quality and *innovate*, as well as continuously to improve operational efficiency and lower costs. No organisation, whether in the manufacturing or service sector, can afford to stand still on quality and innovation. So there is a limit to the long-term effect of mere productivity deals that do not incorporate a system of continuous improvement through employee involvement. For example, a company could be highly efficient at producing an out-of-date product, such as a mechanical typewriter. But however high their productivity, they would be unable to compete successfully; and indeed this 'standing still' aspect has been the downfall of many organisations in the West faced with superior quality and innovation from the East.

McGregor is one who has warned against the usual way of perceiving productivity merely in terms of the *physical* output of employees, and condemns the general cry that if 'people would only do more of what they are told to do, productivity would rise and the economy would be better off'. Such a view, he believes, is narrow and insults the worth of human beings. Productivity, rather, should be seen in terms of the overall effectiveness of an organisation, and everything that contributes to it should be valued. As McGregor points out, the potential contribution of the human being *'at every level of the organization'* surpasses that of the machine, and it, '. . . stems from his capacity to think, to plan, to exercise judgement, to be creative, to direct and control his own behaviour' (1987, p114).

It is a collaborative commitment to this distinctive value of the work-force that makes Japanese managers come to quite different technical and financial decisions concerning automation from Western managers. Automation was introduced to relieve workers of mindless, dirty or heavy work, enabling more creative activity and customer care, and to help increase efficiency by increasing output per worker – keeping costs low, ensuring jobs, and, in good times, ensuring wage rises, as is spelled out by Kenichi Ohmae, consultant at McKinseys, Tokyo, 1974:

> The Japanese . . . have to be married to the work-force. So you don't worry about the work-force – that's a given. In order to increase competitiveness you have to give them [a] wage increase every year, and therefore this means you have to reduce hours worked – in order to assemble a TV, if it takes 120 minutes [and] now it's 20 minutes – you can absorb six times [the] wage increase and cost will be still the same. Therefore driving the hours, the man-hours down, was the major way. This meant automation (*Nippon*, 25.11.90).

In Japan, therefore, automation was introduced to help people in their work to increase efficiency – not to cut jobs – indicating an underlying respect for people, which increased motivation – the ultimate key to increased efficiency, quality and innovation in the long term. In the West, automation is usually introduced to cut jobs – indicating an underlying lack of respect for people, decreasing motivation, quality and efficiency in the long term. For this reason, auto-mation and new technology, does not in itself increase efficiency/productivity (cf Deming, 1986, p12). For example, car manufacturers in the West have been shown that technology itself does not solve problems:

> They thought they were catching up with the Japanese by introducing new robots to their factories, but there's a lot more to Japan's flexible revolution than that . . . [it depends on] the way the Japanese car companies have used new technology (*The Money Programme*, 6.1.91).

And 'the way the Japanese used new technology' rests on their collaborative treatment of the human resource – the way they respect and trust that resource and their abilities, involve them in the decision-making process, and invest in their skills development – as a result of underlying collaborative attitudes, which lead them to perceive automation as a human-resource *aid* not *substitute*.

Understandably, therefore, automation was not seen as a threat to the work-force as it is in the West, and in fact workers looked on the robots installed with affection. Again, there was help from the government in the form of cheap loans for companies to buy robots. The highly successful programme of energy saving, restructuring and automation to meet the energy crisis, therefore, was made possible by workers, unions, managers and government working together in a collaborative partnership.

Generalising, it can be said that when organisations in more collaborative national cultures get into trouble:

- Managers and government see cutting production costs and raising efficiency (to improve competitiveness) *first and foremost* in terms of increasing long-term operational efficiency through, eg, waste reduction, energy/raw material savings, increasing capital spending (or reducing it very little), increasing investment in education and training, and increasing R&D; and in terms of restraining wage increases only in the short-term.

- Government intervenes to collaborate with organisations in short-term and long-term strategies.

- Unions do not resist restraints in wage increases when necessary.

- Investors look for long-term gains and do not pull out when the going gets rough, but invest more.

This directly contrasts with the predominantly non-collaborative British approach summarised on p211.

More collaborative national cultures – the British contrast

At the time of writing, British Aerospace are faced with a situation not unlike that which faced many industries during the oil crisis, and Japanese military organisations after the Second World War. This has been brought about by the end of the Cold War, which is leading to cuts in defence spending and a sharp decline in orders for military aircraft. But are the top managers of the company trying to keep people employed 'at all costs' as in more 'collaborative' countries? Apparently not. They have so far announced the loss of 5000 jobs over the next two years, and more are expected, although the company sub-contracts large amounts of civil work overseas:

> The company says the cuts are inevitable – part of a major re-structuring and rationalisation programme to cut costs and so stay competitive in the military aircraft business. (*Newsnight*, 30.11.90)

Are the top managers collaborating with investors to increase investment in training and R&D as in more 'collaborative' countries? Apparently not, although workers have been calling for it for some time:

> We believe this site could have been saved and can be saved for aircraft production providing there is a programme of investment which will enable it to convert to civil aircraft production. We believe that process should have started some eighteen months ago (shop steward on *Channel 4 News*, 30.11.90).

Are the government planning to intervene to help the firm diversify into civil markets as in more 'collaborative' countries? Apparently not. The government instead has made large cuts to the defence budgets and believes:

> If there are changed market conditions, it is for the company to decide how to react to them (Leader of the House of Commons, 29.11.90).

In contrast, the governments of other countries in Europe are intervening to help their defence industries through a restructuring period. The workers within the British industry, quite understandably,

have a perception more in line with the Japanese and general European ways of doing things:

> But why should we close such factories with skills, capacity, world
> leaders in terms of design teams when if employers, with support
> from government, put their minds to it, they could move into
> expanding civil markets? (Jack Dromey, Transport and General
> Workers Union on *Newsnight*, 30.11.90).

Why don't they 'put their minds to it'? According to Trevor Taylor
of the Royal Institute of International Affairs, converting the
defence industry to civil industry is extremely difficult to organise
because of the diverse elements within a company, and so, 'Many
business people believe that it's simply better to close up a defence
plant than start again' (*Newsnight*, 30.11.90). One wonders where
the Japanese would be now if they had thought in that way. Far
from avoiding 'difficulties' they describe themselves as people who
'love a challenge' (*Nippon*, 25.11.90); and it has been considered in
previous chapters of this book how they are eager to learn. The
more persistent, less short termist, less defeatist attitude of the Japanese compared to Western attitudes, is illustrated by Hiroshi Chino,
president of Chinon Cameras in Japan. He refers to the time when
Kodak, the major shareholder in the company, decided not to
develop camcorders:

> They did make a camcorder at the very beginning . . . But it was a failure
> and they took fright, never touching it again. As far as I am concerned, if
> you make one mistake you should try again (*Business Matters*, 19.9.91).

Despite the offer by Sony to work collaboratively with Chinon to
help produce a camcorder, Kodak, much to Mr Chino's dismay and
future concern, remained defeatist and did not take up the challenge.

A major underlying reason for the Japanese not being defeatist,
and, in the past, fighting hard to save and build organisations, has
been, as considered above, their commitment to people and their
skills as a resource (see also Chapter 6). This 'human' factor, however, does not seem to figure in the financial and technical decision
making of British managers, despite the increasing rhetoric:

> . . . they [the management] give the attitude that they care for their
> work-force and their employees – we know that is not true (Terry
> Stevens, shop steward, British Aerospace, on *Newsnight*, 30.11.90).

And the non-colloborative lack of respect and consideration for

244 • THE HUMAN FACTOR

people is reflected in the fact, according to Terry Stevens, that the world press were informed of the particular job losses before the work-force (see also next section).

At the same time as British Aerospace are having trouble, Dowty have shown more commitment to their enterprise and their work-force by diversifying out of defence. They are reported to have 'a carefully worked out strategy for reducing reliance on defence-related business' (*Newsnight*, 30.11.90). But this is unusual. Other defence-related industries, besides British Aerospace, announced jobs at risk and lay-offs, and some estimated that 300,000 workers could lose their jobs overall (*Newsnight*, 29.11.90). Not surprisingly, therefore, the unions were concerned about the loss of skills it would represent, and rightly claimed it would erode Britain's manu-facturing base.

Losing your job the non-collaborative way

The manner in which organisations contract or collapse reflects, and accentuates, the kind of non-collaborative culture that has caused them to reach that position. *World in Action* report five clues which warn employees of impending contraction or collapse and worker redundancy;* and each strongly reflects non-collaborative practices.

Clue 1

The first clue is the reduction in enquiries, which is an indicator of reduced order intake. According to David James, 'a company surgeon', workers on the floor are better placed than the people in the boardroom to spot this, and he says they should be banging on the management's door as soon as they notice it. But would the kind of management that does not regularly communicate with employees to the point of being ignorant for many months of drops in enquiries, be realistically expected to *listen* to employees who 'bang on their door' with the message? Not that an employee is likely to do so where everyone has, and knows, their place in the hierarchy,

---

* The quotations and factual information in the ensuing section are taken from *World in Action*, 11.3.91, unless otherwise stated. The interpretations are this author's.

and where communication is a one-way process only, ie top down. For example, as already mentioned, David James remembers one 'vivid occasion' when he spoke to a shop steward who said he could tell the organisation was going under 'long ago' because the enquiry level had fallen off. When he asked the shop steward what he had done about it, he recounts: ' "Do about it?" he said. "It wasn't our job to do anything about it." Goldsmith and Clutterbuck refer to just this situation in their book *The Winning Streak* (1985). They report that the usual finding of a company of receivers when called in to a troubled company, is that the managing director is very unlikely to have the information they need, 'But somewhere there is George who does know. George is dying to tell somebody, but no one will listen to him.' (p153) The company of receivers believe that if the management had talked to George, then it would have fared much better.

Clue 2

The second clue is when the boss's anxiety begins to show through, and a flurry of cuts are made. David James believes managers first look for all kinds of minor cuts to avoid more drastic cuts. But it is not just the kind of cuts that are made initially that are inadequate, but the fact that they are management-driven, imposed on employees without their involvement. Collaborative cultures would involve workers in coming up with ideas for more radical cost savings – they know more than anyone else the work processes involved and how to improve their efficiency.

Clue 3

The third clue is 'when the economy drive stops and management goes very, very quiet'. A time of intense *secrecy* is reported to be common in firms about to cut jobs. Lack of openness is a characteristic of hierarchical cultures, and, as with other characteristics, it gets accentuated at times of difficulties. Michael Dixon of the *Financial Times*, compares the situation to 'a sort of vast military operation, but carried out by the secret service'. Consultant Peter Trigg believes secrecy is necessary in order for management 'to maintain the initiative'. This, of course, is what management generally does in 'good' times, and is mistaken.

Clue 4

The fourth clue that you might be about to lose your job is if you are too bright or non-conformist, which is dangerous. *World in Action* cite several studies that suggest that redundant managers are often more intelligent, more imaginative, more venturesome and more independently-minded than those 'don't-rock-the-boat' people who are retained. What times of difficulty in fact reveal, is how hierarchical cultures do not value questioning people, people with intelligent, new, 'non-conformist' ideas. This, as considered previously, contrasts with more collaborative, 'learning' organisational cultures.

Clue 5

The fifth clue that you are going to lose your job is your boss's attitude to you, which may suddenly get colder or warmer. The reason for this behaviour change in bosses is believed to be because they feel embarrassed; because they feel anxiety. No doubt they feel embarrassed – guilty might be a better word – because of the underhand and apparently unfeeling manner in which the matter has been dealt with. No communication with, and involvement of, the employee in the organisation's problems, until he or she is told to go, is always a hurtful and devastating shock to the employee, who feels totally betrayed. This dismay and betrayal felt by employees, strongly shouted through the rapidly written lines put up in the window of a closed travel agent:

> Sorry,
> Closed due to Company Liquidation
> Staff only told at
> 8am this morning!

Again, the manner in which people are told they have lost their jobs is a caricature of employees' non-involvement, non-collaboration, in the workplace.

All this contrasts sharply with more collaborative cultures who show more respect and commitment to employees, particularly Japanese organisations, which go to great lengths to find alternatives to sacking people, and involve them collaboratively in the process of making savings (see also previous section). Kanter is one who believes that, for a number of reasons, a collaborative process works

better in times of difficulties than when a decision is made at the top
– such as 'we've got to take out 10 per cent of employees', ie mindless cost cutting. She points out that this way fails to ask 'what work
are we really trying to produce, and what other opportunities do we
have to use people'; and she claims that if jobs are eventually cut,
then a more collaborative process will not only be a more 'humane'
way, but a more 'sensible' way from the point of view of the business
itself, because:

> . . . you also have to work with the survivors, and . . . if they see that
> the process was unfair, or that it hurt people, or that it didn't involve
> them, the survivors on whom you are counting for future production,
> the survivors lose faith (*Business Matters*, 14.6.90).

For example, the personnel director at Rolls-Royce acknowledged
that the announcement of 6000 redundancies would reduce worker
morale in the short term. Rolls-Royce went even further in making
the remaining workers 'lose faith' by, less than a week after
announcing the redundancies, sending a letter to all their 34,000
workers dismissing them under their present contract, and offering
them new terms including a freeze on the annual pay rises. Later the
company withdrew the letter, but employee trust and commitment
will have been further undermined. And this kind of non-collaborative
treatment was not restricted to the manual worker. When 'push
came to shove' in the height of the latest recession, non-
collaborative attitudes permeated even the professions, and loyalty
and commitment went out of the window. For example, it came as a
tremendous shock to an accountant who was employed by one of
the large firms of accountants, to be sacked only four years after
joining the organisation. He said, '. . . I certainly wasn't expecting
anything when I went into work that day' (*The Money Programme*,
19.5.91). Two hundred other employees were put through the same
pain, yet the organisation was taking on 900 new graduate recruits.
How can there be trust and commitment in the remaining work-
force? Everything will be tainted, and motivation, innovation and
quality eroded.

As Kanter points out, organisations in difficulties should start by
saying 'What are our goals?', and scrutinise work activities using
those goals; and they may realise that some departments should be
adding staff because they really contribute value. Further, by asking
and involving the people themselves, 'they often come up with
many ideas that end up saving jobs' (*Business Matters*, 14.6.90). And

it is not just management experts that see this truth. For example, Gavin Laird of the Engineering Workers' Union, in a comment about the manner in which Rolls-Royce management have treated the work-force, summarises:

> . . . the only way they are going to get out of that [financial trouble] is by the help and co-operation of the work-force. And they're not going to get that by sacking everyone and then re-employing them (*BBC News*, 23.5.91).

And employees also know it. For example, an employee at a college of higher education that was undergoing restructuring, where fear and rumour about job losses were rife, and where management did nothing to dispel that fear and rumour, commented:

> Nobody will talk to us. I don't know why we don't all get together and have a meeting to talk about what is going to happen and what we can do.

This employee, as all employees in this situation, was totally demotivated and did not see why he should bother much with his job – after all, as he said, 'I may be sacked in a few weeks'. Quality dies with creativity – a dreadful waste of human potential.

Organisational collapse the non-collaborative way – Example*

Organisation The International Leisure Group (ILG), which included the second biggest tour company in Britain, Intasun, and the second biggest airline, Air Europe. It had taken decades to build up.
Chief executive Harry Goodman, described as a character and trail blazer. Had absolute power of veto. Unpopular in the industry because of his savage cost-cutting and ruthless price wars. His ambition was to build a pan-European airline by expanding Air Europe to take advantage of deregulation.
Underlying problems A lack of capital to fund the company's very rapid expansion since 1989. Insufficient skills in the existing business to support the rate of expansion into the new area of scheduled service.
Consequence The company was in an inadequate state to meet the

---

* The quotations and factual information for the ensuing example are taken from *The Money Programme*, 24.3.91; the interpretations are this author's.

effects of the recession and the Gulf War. It lost £50 million in the three months to the end of January, 1991.

In such financial difficulties did all those involved rally round and collaboratively try to save the business and jobs? Unfortunately, what *did* happen was rapid, secretive, and characteristic of a non-collaborative organisational and national culture.

In the early hours of 8 March 1991, the board of shareholders decided to put ILG into the hands of the administrators. That same day bank creditors acted to ground planes as security, and withdrew support. The Civil Aviation Authority moved in to secure their interests and impounded more aircraft. Air Europe staff were reported to be totally ignorant of the events and therefore shocked to discover they were grounded. Friday, 10 March the Tour Operators Study Group decided to call on the bond (from a special fund run by 19 leading travel companies, to refund and support stranded holidaymakers). But under ABTA's rules, *all* ILG's tour operations had to cease trading. The chances of the administrators finding a buyer for those companies, which they were working hard to achieve, faded. On Wednesday 15 March, the tour operation was put into liquidation.

A former director of ILG believes that inadequate consideration was given for the survival of the group, and that hasty action was taken by a number of parties. *The Money Programme* reporter sums up the inexorable momentum of a non-collaborative national culture:

> Without doubt ILG was in bad financial shape. But once the crunch came the system was impossible to stop. But then, it was clearly not in the interests of the rest of the travel industry to halt the process which helped to remove a significant competitor. In the end Harry ran out of both money and friends.

Collaborative partnership – industry, education, unions, government

In collaborative national cultures, partnerships are forged between industry, education, unions and government. In Britain, however, there is a general lack of collaborative dialogue, consultation and commitment, which stretches from the classroom to the boardroom and beyond. Concern over this is being increasingly voiced. For example, James Watson, the then chairman designate of the National Freight Company, commented:

> I'd like to see more *dialogue* between government and industry . . . we've reached a stage where we want to see more consultation, more dialogue . . . I'm looking for [government] *involvement, participation, and understanding industry* (*The Money Programme*, 25.11.90; my emphasis).

And Ray Cowell, director of Nottingham Polytechnic, believes there should be more dialogue between education and industry to ensure that '. . . academic standards are defined jointly with industry, and that academic excellence goes with vocational relevance' (*The Thatcher Audit*, 4.9.90).

The next chapter looks at the nature of the relationship between industry, education, unions and government, and the need to develop a more collaborative partnership between them in order to improve industrial and educational performance.

13
Collaborative partnership between industry, education, unions and government

Collaborative partnership between organisations and unions/workers

Collaboration between unions and managers is generally missing. For example, John Chisholm, UK managing director of the computer services company SEMA, progressively acknowledges the need for more investment, research and development, improving education and skills, and the need to play a full part in Europe. At the same time, however, he says of the 1980s:

> What we've done is lick the power of the unions. We have got together a base for industry where management is firmly in charge. We've got – well, we had inflation under control. We've done a lot of things to establish a base for industry for the future (*The Money Programme*, 25.11.90).

Leaving aside the need for some kind of union reform in the past, it is doubtful whether the use of inflammatory language such as 'licking the power of the unions' at this present time, and the attitudes that underlie such hostile and confrontational language, is conducive to a sound 'base for industry'.

The attitude of most European and Japanese managers to unions is quite different, and there is much more of a cooperative partnership between them than in Britain, as exemplified in the previous chapter. An example of the non-adversarial attitude of Japanese management towards unions in Britain is provided by the Nissan plant in

Sunderland. They have a single union agreement with the AEU – it is not a 'no-strike' deal, and all staff are actively encouraged to join the union (Nissan, 1985, 'Facts Against Fallacy', p1). The collaborative attitudes of management towards employees, which respects and trusts employees and their abilities, means that they strive to give employees the fairest deal possible. There is, therefore, generally excellent industrial relations in Japanese organisations, and in that sense the need for unions becomes less necessary. This point is expressed by a Toyota employee in the US:

> I really don't think that the union would have a chance of getting in for the very simple reason that Toyota doesn't fight. They're like – if you want a union you can have a union. But whatever the union could give you Toyota would already have given you – pay rises on a regular basis, they're willing to listen to any grievance . . . (*The Midlands Report*, 25.10.90).

Nevertheless, many Japanese plants are unionised, and there is a positive relationship between managers and unions. The 1991 TUC Conference's backing of the view that Japanese companies brought an 'alien' approach to British trade unionism, suggests that the traditionally confrontational approach between management and unions in Britain does not all stem from the former. Certain union leaders, however, strongly criticised this stance, and welcomed Japanese investment in Britain. And some accused the 'alien' view as racism. Indeed, the union leader who led the debate, seemed confused in his attack of the way unions were having to compete to represent workers at the new Toyota plant being built in Derbyshire, by including, 'We wouldn't need Nissan and Toyota to fill a technological gap if British Leyland and Austin Rover were thriving.' True. But that is a separate point, and should not be allowed to colour one's judgement.

Some management–union relationships are becoming more positive and constructive. For example, the general manager at Lucas Heating and Engineering Systems contrasts the time when he managed a different business in the 1970s with now (1991). In the 70s he spent 20 per cent of his time 'arguing with the unions, debating with the unions whether we could move people'. In contrast, now he claims to spend 20 per cent of his time 'looking at education and training, involving the unions, and indeed getting a lot of support from the unions' (*State of Training*, 29.9.91). The key to constructive cooperation is genuine collaborative involvement and consultation.

Consultation, however, is decidedly missing in the main in the management–union relationship. The generally poor nature of the relationship came to the fore in the autumn of 1991, with the speculation that the electronics company GEC were going to merge with or make a bid for British Aerospace. GEC were reported to have had 'friendly' talks with BAe, but despite their denial that they were going to make a hostile bid, and despite the denial by BAe chairman, Sir Graham Day, that there had been any discussions with potential bidders and his reported annoyance over GEC's moves, the unions (and the employees and opposition political parties) showed great concern and distrust. The reason was strongly expressed by John Edmonds, general secretary of the GMB, in an address to the Labour Party Conference at the time of the speculation:

> What the hell is going on!? This is all good fun if we were playing some childish guessing game in innocent amusement. But we're actually playing with the future of a large part of our engineering industry, a massive part of our defence industry, a big car company, and the lives of 200,000 people.

The statement reveals the general lack of collaborative openness and unwillingness to consult on the part of management, which explains, and justifies, the unions' and others' distrust that management would be acting collaboratively in the best interests of the employees and the integrity of the company (cf examples p234–6, Chapter 12). The non-collaborative way in which people, and the overall health of organisations, do not generally figure in the activities of top managers and shareholders, is condemned by Bill Jordan, president of the AEU, in the following comment concerning the plight of Rover, a subsidiary of BAe:

> ... it's disgraceful that the boardroom shenanigans and the speculators of the City can threaten the livelihood of 35,000 people in Rover who are doing a splendid job for the country – I only wish the City had as much responsibility (*Newsnight*, 3.10.91).

Anxious workers at the Rover Longbridge plant complained about being 'left in the dark'; and the harmful effect of the secretive, non-collaborative way management treat employees was recognised by a worker at the Rover plant:

> It'll damage the lads ... we've been having letters come round saying about how they want an *even* work-force, and a happy work-force

and all the rest of it. Now this has come on again and so nobody knows what we are doing now (*Newsnight*, 3.10.91).

No amount of letters and words will bring about an 'even' and 'happy' work-force. The latter will only happen if management shows a genuine collaborative commitment to the work-force, openly and fully involving them, informing them and consulting them about the state of the organisation. And only then will workers stop feeling they are other than insignificant pawns in some remote and uncaring financial game.

That the poor relationship between management and unions/ workers is part of a more general non-collaborative national culture was reflected in the fact that GEC – a major supplier for BAe – did not trust BAe's future intentions. According to defence analyst, Keith Sykes, GEC 'put down its marker' because of fears over the possibility of joint ventures between BAe and other European companies:

> GEC and Aerospace are major trading partners, and there's always been a suspicion in the GEC going back really a fair number of years now, that British Aerospace would . . . do a deal with other people . . . Now clearly GEC must make sure . . . that it doesn't see business drifting away in this fashion (*Business Daily*, 7.10.91).

'Trading partners' maybe, but not the long-term, open, lacking in suspicion, collaborative partnership between organisation and supplier organisation that generally exists in Japanese organisations and other more collaborative national cultures (see Chapter 9).

Collaborative partnership between government and unions/ workers

Government leaders in Europe and Japan generally have a constructive partnership with unions (Chapter 12, examples p234–6). Within Europe, German government leaders in particular, following a tradition that began after the Second World War, believe that a key element for a sound economy is for government to cultivate good relations with union leaders, and to create a business environment of cooperation between management and labour. It is based on the attitude that more consultation, co-determination and partnership create more humane working conditions and give workers more pride in their work. This way, by having more dialogue between worker and managers, and between the 'work partners' and government, they have tried, with some success, to overcome the counter-productive, adversarial struggle of class conflict.

In contrast, class conflict largely characterises the British way of doing business, and dialogue between management and workers, and government and organisation, is largely absent. There is basically a hostile attitude of government towards unions. In the autumn of 1991, John Edmonds, General Secretary of the GMB, offered to hold dialogue with the government and employers over pay and the ERM, but it was rejected by both the CBI and Michael Howard, the Employment Secretary. The government believes that pay levels should be decided between individual employers and their workers. But, as was considered at the beginning of this section, workers are asking for rises in line with inflation, and this will put up unit costs and make us uncompetitive abroad. The reason why the unions do not step in and support and urge wage restraint, as the Belgian and Japanese unions did in the two examples cited above (p234–6), has a great deal to do with the lack of collaborative dialogue and partnership that exists in Britain between government and unions, and the underlying interpersonal attitudes that underlie it.

The workers and the unions, in both industry and education, generally see a remote and greedy management, often uncaring of the work-force; and a remote and uncaring government that does not help industry or its work-force. These views are expressed, for example, in the following statements by a managing director, and an industrial employee respectively:

> It's not easy [to reduce pay rises]. And it's particularly not easy when some of the captains of industry have grabbed so much for themselves.

> Oh, I don't think he's [the Chancellor] on this planet really. It's alright saying that [people should moderate their pay rises], but I mean, he's in a different position than what we are . . . I mean, he's on a lot more money . . . I mean Germany, they might have a higher cost of living over there, but they have their wages to compensate for that. I mean they – well I don't know, I think they have a better all round way of living . . . these European countries. (*Panorama*, 12.11.90).

This perception will have been enhanced within the latest recession with the high job losses, and the relatively low wage rises for employees compared to that for top managers. If unions and employees could *trust* that managers were *committed* more to the value of the work-force, keeping them on and giving them the *fairest* deal possible both within an existing problem, and in the future when things improve; and saw government more committed to industry, education, and the work-force, then ERM entry and the recession might not have been the problem they have been, and employees would have been more cooperative in surmounting problems by, for example, immediately accepting a reduction in wage rises and initiating and cooperating in other efficiency gains. But unions and employees will not have that trust until the attitudes and skills of top management become more collaborative, involving them more and directing funds more towards their training, equipment and R&D, and less to their personal salaries and dividends; and until government gives more support and incentive for education and training, and acknowledges its responsibility for inflation and creating adverse conditions affecting industry and education, and enables rational open dialogue concerning the economy and wage levels (see also next section). In short, until managers and government begin to work together *collaboratively* with unions and employees on *everyone's* behalf, for UK incorporated. The point is contained in the following statement, by ITN's industrial correspondent Ian Ross, which contrasts the German situation, and the advantages of a German car worker over his British counterpart:

> He's better paid, better trained, more productive with more investment at his elbow, and also better protected against inflation . . . British pay bargaining might be rather different if our inflation was as low as theirs, and our investment and productivity as high (*Channel 4 News*, 29.10.90).

Collaborative partnership between government and industry

The relationship between government and industry/business in Japan and much of Europe, is much more of a constructive partnership than in Britain, just as their organisation-union and government-union relationships are. In contrast, the relationship between the employers' body, the CBI, and the government has been described by industrialist Sir Peter Parker as a 'nervous relationship', an 'arm's lengthy relationship' (*Channel 4 News*, 13.9.91); and there is no forum for constructive dialogue where they can become involved, along with the unions, in the formation of national industrial and commercial policy. Significantly, a Mori Business Poll in September 1991 indicated that 65 per cent of businesses approached expressed a concern over government economic and industrial policy. There would be no such concern if these policies were jointly arrived at through a process of consultation involving employers, unions and government, as is the case in Japan and Europe. In line with the wishes of the unions, the CBI, in a report published in October 1991, called for more government support for industry, as occurs in Europe and Japan, and for the reconstitution of the National Economic Development Council to provide an effective forum for government and business dialogue.

Collaborative partnership between industry, education and government

Education – a reflection of the non-collaborative national culture

The educational system is not separate from, and immune to, these 'non-partnership', 'non-collaborative' ways of working. Admittedly, in the constructive collaborative sense, there has been very little link for example, between schools, colleges, and industry, although there is now some action to create bridges – mainly by the polytechnics. In another sense, however, there has always been a link between education and the outside world, in that educational organisations, often without being aware of it, strongly reflect the general non-collaborative, hierarchical culture of society (cf Lane, Lane & Pritchard, 1986). It is perhaps most obvious in the area of resource and pay negotiations. In education, although pay levels are set nationally, there is, as is the case for industry, a lack of collaboration between the government, local managers and unions. But the similarity between education and the outside world does not stop there. Significantly, John Edmonds, General Secretary of the GMB, says of the fragmented nature of pay negotiation in the UK:

> It soaks up our resources, it builds up and then frustrates the expectations of union members, and *it ensures that industrial relations' focus never moves off the pay issue* (TUC Conference, 5 September, 1990; my emphasis).

The trouble surrounding pay negotiations is, in fact, not only a sign that government, local managers and unions do not negotiate collaboratively over pay, but also a sign of a deeper non-collaborative approach *within* industrial and educational organisations. Thus, according to McGregor, insistent demands for more money are a sign of what he calls 'egoistic and self-actualisation' needs not being satisfied in the work-place:

> It becomes more important than ever to buy the material goods and services which can provide limited satisfaction of the thwarted needs . . . [money] can become the focus of interest if it is the *only* means available (1977, p209).

The view supported by this book is that ego and self-actualisation needs are best met through collaborative involvement of employees in the work-place, giving them more say and self-determination (see Chapter 8). Blumberg spells the situation out as follows: power (self-determination, control) ➡ increased status (decreased social distance from management) ⬅➡ increased sense of responsibility and identification with the job ➡ improvements in morale and efficiency/productivity (Blumberg, 1968, pp 27, 43). It is the reason, therefore, why people in collaboratively run organisations are not so obsessed with the pay issue, with demarcations between jobs, and with strict time-keeping, found in hierarchically run organisations, but instead feel rewarded in terms of involvement in the job, willing to flexibly interchange between roles, and willing to work for as long as it takes to get a job done – doing work in their own time both in the work environment and by taking it home to think about.

Employees' needs for self-determination and control, and the status that goes with it, seem to be very much thwarted in the educational sector. Significantly, the Education Secretary, while denying that our lower standards of education compared with Germany are due to lower teachers' pay (which he claims is on a par), acknowledges, '. . . that we need to raise the morale of teachers in the country. I agree we need to restore to them their self-esteem' (*Channel 4 News*, 13.11.90). The relevance of control and involvement – or the lack of it – to low self-esteem and morale, is strongly voiced by Peter Sampson, a former head of sixth form at a comprehensive school. Of the three most common criticisms made of head teachers by teaching staff he maintains, 'The most serious charge of all is . . . that they reserve all power to themselves or, share it, if at all, only with a small group of cronies' (1990). Lack of control and involvement was also found to be a major factor by a research team project undertaken at Nottingham University into school stress, commissioned by the National Union of Teachers. On the basis of the survey and discussions with teachers, the NUT 'action plan' recommends: improving leadership and management styles used by heads; developing a more cooperative and supportive culture; requesting senior teachers to share information; encouraging teachers to work together as a team; improving training and making it more relevant (NUT, 1990). There have been similar findings by the Health and Safety Executive, who point to: lack of consultation in teachers' job descriptions; changes in management styles; work overload without reward; dealing with aggrieved parents; inadequate training; a feeling of low status in society; as a source of stress on teachers (HSE, 1990). Their figures indicate an increase of almost 300 per cent in the numbers leaving the teaching profession through ill-health during the previous 10 years, and insurance companies are warning schools to prepare for rising premiums to cover the cost of staff absence through illness. Generally they warn of rising costs, falling standards, and personal suffering if stress is not dealt with.

The picture in higher education is the same. For example, in 1990 a 'confrontational' industrial relations strategy was reported to exist in Birmingham Polytechnic, where, of a survey of almost half the academic staff:

> 32 per cent said they felt stressed most of the time at work and more than 80 per cent disagreed with the statement that their relationship with senior management was supportive and mutually trusting . . . More than half the respondents said senior management regarded them as 'not important' (Utley, 1990).

This situation is not untypical. In British education, as in industry, there is a general lack of collaborative involvement of employees, where people are under-valued and under-used. (This is less so in Scotland, Northern Ireland and Wales than in England.) Also, as is the case in industry, the social distance between management and workers that the lack of involvement brings about, and the general lack of commitment of top managers towards the work-force, is 'rubbed in' further by the disproportionately increasing pay of education managers. Concerning this Sampson refers to head teachers' '. . . greedy concern with status . . . Their determination to increase the salary differentials between themselves and their staff does not make them any more attractive.' (op. cit.) Similarly, a large discrepancy between the salaries (and perks) of top managers in higher education and employees' salaries has been reported in various local newspapers. This, and the fact that many college directors are keeping their salary a secret, exacerbates the poor personal relations that exist between them and employees, and undermines the latter's trust that management are acting collaboratively in the best interests of employees and the organisation as a whole.

In this context, therefore, it seems that it is not so much absolute pay levels that are important, but *relative* pay levels. Significantly, in Japan income is distributed much more equitably than in Britain, and employees' pay in the educational sector, for example, relates favourably with other professions, reflecting their higher value and status in the eyes of society (see below).

Sampson, recognising that very few head teachers act as 'facilitator', enabling colleagues' involvement, and that vast numbers of schools are run on 'strict hierarchical lines', observes: 'A cynic would argue that this is the perfect preparation for the pupils for a world run on the same lines.' (op. cit.) Indeed so – at least as far as Britain is concerned. The predominant hierarchical school/ college culture is a mirror of the unhelpful, 'not-care', non-collaborative culture in society generally. Non-collaborative, hierarchical attitudes, preventing people acting as partners in a common enterprise, are endemic and go right through the very fabric of society. Of course, people take these attitudes to the workplace. However, it was considered above (Chapter 7), that a top manager with genuine collaborative attitudes can work to overcome hierarchical attitudes in employees and bring about a collaborative organisational culture.

In the case of schools, teachers, pupils and parents will all be affected by non-collaborative, hierarchical attitudes in society generally, including a distrust and judgemental disrespect for education and teachers. They therefore bring both hierarchical attitudes and low self-esteem to the school environment. Consequently, there is a hierarchical relationship between teacher and pupil, teacher and parent, and parent and pupil. This involves a lack of trust and respect on all sides, leading to a judgemental intolerance of others and an inability for self-appraisal. The low value put on education and teachers by society, and the generally hierarchical attitudes found in teachers, parents and pupils, was reflected, for example, in some comments made in a television debate on education (*The Great Education Debate*, 19.11.90):

> I think we're all to blame [for low standards], because this country does not have an ethos which says that education is important – other countries do (Bryan Symons, president, Bristol Chamber of Commerce).

> The thing that concerns me is that we've heard from some 150 teachers here tonight, and I find it difficult to recollect any word of doubt or self-criticism from them (Bryan Symons).

> I think the salaries of various key teacher areas is getting way out of line, and there ought to be more money put into some of the key areas . . . so that we can raise the level of people in those areas who otherwise actually can go off to industry and get much higher salaries (David Sainsbury, deputy chairman, Sainsbury PLC).

> I felt that children would not learn unless you had some kind of respect and mutual regard between parents and the pupils (ex-teacher).

However, hierarchical attitudes taken to the school environment by teachers, pupils and parents, could be overcome by a head teacher with collaborative attitudes and skills. Instead, school heads predominantly have strong hierarchical attitudes, and this reinforces and develops the hierarchical attitudes teachers and pupils generally bring to the learning environment. A head teacher's lack of respect and trust in people will pass right through the school. As a result, teachers, rather than working together cooperatively, generally lack respect and trust towards their colleagues and pupils. There is often back-biting and politicking rather than team work in the staffroom. And the non-collaborative, hierarchical head teacher–teacher relationship reinforces a hierarchical teacher–pupil relationship (see also Chapter 9), irrespective of the less formal, more 'democratic' arrangement of classroom furniture that mainly exists today in schools. The same general situation obtains in higher education.

Education in more collaborative national cultures*

Likewise, Japanese and German schools, for example, reflect the general culture of their societies. There, just as industrial workers are more respected and valued by their managers and by society generally than in Britain, so too are teachers more respected and valued by their managers and by society generally. Teachers are particularly highly valued in Japanese society, which is reflected in the fact that they are paid better than the police or the armed services, and as narrator, Philip Tibenham, observes, 'Competition for jobs is intense. There are five times as many applicants as there are teaching posts.' Teachers in countries such as Japan and Germany are not, as they are in Britain, 'the whipping boys of the nation . . . they don't get blamed for every little thing that goes wrong', as one head teacher put it (*Channel 4 News*, 13.11.90). They are not part of a hierarchical, judgemental culture, but a general collaborative culture, based more on respect and trust. From the fact that the Japanese Ministry of Education controls details such as the size of classroom, the textbooks to be used, and what children should study and for how long, it might seem that the teachers' needs for control are highly thwarted and morale low. As the Japanese themselves are aware, there are things wrong with the system, and the teachers' union, for example, criticises the non-consultation of practising teachers by government in curriculum reforms to date. Yet, within this overall rigid structure, there is mutual respect and cooperation, more equal involvement, and more equal sharing of power within schools, as is the case in other organisations in society generally. The gap between management and worker is not as great as in Britain, and there is correspondingly more responsibility, morale, motivation and efficiency amongst employees.

In Japan, just as the teachers are generally treated non-judgementally and with respect by their managers and society, so in turn teachers generally treat pupils non-judgementally and with respect. Therefore, although the teaching methods used in Japan are mainly traditional – and as a result of concern over this a new school curriculum placing more emphasis on enquiry and practical work is

---

* The quotations and factual information for the ensuing sub-section are taken from *Nippon*, 11.11.90, unless otherwise stated. The interpretations are this author's.

to be introduced in 1992 – the relationship between the teacher and the pupil is not such an unequal, judgemental, hierarchical one as is mainly the case in Britain. This is borne out, for example, by a comment of a junior high school principal in a talk to his new pupils (12-year-olds):

> Well, now you have become junior high school students, I want you not *just* to do whatever your teachers and parents say. Try to think for yourselves what you should be doing, and then do it.

The culture of collaborative equality is extended to the children in two other ways. Firstly, there is no streaming – all children study together. Toshihiko Zenke, a maths teacher, explains the philosophy behind it:

> We want every child to do well, so we put a lot of effort into teaching the basics. But because we also want to stretch them we give them some very difficult problems. And so the ones who are not good at maths don't lose out, we get them to study in pairs to work it out together.

The possibility that the 'brighter' pupil will dominate and therefore not help the 'less bright' pupil, and that the less bright pupil will hold up the brighter pupil – often a concern of British teachers – is not likely in the Japanese system where children are part of a less hierarchical, more cooperative, and more caring, non-judgemental culture. The teachers, and therefore the pupils, genuinely believe in *everyone's* worth, they expect *everyone* to achieve, and they genuinely help each other in that goal. A word that encapsulates the nature of the Japanese system and its contrast with Britain, is 'expectation'. The Japanese culture is characterised by high expectation – of the ability of all children in school, of teachers, of students, and of employees in business and industry. Conversely, the British culture is characterised by low expectation – a low expectation of the abilities of the majority of schoolchildren, of teachers, of students, and of employees in business and industry. And, of course, the difference in expectations rests on the underlying difference in attitudes towards people – collaborative ones of respect and trust, etc, in the case of the Japanese, hierarchical ones of disrespect and distrust, etc, in the case of the British. High expectation is also a characteristic of much European education and industry.

Secondly, the culture of equality in Japanese schools is extended to the children by involving them in the running of the school. For example, Philip Tibenham relates how *elementary* schoolchildren take lunch duty:

> Like most school activities, it's organised in small groups who take it in turn. Serving lunch to their classmates teaches them how to get organised and have concern for others.

Also, he observes that, at the end of each day in all state schools, the cleaning is done by the children:

> It's part of a continuing effort to put across a set of public values and encourage frugality, self-help, and working as a group.

The schools beyond the elementary stage are disciplinarian concerning dress, punctuality, etc, but again the 'discipline' is imposed by the children themselves in the form of children's committees.

Self-help, self-discipline, and concern for and working cooperatively with others within a tight social group, are stressed again and again. They are the basis of the school culture, as they are of society generally, which the school culture reflects. It is to be hoped that the current moves to reform the Japanese system, including putting a greater stress on individuality, will not be at the expense of group cooperation, as is generally the case in the West. The result of the traditionally strong group ethic has been a highly successful, highly efficient educational system and national economy. For example, in maths and science they do work which is reckoned to be two years ahead of British children at 13. The BBC programme *Nippon* reported that 94 per cent of children stay on in full-time education until they are 18, compared to less than 50 per cent in Britain. British government figures in 1990 for participation rates in full-time education and training of 16 to 18 year olds were 77 per cent for Japan, and 35 per cent for the UK. In 1990 60 per cent of all Japanese children were reported to go on to higher education, 30 per cent to university. But despite the impressive higher education figures, Philip Tibenham rightly concludes that:

> . . . the real accomplishment of Japan's schools is . . . the high level of schooling it gives to the mass of ordinary children and the way it prepares them for a modern industrial society.

In contrast, in Britain, where only about 20 per cent go on to higher education and 45 per cent leave school with no recognisable qualification, and only about a third of 16-year-olds stay on in full-time education until they are 18, the system is élitist. It has been claimed by the director general of the Institute of Directors that the 'big inequalities' of the system are fundamentally wrong', and they mean that 'we fail abysmally' with the majority of children 'so that they're under-qualified, under-extended, under-developed, and they under-achieve' (*Fighting Talk*, 22.10.90). It is also believed by some that the problem will not be removed by the National Curriculum but, 'under current plans Britain will still remain as it is, under-educated and under-trained' (*The Thatcher Audit*, 4.9.90).

The academic-vocational divide and the non-collaborative culture

The general educational underachievement and underskilling of British society, represents not only a loss in personal development and fulfilment, but also undermines international competitiveness as considered earlier in this chapter. Many of those in industry will know that this is not a recent phenomenon, brought about by the 1990–91 recession, nor even the 1980–81 recession – although these of course made matters worse. It has, in fact, been a feature of the British climate for many years. For example, Vivien Marshall of the Engineering Employers Federation pointed out, 'We are very, very short of technicians. We've been short of engineering technicians, I don't know, for 20 years maybe' (*BBC News*, 20.5.91). There is a general consensus over the reason for poor educational performance and the consequent underskilling that exists. At the root of the problem, it is believed, is the divide that exists between academic and vocational education, where the 'academic' is given more status by both people in education and employers. It is generally acknowledged that students only take the vocational route – if at all – if they fail the academic route.

The academic–vocational divide is based on the way theory and practice have come to be separated traditionally in education. Academic courses are 'theory biased' – either practical aspects are neglected, or, if present, as in medical, science and engineering subjects, they are underpinned by a strong theoretical component. Somehow the 'practical', using one's hands, is considered to be inferior. Yet, in truth, the 'practical' is inextricably bound up with some theory or another, and the divide made is quite artificial. Conversely, vocational courses are 'practice biased', often with what is considered a watered-down theory component, and so considered as inferior. The emphasis on 'academic' qualifications, and the undervaluing of 'non-academic' qualifications, alienates many young people from education, and is believed by many to be the reason why only about a third of 16–18 year olds remain in full-time education, and why only 64 per cent of 16–18 year olds are involved in any kind of education or training compared to 79 per cent in Japan and 90 per cent in Germany (DES, 1990).

Because of the dire situation concerning the resulting skills shortage and the great competitive disadvantage it puts the country in, the government introduced a series of White Papers in May 1991 aimed at achieving 'mass participation' in higher and further education and training, by:

1. giving vocational qualifications equal status with academic qualifications such as A' levels;
2. abolishing the distinction between polytechnics and universities;
3. ending local authority control of sixth form colleges and further education colleges (to give institutional freedom so that they are able to respond more flexibly to the demands of young people and employers).

But doubts have been expressed on how exactly the central aim (1) is to be achieved in practice. Professor Alan Smithers, who made a two-year study of bridging the gap between academic and vocational studies (1991), rightly points out: 'it's no good just declaring' they want vocational qualifications to have the same esteem in which academic qualifications are regarded. He maintains that vocational qualifications will have 'to open doors'; there will need to be a 'bridge' formed between the academic and vocational; there must be a direct link with employment, not the indirect link as at present; there must be a link in terms of extra money and in terms of getting employers to provide the training. Most significantly he comments, 'Why do vocational qualifications when by taking academic qualifications you can become that person's boss?' (Newsnight, 20.5.91).

This relates to the point made earlier in this section that educational organisations reflect the general non-collaborative, hierarchical national culture – what happens within the educational sector cannot be separated from, and indeed is a reflection of, what happens in industry and society generally. For example, at the time the White Papers on education were published, the Prime Minister, John Major, said:

What I believe we have to do is to break down the artificial barrier which has far too long divided an academic education from a vocational one – the blue-collar worker from the white-collar worker (*Channel 4 News*, 20.5.91).

The point indicates that as long as the kind of pay/status differentials that exists between the blue-collar worker and the white-collar worker, between 'professionals' – such as solicitors, doctors and managers – and people in other occupations – such as mechanical engineers, catering staff and bricklayers – then it will not be realistically possible to give 'vocational' qualifications *equal* esteem with 'academic' qualifications. A move towards less hierarchical, more collaborative working practice, therefore, where manager and employee roles merge, and people work in equal teams along the lines referred to in Chapter 6, would be a necessary part of removing the status difference between blue- and white-collar workers, and equalising vocational and academic qualifications.

Industry and education – the basics of collaborative partnership

If the vocational-academic gap is to be truly bridged, therefore, first and foremost there will need to be a more collaborative culture in the workplace.

Secondly – and this would be an outcome of the first requirement – there would need to be more collaborative dialogue between school/colleges and industry/business, to ensure that the 'academic' (theoretical) cannot stray from 'vocational' (practical) relevance in the way that it has done in the past – not only in management and teacher training courses (see Part III) but also throughout education in all subject areas – reducing the esteem of vocational qualifications, removing the relevance of the bulk of the subjects offered, and, in turn, removing interest, self-esteem and motivation in the bulk of the school population. The importance of having a collaborative partnership between education and industry is recognised by, for example, Ray Cowell, director of Nottingham Polytechnic, who deplores the exclusively academic nature of higher education in Britain:

In many ways what the polytechnics are doing is bringing British higher education into line with European best practice, by ensuring that academic standards are defined jointly with industry and that academic excellence goes with vocational relevance (*The Thatcher Audit*, 4.9.90).

Thirdly – and this would be part of the first requirement – schools and colleges themselves will need to be run more collaboratively, both to ensure that they are open to, listen to, and collaboratively respond to, the needs of students/trainees and employers; and to enable collaborative involvement in the learning process needed to ensure relevance, interest, self-esteem and motivation in both teachers and students, trainers and trainees. In short, there needs to be a more collaborative culture of partnership within the business/industrial workplace, between the workplace and schools and colleges, and within the schools and colleges.

It is unlikely that the government's declaration that they want vocational qualifications to have equal esteem to academic qualifications, together with the particular framework they lay down ((2) and (3) above), and the imposed National Curriculum, can in themselves have any *fundamental* effect on the inequalities of the system. These latter cannot be removed without a change in the underlying hierarchical attitudes, skills and practices of head teachers, college heads, heads of other organisations, and heads of government.

In the context of education and training, the following broad viewpoint was expressed by the shadow Employment Spokesman, and agreed to by the Parliamentary Under Secretary of State responsible for training:

> . . . there is a long-term problem of attitude, a question of culture, and I think we've got to shift Britain into a situation where people want to seek skills, they want to acquire, they want to own, they want to then enhance them. Now the Germans can do that, the French increasingly, the Japanese historically have been doing that. That's the long-term aim I think of *any* government, but that again comes back to the partnership model – it is about individuals, it is about companies, and it is also about the leadership the government can give. The *culture* is the key issue (*State of Training*, 7.4.91).

Fine rhetoric and sincerely meant. But *action* will be needed to shift Britain into a culture where people generally value education and training as they do in other more successful countries – action both on the part of heads of industrial and educational organisations to develop underlying collaborative attitudes, practices and partnerships; and on the part of the government to provide a framework to encourage and enable such development.

Summary – collaborative national partnerships and UK incorporated

The approach of the Japanese, and many European countries, where people work less selfishly and more collaboratively, both within and between organisations, is central to their success. The collaborative approach has probably been taken further by the Japanese than any other industrial country. The unique and close relationship between government and industry since 1880, now in the form of MITI, is testimony to this. As Example 2 (Chapter 12, p236) and the school situation discussed above exemplify, a strong characteristic of Japanese culture, and Japanese organisations, is the commitment by *everyone* to the group, top managers included. This involves a more equal treatment of people, and it is reflected in the equitable distribution of income already referred to. Deming, who has had much involvement with Japanese organisations, advises Western managers that, '. . . without a management commitment to the personal welfare of its workers, it will be impossible to inspire employees' interest in company productivity and product quality' (1986, p148).

Similarly, notice again the statement by McGregor quoted in Chapter 4, where he contrasts collaborative commitment (to people and organisation) with personal gain:

> Only the management that has confidence in human capacities *and is itself directed toward organisational objectives rather than toward the preservation of personal power* can grasp the implications of this emerging theory (1977, p211; my emphasis).

From examples cited above, the claim that 'people are an organisation's most important resource', now increasingly being voiced by managers in British organisations, is not a sham or mere palliative for the Japanese. They have provided proof that genuine collaborative attitudes in top management are the basis for more stable and thriving organisations in the long term.

Generally in Britain there needs to be a change in attitudes – less individualism, less personal acquisitiveness, more collaborative commitment to the organisation and the work-force by top management, and more collaboration between industrial, educational, financial and governmental organisations. The general non-collaborative culture in Britain imposes adverse pressures on individual organisations even if they are well managed, and it does indeed put them at a disadvantage over their competitors abroad. Just as an individual is restricted from developing a fully collaborative approach within a hierarchical organisation (Chapter 6), so an individual company is restricted in its application of a collaborative approach within a broader non-collaborative national culture. But this comparison is not exact. Individual organisations are able to develop collaborative cultures internally given the right kind of leadership from the top, and although there might be adverse external pressures, eg against long-term investment in education, training and R&D, collaboratively run organisations will be fitter and better able to meet, influence and survive those adverse pressures, than organisations run non-collaboratively. And they will be fitter and better able to flourish against increasing competition at times of more collaborative support from government and other organisations. The government should take a lead in society to provide a framework encouraging more top managers to operate collaboratively. However, organisations do not have to wait for government action, and it will be those who act now to develop a collaborative organisational culture, with or without external support, that will survive and flourish in the 1990s and beyond. One top manager, at least, recognises the overriding importance of the organisational culture, when he says:

> I think now we need a more strategic approach, not just involving management but also involving employees in the business ... I regard training, I regard employees participating through shareholding, *I believe that the communication that we develop between managers and employees, to be absolutely critical if we are going to be a successful country* and have a successful strategy (James Watson, then chairman designate, National Freight Corporation, on *The Money Programme*, 25.11.90; my emphasis).

Part II – key points

- Leadership skills can be split into three different levels: an upper *general functional skills* level, a middle *collaborative interpersonal skills* level, and a lower *collaborative interpersonal attitudes* level.

- Effective leadership is dependent on developing the underlying *core* collaborative interpersonal attitudes and skills.

- The skills of effective leadership/management are also the core skills of effective *teaching*, effective *teamwork* and effective *learning*.

- Too much emphasis on *team roles* at the general functional skills level – a central plank of much of the literature and training in leadership and teamwork – risks the possibility of confusing or losing sight of the underlying core skills and attitudes.

- *Shamming* a collaborative approach to manipulate people is cruel, dangerous and counterproductive.

- The core collaborative skills are the basis of effective *consultation*, essential for *all* management tasks, including the key task of dealing with continuous improvement and innovation, necessary for survival and success in the 1990s and beyond.

- A genuine *collaborative organisational culture* is only possible with the *active* commitment of the *top manager* to developing his or her own collaborative skills as the basis for a collaborative organisational structure.

- Caution! Managers, teachers, etc will only be able to translate the growing rhetoric for group/teamwork into practice effectively, within a (developing) collaborative organisational culture.

- A genuinely committed top manager has the means to overcome resistances to collaborative practices by being *flexible*, giving *time*, *allowing mistakes*, *recognising/rewarding collaborative behaviour*, and providing *training*.

- A collaborative organisational culture *cares* for the *employee,* the *customer,* the *supplier, other related organisations* and *the environment* – each increasingly necessary for survival and success.

- Traditional annual or semi-annual performance appraisal has been ineffective and counter-productive within prevailing *judgemental, unequal, fear-governed* hierarchical cultures.

- Collaborative organisational cultures instead enable *self-appraisal,* and *team-appraisal,* essential for effective personal growth, quality and organisational success.

- A collaborative organisational culture invests long term in people, their training and equipment, as a basis for sustainable success; and it is essential for *effective and cost-effective* training and development.

- In Britain there is a prevailing non-collaborative, 'not-care' *national culture* within and between organisations – including government – where top management has mainly a *short-term* outlook; in contrast to the more *collaborative, long-term commitment to organisation, employee, education, training, research and development,* found in more collaborative (and successful) national cultures.

- Prevailing non-collaborative attitudes and skills among top management are *reinforced* by the non-collaborative national culture – characterised by a preoccupation with short-term profit and cost cutting, at the expense of the human resource and the building of organisations.

- Collaborative organisational cultures are fitter and better able to survive both increasing competition and adverse external factors brought about by a non-collaborative national culture.

PART III

DEVELOPING THE CORE COLLABORATIVE SKILLS OF LEADERSHIP AND TEAMWORK

Parts I and II have considered the central importance to all organisations, in industry and education, of 'soft' collaborative interpersonal attitudes and skills – the need for *all* employees to develop these attitudes and skills; the need for top managers to initiate the process as a basis for developing enabling collaborative organisational cultures; and the overriding importance of developing such cultures if organisations are to meet and survive rising competition, depleted natural resources, and adverse conditions produced by a generally non-collaborative national culture. This final part will consider how the core collaborative skills are best developed, incorporating a look at the inadequacy of much present management and teacher training provision, stressing the importance of an enabling collaborative culture for effective and cost-effective training generally, and finally providing a practical 'core skills' guide for practising top managers, middle managers, teachers, supervisors, etc.

14

Learnable skills, team roles and training courses

The learnable skills of leadership and teamwork, and team roles

It was pointed out in Chapter 4 that a central plank of much of the literature and training in leadership and teamwork today rests on considerations of team roles; where, broadly, a person's 'role' is determined by the personal preference they have for undertaking certain of the work functions at level 3, in Figure 4.1 (eg Margerison and McCann, 1985, p16; cf Belbin, 1981, px). This author acknowledges that a consideration of people's preferences for certain tasks can be a useful way of prompting them to reflect on, and discuss, their particular strengths and weaknesses. But, without an overt consideration of the underlying core collaborative attitudes and skills (levels 1 and 2, Figure 4.1), no amount of training exercises and discussions centring on team roles, will fundamentally improve people's leadership/team skills. In fact, too much concentration on team roles has, at best, tended to obscure and confuse the underlying core collaborative attitudes and skills, and how people might go about effectively developing them. And, at worst, it can suggest that people, because they are 'predisposed by nature and ability' to certain team roles only (Belbin, 1981, px), are locked into those roles, with no possibility of them learning and developing the range of leadership and teamwork skills.

The view represented by this book is that the skills of leadership and teamwork are not inborn traits, but are skills that can be learned and coached (cf Adair, 1984, p70, 1986, p195; Smith, 1969; Peters et al, 1985; Deming, 1986; Beck, 1989; McGregor, 1987, pp181, 182). Furthermore, as considered in Chapter 4, it is believed that only through developing the underlying *core* collaborative attitudes and skills at levels 1 and 2 (Figure 4.1), can aspects of the higher level leadership/team functions (level 3) and related team roles, be dealt with effectively.

'Learning by collaborative doing' and training courses

A central message of this book is that people work and learn best in a 'participatory' or 'collaborative' environment. It is on this basis that it is maintained that *the key skills of managers and teachers are those of collaborative leadership and teamwork*. However, apart from a few exceptions (see later in this chapter), this view has not filtered down to the bulk of courses in management and teacher training.

Traditionally too much theory – not enough practice

This has been a growing criticism made against both management and teacher training. In the area of management training it was nearly twenty years ago that Mintzberg made the comment, '. . . although the management school gives students MBA and MPA degrees, it does not in fact teach them how to manage . . .' (1973, p187). The reason he gave for this was that training was not 'participative':

> Learning is most effective when the student actually performs the skill in as realistic a situation as possible . . . One cannot learn to swim by reading about it. The leadership skills, perhaps more than any others, require participative training. (p188–9).

Little had changed by 1987 when Charles Handy reported a total inadequacy of management education and development in Britain (Handy, 1987); and increasingly company personnel, such as Peter Dickson, Head of Management Training at the Sutcliffe Group, are rejecting the 'overly theoretical' and 'academic' nature of training programmes (*In Business*, 12.9.90).

Similarly, in the area of teacher training, the view that there is too much emphasis on the theoretical, and courses are irrelevant and inadequate preparation for the teaching task, has been expressed by newly-trained teachers (see below), observed by HM Inspectors (HMI, 1988, pp10, 29), and echoed by education secretaries and ministers (eg DES, 385, 1990; see also Jones, 1989:b).

It is remarkable that management training, and to a large extent, teacher training (see below), which are – or should be – about developing a *practical skill*, have traditionally contained little or no *effective* practical component. It is an extreme example of the academic-vocational, theory-practice, divide referred to in Chapter 13, a divide that goes right through the education-training sector. It would be unthinkable to expect trainee doctors, builders, engineers, etc to acquire competence and expertise in their particular area by a training process that just *told* them (and asked them to write about) the theory of medicine, house building, bridge building, welding, etc. Yet managing and teaching are equally practical activities. It should be noted here, however, that even with 'practically-biased' courses, what are called 'vocational' courses, there has, to a certain extent, been an 'academic' bias in that the practical element is undertaken in an unreal, artificial, college environment that may not directly relate to a real work situation. It is for this reason that all training in all subject areas – not just management and teacher training – needs to be *work-based*, where there is a close partnership between training organisations and employing organisations (see below).

The irrelevance of traditional training – Example 1

Anita Roddick had no knowledge of economic theory and no management training before she embarked on her now highly successful international business. She believes that this has been to her advantage, and that such knowledge and training – what she calls 'the science of making money' – can stifle the underlying 'human' values required for organisational success (Schumacher, 1990; Burlingham, 1990, p41). Further, Roddick claims that the most intelligent thing her company does is to discriminate against anybody who has been to a business school:

> I *never* employ anybody from Harvard, *ever*, *ever*, and I would be *deeply* reluctant to employ anybody from the system, you know, a standard business school, because they are trained not to think with their emotions or feelings, they are trained not to even *care* about the products, they're just trained to what's like the science of business . . . they run it like a military campaign – the hierarchy of authority . . . (*Walk the Talk*, 7.4.91)

> . . . what I can't get out of a business school is that secret ingredient of euphoria, which is a belief that business can fly a flag of social change. (*Great Expectations*, 29.4.91)

Anita Roddick's attack on traditional business training is endorsed by Deming who claims that courses are 'often watered down to numerical games of inventory control and production flow', in which tight financial budgeting is seen as effective management (1986, p147). Similarly, Peters and Austin accuse business schools of focusing on 'cost control' at the expense of more people-centred service and quality considerations (1985, p63).

What has become a 'traditional' leadership-team skills management training vehicle, namely, the outward bound course can also be challenged. In this approach the traditional theory-biased method has swung to the other extreme where people are expected to learn skills through pure experience. But such an approach is unlikely to succeed (see also Chapter 15, p286). There is no guarantee that experience alone, in the form of outdoor group activities, will change and develop underlying attitudes to more collaborative ones – a necessary precursor to collaborative leadership-team skills development. Indeed, it might even harden existing hierarchical attitudes in that those who tend not to consider the views and feelings of others but instead inconsiderately override and dominate in order to get their own way, might thrive under the guise of being a good leader, dynamic etc in the context of such contrived outdoor activities.

The Body Shop instead sends people out in service. For example, as mentioned previously within their programme of employee involvement in community projects, The Body Shop regularly send a team of people – in their pay time – for two or three weeks at a time to Romania to work in the orphanage project. They have found that this activity, where people are bonded with different age and economic groups, living in difficult physical conditions, and 'doing some good', produces a team who are empowered, and has been 'the most brilliant training project in leadership skills' (*In Business*, 18.9.91). Certainly, it seems much more likely that such activities will influence set underlying attitudes and develop a caring concern for others, and reveal the pressing need for people to work cooperatively with others to achieve effective and constructive help and improvement. Roddick sums up the difference between her organisation and others:

> The way we work is quite simple: we run in the opposite direction to the rest of the cosmetics industry. They train for a sale, we train for knowledge. (NatWest, 1991, p3)

Similarly, a participatory-collaborative group discussion approach, with its supportive, non-judgemental and so non-threatening group framework (see Chapters 15, 16), is a far more effective vehicle than either the chalk (flip-chart, video) and talk or outward bound approaches, for airing and challenging underlying hierarchical attitudes and prejudices, and enabling and developing collaborative attitudes and skills.

The irrelevance of traditional training – Example 2

An HMI view

A 1987 survey by Her Majesty's Inspectors on newly qualified teachers (HMI, 1988), included the following observations:

> ... substantial proportions [of new teachers] felt ... the more practical aspects such as teaching method, classroom observation and teaching practice had received too little [emphasis in their training]. (para 1.18)

> The probationers' views and HM Inspectors' observation of their work indicated that the professional courses which the new teacher in primary schools had followed [at college] were not always adequate preparation for the teaching task. (para 1.40)

> In many lessons the new teachers over-directed the work of their pupils ... Perhaps through lack of confidence ... (para 1.12)

> The fact that in a third of lessons the newly trained teachers showed a lack of skill in a basic teaching technique [open questioning skills] suggests that insufficient emphasis is given to this technique during training and induction. (para 2.25)

> ... 19 per cent of probationers in primary and middle schools and 12 per cent of those in secondary schools were ... less than adequately or poorly equipped for their jobs. (para 1.36)

A trainee's view

A common criticism by new teachers of their training is the feeling of inadequacy it leaves them with. One teacher comments:

> My teacher training lasted for a year. It was very theoretically based and I don't think it prepared me for the practicalities of teaching ... I know several colleagues of mine who I was at teacher training college with who have already left, and several probationers this year have spoken to me about this feeling of inadequacy and just not feeling prepared for the job in front of you (Public Eye, 7.6.91).

A head teacher's view

The irrelevance of much of teacher training is also voiced by head teachers. For example:

> They [training institutions] can't be doing a proper successful job if about a third of all teachers trained actually drop out of the system within five years (*Public Eye*, 7.6.91).

Work-based education and training

Generally in education and training, the wisdom of the old Chinese proverb:

> I hear and I forget,
> I see and I remember,
> I do and I understand

has been missed. Traditionally, much emphasis has been put on the student/trainee learning by being told about things – *hearing*. More lately, importance has been placed on the value of visual aids, eg overhead projectors, flip-charts, videotapes, etc – *seeing*. Some management training goes to great expense in this area to present very 'glossy' courses. Although this is an improvement on the mere aural approach, the student/trainee still remains a passive receptor of information. Understanding really only comes through welding the theory to practical experience – *doing*.

'Learning by doing', making training directly relevant to the practical work needs of the trainee, is the policy, for example, of the Ashridge Management College and the International Management Centres*, which advocate a closer partnership between college and companies, and centre on work-based projects; and there are examples of companies, such as Marks and Spencer, IBM and Unilever, who have opted for part-time MBAs in conjunction with business schools (*In Business*, 12.8.90).

Similarly, in the area of teacher training, there has been some move away from the traditional college/out-of-school courses to more school-based, 'on-the-job' training, with a closer partnership

---

* The Ashridge Management College is at Berkhamstead; see also Handy, L, 1988. The International Management Centres (IMC) operates from Buckingham; founded by Revans, see eg Revans, 1978.

between college and school. This is being experimented under the Articled Teacher Scheme, a new route into teaching for postgraduates where four-fifths of the course is based in school and the training shared between the teachers in the school and college/university trainers. The scheme has been reported to be welcomed by schools and by teacher trainers (DES, 385, 1990), although the extra time and financial burden it puts on teachers and schools makes it unfeasible for every trainee.

Perhaps the most *equal* partnership between school and college so far is within the experimental Internship Scheme at Oxford University. Again, the trainees or 'interns' spend a large portion of their time in school. But this author believes that it is the genuinely close relationship between college staff and teachers, where they share equally both devising and delivering the training, which is the key to ensuring that theory dovetails with practice to a greater extent than with other schemes. And, in turn, it is the more equal and open relationship that is encouraged between trainers and trainee – making the learning a two-way process – which will improve the quality and relevance of that practice.

There is also a growing trend to more 'school-based' training for in-service practising teachers, achieved by working alongside colleagues in classrooms, using advisory and curriculum support teachers, school-based courses, and including on-going evaluation and action research (see Chapter 15). This in-house, 'on-the-job' training has been reported to be thought more effective than traditional college courses/workshops, and to have prompted a growing number of higher education institutions to modify their provision, to become more flexible and accredit classroom-based study (NFER, 1990) – but see Chapter 15 on the set-backs of *pure* in-house training.

The practical and flexible nature of distance learning or open learning provided by the Open University and the Open College, which allows people to study at their own pace and to adapt and apply new knowledge and skills within their own workplace, is becoming increasingly popular. It is not surprising that they are becoming more attractive to the trainee and employer against traditional courses that are less practically relevant, less flexible, more time consuming away from the job, and less economical. This general criticism of traditional courses is not only true of the more theoretically biased ones such as management and teacher training courses, but also of practically biased courses. As a result there are now moves by some colleges to provide more *practically relevant* and flexible courses. For example, the Boating Enterprises skills training manager at Tile Hill College, Coventry comments:

> Initially it was intended that the scheme would run from the college ... We soon discovered that it wasn't possible to do that to have an effective scheme, so that we not only brought in more trainers, other colleges, Calor Gas, even private training organisations – but we started to go *away* from the college, to take the training out to the boat yards to help them in this business of releasing people for training (*State of Training*, 7.4.91).

Most students on most courses, and not just the theoretically biased courses, are eager to centre their training on practising the new theory and skills *in a real situation*. Practical, 'work-based' training keeps the theory firmly rooted in practice, giving relevance and interest, which then motivates the learner; in contrast to the traditional artificial and isolated 'academic' training courses, which are devoid of *direct* practical relevance, removing interest and demotivating the learner. For example, Chris Hayes of The Prospect Centre training consultancy, has found for the training programmes the centre is developing, that the value of sandwich courses is greatly enriched, and the motivation for people to learn increased, by transferring the planning of future development from the classroom to the workplace (Golzen, 1991).

For work-based training to be fully effective, however, much depends on the culture of the employing organisation (see Chapter 15).

Traditionally, however, most trainers, whether in management, teaching or any other skill area, have not been open to the wishes and needs of the student/trainee (or the employing organisation). An example of trainers who have been open to the student's needs for more relevance, is provided by a conversion course run by Jaguar in Coventry.

Effective work-based training – Example

In the mid 1980s Jaguar was faced with a shortage of body engineers that was threatening production. This skills shortage had been brought about by the cutting back of apprentices in the late 1970s and early 1980s, and most motor manufacturers as part of interna-

tional groups, were having body engineering done overseas. Jaguar
had the option of trying to pay more to attract the skilled engineers,
but this would have upset other Jaguar workers and caused dissatisfaction. For this reason they decided to 'grow' their own by
retraining existing workers. *By being open and listening to the views of
the trainees*, they soon learned a key characteristic of effective training that many traditional trainers have not been, and are still not,
open to. The words of the chief engineer of body design and the
head of conversion training illustrate the learning gains of being
open:

> We did early on make that mistake – we did all the training in the sort
> of classroom situation in the training centre, and we took feedback
> after each course to try and make improvement, and we found that
> the guys were very keen to get into the main design office as early as
> possible. And we also felt we could learn more about them and what
> sort of thing they needed to be taught . . .

> The project work that comes through which has been given to us by
> body engineering, actually creates an enthusiasm with the guys. They
> know that they're actually doing live projects, and they are liaising
> *themselves* with people in body engineering, with their future managers
> and principal engineers. That works out very well (*State of Training*,
> 7.4.91).

Because of the success of this course, Jaguar uses the approach for
other areas where there are skills shortages.

Collaborative work-based education and training

By the above claim that people learn best in a 'participatory' environment, however, more is meant by 'participatory' than there merely
being a relevant practical component involved. Indeed, although
traditional training in engineering, building, science, etc contains a
practical component that enables people to 'do' and 'practice' their
skill (although usually within an artificial college environment that
is not directly relevant to the workplace as considered above), it
operates within a *didactic* framework where people are authoritatively
told about the theory and what to do and then, some would say,
blindly follow. In contrast, a 'participatory' approach means involving
trainees *equally* in the learning process, encouraging them, for
example, actively to discuss and weigh up differing viewpoints, to
question viewpoints, to challenge and be challenged by others, to

give alternative ideas, etc. This provides an environment that develops the learner's collaborative interpersonal attitudes and skills (levels 1 and 2, Figure 4.1, the basis of effective communication, decision-making, self-development and self-directed learning, increasingly needed in the workplace.

For example, the manual of the German Federal Institute for Vocational Training states:

> The new electronic technologies are shifting the human-labour fraction ever faster in the direction of tasks which call for decisions, initiative and human intervention.

And The Prospect Centre in London is applying the German principles in training programmes it is developing with leading companies in the UK in partnership with a group of colleges of further education. For example, in manufacturing they believe that more than purely technical skills are needed, and that training must impart knowledge about working in teams, the changing needs of the customer, communication skills, and problem-solving techniques, etc (Golzen, 1991).

Similarly, the CBI strongly believe that national vocational qualifications (NVQs) should include such 'core skills' training; and they consider present education and training in Britain to be 'too narrowly based' – education stressing knowledge, training stressing occupational skills, and both failing to give prominence to 'core skills' (CBI, 1990, p25). Generally, in the early 1990s, prevailing British attitudes to education and training are some way behind the German model. The National Council for Vocational Qualifications does point out that the government White Paper 'Education and Training for the 21st Century' (May 1991), establishes an extra category of vocational training dealing with more general aspects of working methods, such as teamwork. But according to Chris Hayes: 'these merely bolt on concepts that ought to be integrated into technical courses' (Golzen, 1991). As such, of course, they cannot possibly be effective. 'Dealing' with the core skills needed to undertake technical, or any other activities effectively, in a vacuum separately from those activities, is a grotesque example of the theory–practice divide that undermines the quality of so much education and training; and it puts into question the genuineness of the government's willingness to improve employee autonomy, (core) skills and working practices.

Because of the central importance of the core collaborative skills, therefore, learning and training in *any* subject area is most effective when it is work-based *and* when it uses a participatory or collaborative approach. Learning and training in the area of collaborative leadership and teamwork, therefore, should itself be a collaborative process. To hammer the point home, it is no good just being told about, or reading about, or writing about, the skills and attitudes needed for effective leadership and teamwork (or any other skill area).The trainee needs collaborative 'doing' in order to develop them. Management and teacher training courses, therefore, which should centre on leadership-team skill development, should be run on collaborative lines. As was considered in Chapter 9, this will require 'training the trainers' in collaborative skills, and training institutions developing more collaborative organisational cultures.

Dr Laurence Handy, director of the MBA programme at Ashridge, stresses the 'collaborative' nature of the 'doing' that is required within training programmes; and a directly parallel statement could be made about teacher education:

> The traditional MBA had a very high emphasis on the analytical, the hard technical skills, finance, marketing, etc . . . but . . . the ability to work *with* others and *lead* them, the ability to negotiate, to influence, to actually be able to take people with you, and lead in that way is very, very important, and that's an aspect of management development which is not found in the traditional MBA programme. (*In Business*, 12.9.90)

In summary, effective management and teacher development programmes will contain the following key components:

1. an emphasis on collaborative leadership/team skills development. This will be made manifest by:
2. an overall participatory or collaborative team approach, giving practice in leadership-team skills within a theoretical/knowledge component, thereby welding theory to practice;
3. a work-based practical component, to deploy the skills gained under component 2.

The activity under component 2 might be undertaken in the college environment (daytime, evening or weekend sessions), or in the work environment, according to the kind of development programme being undertaken. Basically the same format is needed in all areas of education and training.

15

Training courses, organisational culture and self-team development

Effective training needs collaborative cultures

As well as training courses needing to be work-based and collaboratively run, the point was made in Chapter 11 that training will only be *fully* utilised and extended if the trainee works in an empowering collaboratively run organisation. It is the relevance of the organisational culture in deploying and extending skills, therefore, and not only the need for a relevant practical component, which is the reason why there needs to be a close partnership between training establishments and work organistions for courses to be effective.

Significantly, the Open College, which was set up in 1987 with the idea of providing open learning packages for individuals to enable them to improve the way they did their job, has found that it has been employers (training managers in companies), and not individuals who have approached them. Individuals in organisations might not only lack confidence to take on courses in training, but also know full well that whatever they do to try to improve and develop themselves, without the *active support* of their 'bosses' will be wasted (see also Chapter 6). Both the Open College and the Open University realise the central importance of support for the effectiveness of training, not only from themselves and their tutors, but also from the employers. For example, Lesley Briggs, account manager of the Open College, describes their approach in providing management training for the Sports Council as, '. . . a sort of process that involves everybody, line managers, tutors, the Open College and the training department' (*State of Training*, 7.4.91).

Sheffield City Council, is an example of an employer that realises the importance of training *and* their active support in the process. They use Sheffield Polytechnic for the training of their managers, as it is able to provide a flexible course involving the business school, in-house learning – learning on the job, and open learning packages. And, as the assistant chief personnel officer comments:

> . . . above all else, it involves management who are in the organisation, and they have to be part of the programme, they have to be the mentors so that we can put the learning in context (OU 1991a).

It is through the use of mentors, the training manager points out, and the assistance they give to the trainee to apply the learning in the workplace, that they are able to 'ensure that maximum benefit accrues from the course'. And specifically in the area of teacher training many are advocating not only more relevant school-based practice, but also better support for that practice (*Public Eye*, 7.6.91).

In the case of management and teacher training, therefore, no matter how effective a training course might be in developing collaborative leadership/team skills in the trainee, it will be difficult for an individual to deploy and continue to develop these skills in a hierarchical organisational culture (Chapter 6). In other words, if an organisation is not *genuinely* and *actively* sympathetic to developing a collaborative team approach it will clash with the aims of a course centring on collaborative leadership-team skill development; and sending individuals on courses (apart from the top management), is likely to be a costly waste of time.

'Through-the-job' training

Because of the importance of organisational culture to individual management and teaching development, and the fact that: '. . . natural learning, and self-development with which it is associated, has the virtue of being relatively cheap to foster – provided this is done effectively' (Davies et al, 1984, p169) it might be argued that natural or 'on-the-job' training could take over completely, and training schools and colleges be dispensed with altogether. And the call for purely on-the-job training for both managers and teachers has been a natural backlash to the theoretically biased traditional training. But there are strong counter-arguments. The main one hinges on the warning given by Deming that, 'Experience without theory teaches nothing' (1986, p317). There is the danger that in-house 'training' that relies solely on experience on the job for initiating and developing new recruits, and for further developing other employees, will lead to organisations becoming very inward-looking and stagnant, with the likelihood of perpetuating bad practice (eg Handy, L, 1987, p8; Jones, 1989b, p91). Even in-house training that does have a theory input, is likely to be introspective and unprogressive – unless the organisation has the resources to fund training personnel and extensive R&D, and has an *open* collaborative organisational culture, which, among other things, would enable collaborative 'networking' with other organisations in industry and education.

The inadvisability of pure in-house training is recognised, for example, by Shell UK who use a combination of in-house training with business schools in order to avoid 'introspective' managers. Similarly, within teacher education the government is sceptical about teachers and schools taking over completely the job of teacher training. They acknowledge that the new trainee does not want to be 'thrown in at the deep end' but wants and needs training, but better training (DES, 385, 1990), which combines practical relevance with theoretical understanding (Jones, 1989:b). Busy, under-resourced teachers working within mainly traditional, closed hierarchical cultures, are unlikely to be able to provide this.

The examples of closer cooperation between colleges and companies, and colleges and schools, referred to in the previous chapter help counter the inwardness of purely on-the-job training, while at the same time offering employees training that is more relevant to their job than traditional courses. It is what the Ashridge Management Research Group refer to as learning 'through the job' (Willie, 1991, p27).

Even if one does not go to the extreme of saying that courses (provided by external organisations) can be of no value, however, it is important to realise that *any* training course/programme can only be a *starting point* to leadership/team skill development, which should be an on-going self-development process in the workplace. The point is made by Mintzberg, for example, who said, 'most important, students should be encouraged to develop the skills of introspection needed to continue to learn by themselves on the job' (1973, p193). As considered above,the organisational culture would need to be collaborative in order to enable the deployment (and further development) of such learning skills.

The progressive American organisations observed by Beck (1989) are aware of the need for continual on-going development of the leadership/team skills in the workplace, as indeed they are for technological skills, etc. To this end many of the companies have instigated a corporate training centre, which is responsible for developing leadership/team skills for all layers of management; which offers tailor-made courses contributing to the solution of work issues; which includes broader components as a basis for facilitating personal development; and which encourages networking with external organisations.

Performance appraisal and self-team development

The skill of introspection referred to at the end of the last section, or the skill of self-reflection, encorporating self-evaluation or self-appraisal, is a key collaborative interpersonal skill (Figure 4.1). The ability effectively to question and evaluate oneself rests on underlying collaborative interpersonal attitudes such as *humility* and *honesty*, and without the development of such attitudes self-appraisal and a programme of self-development of the leadership/ team skills would not be able to get off the ground. It is important, therefore, that both courses and organisational cultures are run on collaborative lines in order to encourage and support the development of the underlying collaborative attitudes.

It has been suggested above (Chapter 8), that the judgemental characteristic of hierarchical organisational cultures makes semi-annual or annual performance appraisal systems ineffective for developing employee motivation and learning (cf Deming, 1986, p101ff; McGregor, 1987, p77ff). It also opposes the development of self-appraisal in the employee. The legitimate feeling of dejection and fear of reprisal, rather demotivates employees and prevents them from dealing with critical feedback constructively; and it is the related fear of making and admitting to mistakes that prevents the development of their self-appraisal skills.

The old saying: 'The man who never made a mistake never made anything' simply but forcefully brings home the non-learning, non-developing nature of judgemental, hierarchical institutions. There is increasing acknowledgement of the importance of making mistakes and experiencing failure for personal growth, and therefore for organisational growth (eg Adair, 1986, p195; Handy, L, 1987, pp7, 8; Peters et al, 1985; McGregor, 1987 pp152, 153). But, as considered in Chapter 8, to translate this enlightened view into action, where mistakes and failures can be openly and rationally discussed without any possibility of judgemental reprisal, will require a big change in the prevailing hierarchical organisational structures, and the corresponding underlying non-collaborative attitudes in top management.

Within a collaborative organisational culture an 'add-on' appraisal process at periodic intervals of six months or a year, becomes redundant. By tolerating mistakes, such a culture removes fear (see Chapter 8) and provides an environment where people can *continuously*:

1. openly admit to and learn from their mistakes;
2. respond constructively to and learn from team feedback (see also next section);
3. take responsibility and try out new ideas, etc;
4. be open to and learn from customer feedback (Chapter 9).

This applies as much to management as to other employees. In hierarchical cultures management also fear making, or admitting to, mistakes because they believe it would lead to a loss of control and authority (see also Chapter 7). The prevailing attitudes of respect, humility, honesty, etc, within collaborative organisational cultures, however, enable skills of self-appraisal in both employees and managers, and also an ability to deal constructively with critical feedback. Significantly, Beck found that a number of the high performing companies he observed operated some system of evaluation of their managers by, or feedback from, subordinates and he advised, 'Make it right for management to be criticised. This is bound up with unleashing personal initiative and creativity' (1989, p25).

In the same context of people development, Sir John Harvey-Jones gave the following advice to the top managers of a pottery firm concerning the involvement of their middle management:

> Well, I suspect they may produce what they think you want. But the art honestly is, to keep pressing them *until they tell you that you're wrong* (*Troubleshooter*, 30.9.90; my emphasis).

Put simply, everybody in an organisation, both management and non-management, should be able to say 'I am wrong', and be able to react constructively to the feedback 'You are wrong'.

From the first three points above, therefore, it can be seen that within a collaborative organisational culture, appraisal is a continuous and integral part of *self-team* development during day-to-day work activity. Within this culture the head of department, line manager, supervisor, etc, instead of acting as judge, will be a colleague, learning *with* team members, and encouraging and facilitating their involvement and control over their own personal goals, thereby welding personal development with organisational objectives (cf Beck, 1989, p26; Deming, 1986, p117; McGregor, 1987, p152). Initially this 'self-team' growth process can be facilitated by higher levels of management recognising/rewarding line managers, etc, for developing their subordinates (and themselves) in this way (cf Handy, L, 1987, p8; McGregor, 1987, p201); and by the use of learning aids for the development of collaborative interpersonal skills (see next two sections). Ultimately, as was mentioned above (Chapter 7), the development of subordinates by managers will be a natural consequence of the underlying collaborative attitudes and skills (which they should be able to develop in a truly collaborative organisational culture), and this brings its own rewards in the form of loyalty, commitment, personal growth and quality of performance.

Self-team development and the 'action research' cycle

It has been said above that the most effective form of learning is through collaborative 'doing'. In turn, the most effective form of collaborative doing is 'action research'. This has been proposed both in the area of management training, eg:

> . . . further progress can best be made by a form of 'action research', ie by seeking to change what we do by reflecting *before* and *after* some identifiable piece of communication, if possible with the help of others (Adair, 1984, p258)

and in the area of education, eg:

> Action research is a form of self-reflective enquiry . . . It is most rationally empowering when undertaken by participants [teachers, students or principals for example] collaboratively (Henry and Kemmis, 1985).

The next chapter provides a checklist of the core collaborative leadership/team skills, and a basic team format list, and these are designed to help a team leader (top manager, line manager, teacher, supervisor, etc) develop the relevant skills and practices, by providing a basis to reflect (and plan) before an encounter (with a group or individual);

and to check against his or her performance after the encounter. This will then indicate where and how changes should be attempted for the next encounter.

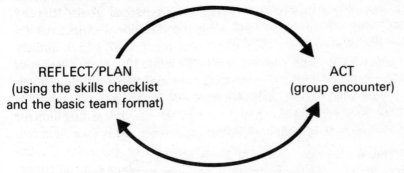

REFLECT/PLAN
(using the skills checklist
and the basic team format)

ACT
(group encounter)

Figure 15.1 *The 'action research' cycle*

A double-headed arrow is used on the lower part of the diagram to indicate the use of *group feedback/appraisal* within the group encounter. Open feedback is being increasingly recognised as important in the learning/development process (eg Kemmis et al, 1982, p13; McGregor, 1987, pp87, 232ff). Yet, because of the personal and judgemental way mistakes and failures are treated within hierarchical cultures, people avoid giving open, honest, feedback – a fact recognised by management expert and headteacher alike:

> But what is more important, we normally get little feedback of real value concerning the impact of our behaviour on others . . . Above all, it isn't considered good taste to give this kind of feedback in most social settings. Instead, it is discussed by our colleages when we are not present to *learn from it* (McGregor, 1987, p220; my emphasis).

> Any headteacher knows that appraisal has been going on by the visits of advisers and inspectors. The unfortunate thing about that is there hasn't been a feedback. In many cases advisers and inspectors have been along, spent a lot of time in schools with heads, and have at no time told them what they think of heads or where heads are doing good work or where heads are on the wrong track, and that's a problem (view of headteacher in, Hellawell, 1990, p7).

Basically people *need* open, honest feedback – critical feedback – both positive and negative, in order to learn. Receiving positive feedback is rewarding and reinforces good practice. Having failings and mistakes non-judgementally indentified and rationally discussed motivates and supports us in formulating different and improved strategies for the future. The need for constructive, collaborative, 'negative' critical feedback to know where you are, is exemplified in a comment by a Komatsu employee about his supervisor, 'He tells you everything that's gone wrong, you know, he doesn't keep nought in the dark off you, you know. Yes, he's a good bloke' (*Business Matters*, 27.9.90).

In short, in the right collaborative environment, receiving critical feedback is both mentally challenging and psychologically supporting. The mutual support and learning aspect of teams has been observed by Prideaux and Ford, in their development of a group/team approach to management training:

> The teams were often spoken of [by participants] as a powerful vehicle for learning ... some participants spoke of the high level of challenge and critical evaluation provided by their teams. Feedback ... in the team was a significant cause of growth. In addition, teams were highly supportive ... one member used the word 'sanctuary' ... (1988(b), p17).

On the above basis the following broad approach is recommended:

1. Use the leadership/team skills checklist, and the basic team format list (Chapter 16), *as soon as possible after group interaction*, to assess your own performance. Record points and plan where improvements could be made for the next encounter.
2. Set some time aside during the group encounter to obtain feedback from the group on your performance.

Point 2 will of course require team members to be involved in the underlying goals summarised by the collaborative skills checklist and basic team format list. In reality, self-team appraisal of the leader's collaborative skills performance will, at one and the same time, overlap with the self-team appraisal of each team member's collaborative skills development. This 'group appraisal' is seen as a central characteristic of an effectively functioning team, eg:

> A highly effective team is characterised by its tendency towards regular and searching self-evaluation of performance (Adair, 1986, p135).

> The group is self-conscious about its own operations. Frequently it will stop to examine how well it is doing or what may be interfering with its operation (McGregor, 1987, p234).

This again indicates, as considered in the previous section, how the team leader's development is tied up with the team members' development.

A re-cap of the obstacles to developing leadership/team skills

The biggest obstacle to people effectively developing the collaborative skills of leadership and teamwork is the nature of the organisational culture. Within a hierarchical organisational culture where the top manager has deeply embedded hierarchical attitudes, his or her collaborative skills development will be grounded, and individuals lower down the hierarchy will have difficulty in effectively introducing collaborative practices in their workplace (Chapter 6). Use of the skills checklist and basic team format list given in Chapter 16, therefore, would have limited value. Where hierarchical attitudes are not so deeply embedded in top management, however, the growing competition of the 1990s, coupled with the growing awareness of the need for less hierarchical, more collaborative, working and learning cultures, is likely to persuade these managers to develop such cultures. The aids given in Chapter 16 will be of value to top managers wanting to take the first steps in this development.

Within a collaborative organisational culture, or one where the top management is already *genuinely* committed to developing a collaborative culture, as was considered in Chapter 7, most people 'lower down' the hierarchy will quite readily adapt to a more tolerant, open, honest collaborative team approach in the workplace. It was also considered that people in management/supervisory positions, however, who are likely to have more deeply embedded hierarchical attitudes of arrogance, disrespect, etc, will be more likely to fear a collaborative approach and resist the development of collaborative attitudes such as humility, honesty, trust, respect, etc, and the related collaborative interpersonal skills. They, therefore, will need to be given more *time* to develop collaborative procedures. Top management will also need to ensure the following:

- Regular informal meetings with groups or departments, where genuine respect, listening and non-judgemental tolerance by top management of people's ideas, encourages group listening, the interchange of ideas, the airing of concerns and anxieties, and the general enabling and development of collaborative attitudes and skills.

- A training programme for managers/supervisors centring on collaborative skills development.

- Definite recognition-reward from top management for middle managers/supervisors as an *incentive* to begin to attempt to apply collaborative practices, – perhaps in the form of public praise, feature articles in house or public journals, or asking managers who are using (or attempting to use) collaborative procedures to give seminars to other managers within the organisation and externally, etc. Once those managers/supervisors not using a collaborative approach feel obliged by this to begin to develop the approach, the collaborative skills checklist and team format list given in Chapter 16 will provide useful learning aids in the development process.

The person who operated in an authoritarian way, cited in Example 1, Chapter 6, p75, confirms the need for a supportive environment for changing attitudes, when he acknowledges that people do need help, and it is 'absolutely crucial' to have a positive organisational ethos which encourages people to behave less autocratically.

And the writer and Radio 4 presenter, Andrea Adams, points to the need to 'understand rather than blame' people who operate autocratically, in order to change their attitude towards others (An Abuse of Power, 2.5.91). Tolerance and understanding, therefore, is important, and a constructive, supportive, collaborative culture that encourages people to behave less autocratically, is likely to be more successful in changing attitudes than one that judgementally blames people for having hierarchical attitudes. This is in line with what a manager at Steelcase, where there has been a training programme for middle managers/supervisors, would call the 'gentle way' of training. The same manager, however, maintains that if the 'gentle way' does not work, there will come a point when it is time to be more firm and say:

> It absolutely isn't working out. You have to change. Here's how you have to change, and you've got so much period of time to do it, and if you don't do it, you may not be a manager any longer. (*Business Matters*, 8.8.91)

However, tolerance will need to be shown and time given for the points above to take effect before resorting to this less gentle way.

Initially, as the attitudes of humility, honesty, respect, etc and related collaborative skills such as self-appraisal and listening, are likely to be poorly developed, or perhaps totally absent, most managers/supervisors are not going to be able *genuinely* to apply the skills checklist and team format. Such learning aids, however, can begin to develop underlying attitudes. For example, the mere setting up of a team, gathering them together in a room and acting out the procedure recommended by the team format list given below – including *asking* people their views, and visually recording them – can produce a positive response in team members, even though at first the team leader might find it difficult *genuinely* to listen and value their views. A positive and intelligent response by team members, however, can begin to increase the team leader's respect and trust in people, which in turn will increase his or her ability to listen, which will produce an even more positive response from team members, in a reinforcing cycle (See Figure 15.2 and cf Kendall, 1982, p110). The 'bully' referred to above explains his experience of a shift from authoritarian to more collaborative attitudes towards people, which incorporates this point concerning reinforcement. He recounts how he started to value the opinions of others and not just his own, and believes that was crucial to making it easier for him to delegate work. Then, by involving people, he began to notice how their abilities and creativity started to flower.

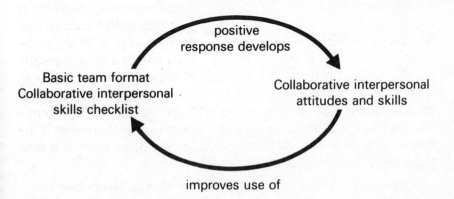

Figure 15.2 *A reinforcing cycle*

Even a negative response from people in the team – perhaps the team leader's inability to communicate a point and bring the team along with him or her – can be of value in 'un-learning' hierarchical attitudes such as arrogance, and learning collaborative ones, such as humility. In this context Laurence Handy talks about the need to '. . . provide the opportunity for the over-confident (not to say, arrogant) high flier to learn from a few rebuffs . . .' (1987, p7). And Adair, summarises: 'Failures teach success. They also teach humility' (1986, p195). This is true. Provided, of course, one is in a collaborative culture.

16

A practical guide to self-team development of the core collaborative skills of leadership and teamwork

The core collaborative skills checklist and basic team format

A summary of who they are for

The collaborative interpersonal skills checklist and basic team format below, have been compiled by taking the bare bones of what is needed to develop the core collaborative attitudes and skills essential for effectiveness and efficiency in both the industrial and educational settings. Much of the basic team format, for example, is distilled from Tom Peters' recommendations to managers/group leaders for conducting effective meetings/discussion in the workplace, an almost exact core of which is recommended by Matthew Lipman to teachers for conducting effective discussions in the classroom. The checklist and basic team format can be used to good effect by everyone in the working and learning environments, but the following people need to take the lead:

Top managers: (in industry and education) who want to develop their collaborative leadership-team skills as a basis for developing a collaborative organisational culture.

Trainee and practising managers/supervisors: (in industry and education) who want to develop their collaborative leadership-team skills with their immediate team(s) within a (developing) collaborative organisational culture.

Trainee and practising teachers/lecturers: who want to develop their collaborative leadership-team skills with colleagues (and pupils/ students) within a (developing) collaborative school/college culture.

Trainee and practising health personnel.

A summary of how to use them

The skills checklist together with the basic team format below should be used to plan *before* a meeting, and *as soon as possible after a meeting*, to appraise one's performance and plan before the next encounter. Writing down one's impressions of a meeting as soon as possible afterwards, and the use of audio or video recordings if acceptable to the group, will help in the appraisal process. The checklist and team format should also be used *during* meetings for everyone in the group to reflect on and appraise their own and the group's progress.

Remember:

1. Collaborative skills determine the way in which we do things, and cannot be learned independently of everyday activities in the workplace. But *never let the subject of those activities make you lose sight of the central importance of interpersonal attitudes and skills for achieving efficiency and effectiveness*. The checklist and basic team format should help you keep one eye constantly trained on the core skills.

2. Collaborative skills are dependent on underlying attitudes towards people. The following checklist, basic team format, and list of open questions, therefore, cannot be learned and applied to a formula, but they will require a fundamental change in the underlying hierarchical interpersonal attitudes that now prevail in the West. They are, however, useful props for beginning the process of developing the core collaborative attitudes in a reinforcing cycle.

3. Give yourself time, give other people time, be prepared to make mistakes.

4. The collaborative interpersonal attitudes and skills manifested in the following checklist are not trivial – an optional extra. They are central to individual and organisational success, and continuing success.

The basic team format – fine tunings

The exact way you apply the team-group format will depend on the particular group you are using it with. For example, under the 'friendly' rules component, teachers using it with children will probably need at first to ask the children to put their hands up before they contribute in order to prevent them talking together and to get them used to the habit of listening. On the other hand, adults in the workplace will generally not need to be reminded not to all talk at once. Again, teachers with very young children of five or six years will need to present some material as a basis for discussion (see eg Lipman, 1980), and plot the progress themselves rather than appointing a group member to do it. And again, adjustments might be made according to the size of the group, and the purpose of the meeting. But these aspects are just the fine tuning, and the basic principles of group procedure are the same for all 'group' encounters from the classroom to the boardroom.

The 'group' may be a one-to-one encounter between manager/team leader and one other person. There are differing views on the optimum group size to achieve effective discussion. Peters refers to research that shows that groups work best with four to seven members – any less might not generate enough energy and enthusiasm, any more might not let everyone get the chance to get really involved. In the classroom setting Lipman maintains an optimum number is 12–15, although teachers have used the approach effectively with groups of 30 or more (Jenkins, 1986). Nissan car workers at the Sunderland plant are grouped in teams of about 20 people.

The basic team format – two major pitfalls

The two major pitfalls that people who are starting out to apply a collaborative team approach fall into are the result of ingrained hierarchical attitudes, which, of course, cannot be shaken off overnight. It is important, therefore, for people to be aware of them.

The core collaborative interpersonal skills checklist*

Am I relaxed, non-abrasive?

Do I make eye contact?

Do I look attentive?

Do I begin (after a brief statement of what the meeting is about – see team format below) by asking open questions to elicit the group's views and feelings?

Do I patiently give time for their response?

Do I concentrate on the answers?

Do I avoid interrupting with my own views?

Do I avoid passing judgements against the person?

Do I help to further elicit people's views and feelings by reflecting (repeating) their response?

Do I periodically accurately summarise what has been said to clarify matters and elicit more response?

Do I make sure the main points are visually recorded?

Do I encourage openness and tolerate differing and opposing views?

Do I ask open questions to:
- encourage appraisal of their underlying reasons and assumptions?
- help people to keep to the point and be consistent?
- encourage appraisal of the implications of their views?
- encourage them to find out, question and value the views of others?
- encourage people to appraise the overall situation and suggest solutions?

Do I inform and fill in where necessary?

Do I take criticism without defending or apologising?

Do I take action, and/or delegate action, on the basis of the decisions reached by the group?

* Compiled and adapted mainly from Margerison, 1988; Lipman 1980; and Kendall, 1982.

The basic team format*

- **Encourage the group to form a circle**
  preferably with people sitting at tables.

- **Agree on 'friendly' rules for proceeding**
  eg don't all talk together, value and listen to others or they won't value and listen to you, build on agreement, avoid dominance by one member, avoid negative personal disagreement, behave courteously.

- **Brief consideration of the material/problem to be discussed**
  presented either by group members or the team leader.

- **Encourage participation**
  sometimes called 'brainstorming' – gather as many ideas as possible along the lines suggested by the above checklist.

- **Plot progress visually**
  appoint someone to write up group members' ideas.

- **Encourage evaluation of ideas**
  avoid side-tracks, irrelevancies; frequently summarise, etc along the lines suggested by the above checklist.

- **Write up conclusions/immediate future plans/actions**
  round off in a positive manner.

---

* Compiled and adapted mainly from Peters, 1989; and Lipman, 1980.

Pitfall 1

The first is the hierarchical skill of talking rather than listening, what might be called an 'occupational hazard' of both managers and teachers. It is incredibly difficult for managers and teachers to feel satisfied with a brief consideration of the material or problem to be discussed, and to hang back themselves at that stage, in order to find out the views of the group. Lacking respect and trust in others and their ability properly to consider a situation, they are likely to feel it is necessary to talk more about the subject, give their views and opinions, and their decisions and solutions. What they are perhaps not aware of is that this is highly impositional on the group members, and greatly reduces their self-esteem and confidence in any ideas they themselves might come up with, so that if or when their views are eventually sought, they will be inhibited and demotivated.

Never go into a meeting giving decisions that have already been made about the subject to be discussed, unless they are decisions reached previously by involving members of the group. A ploy often used to give the semblance of group involvement is to hand out typed sheets of views, opinions and decisions made by people higher up the hierarchy, and then to ask for the group's 'comments'. This, of course, is equally as inhibiting and demotivating as having decisions orally imposed. Dishonesty and manipulation will be suspected by the team members and they will have little trust that the decision makers will take any notice of their comments – after all, they were not interested in finding them out previously.

The use of typed sheets can be useful but purely as a source of information and/or to pose the problem, with no preemptive solutions or decisions. Also, depending on the amount, it is important to let group members have the information *before* the meeting to give them time to look over, digest, and come up with ideas.

Initially, because trust in others' abilities will be poorly developed, it will be difficult for managers and teachers to hang back with their views and seek the views of others – it will require if you like a leap into the abyss, a leap of faith. As the collaborative attitudes of respect and trust develop, it will become a much more positive, constructive and rewarding experience.

Pitfall 2

A second major pitfall is the tendency to attempt to over compensate for a judgemental hierarchical approach by believing it is possible to encourage participation by giving a great deal of praise. It ends up, however, being equally judgemental and ineffective. All people, children and adults, need praise. But reacting to group members' responses with too many 'Yesses' and 'Goods', etc, is just as closed – in that it can inhibit alternative views – and becomes just as judgemental and teacher- or manager-centred as categorical 'Noes'. The most effective praise and encouragement to participate, whether one is child or adult, is to be *genuinely* listened to and valued, having one's view taken up for serious discussion and action. The point is contained in the following advice from Kendall on effective 'active listening':

The listener's manner and tone should almost always tend to be facilitative, listening rather than reacting either positively or negatively . . . (1982, p109)

The use of open questions – a caution

Care must be taken in the use of questioning. According to Kendall, questioning as well as making judgements and giving advice, tends to interrupt the communication process, preventing effective listening and inhibiting the person being questioned. She, as others, maintains that open questions are useful to the listener, but leading questions such as: 'So would you say you can deal with difficult situations?', and closed and forcing questions: 'Do you want to stay here or do you want a transfer?' will retrieve limited information (1982, 110). Closed questions are those where the questioner already knows, or thinks he or she knows, the answer, so often used by teachers in the classroom: 'What is two plus two?' A teacher will rarely ask a question in the classroom with a genuine wish to find something out from the pupils and to explore their views. Questions are usually closed and used with the aim of prompting the pupil to come up with one particular answer already known, or thought to be known, by the teacher. Closed, leading and forcing questions rarely elicit a searching open response, and therefore should be avoided as much as possible.

However, the dividing line between closed and open questions is a fine one. As in the case of the collaborative skills checklist and basic team format above, effective open questioning cannot be learned to a formula, but ultimately depends on the questioner's attitude towards people. As in the case of the checklist and basic team format, however, they can be a useful aid for someone wanting to develop a collaborative approach, but it should be remembered that one's underlying interpersonal attitudes are paramount, and that whether or not a question is *genuinely open* does not depend on the words being used, but on *how* they are used. For example, what on the surface might look like an open question, such as 'What makes you think that?', becomes a closed, judgemental attack when uttered abrasively with anger, with emphasis on the 'What' and 'that'. One needs collaborative interpersonal attitudes of respect and humility in order *genuinely* to value and want to know what the other person thinks; to suspend one's own views, rather than impose them, by believing they could be mistaken; and thereby to be able to question in a genuinely open manner.

Examples of useful open questions*

Open questions to elicit views
What are your views on . . . ?
Tell me something about your experience of . . .
Tell me a bit more about that.
Can you give an example of that?
How did you feel when . . . ?
Could you explain what you mean by what you've just said?
Open questions to reflect and summarise and to elicit further views
As I understand you, what you're saying is . . .
As I hear you, you're saying that . . .
So am I correct in assuming you are saying . . . ?
Open questions to elicit underlying reasons and assumptions
Would you like to say why you think that is so?
What is your reason for saying that . . . ?
What makes you think that . . . ?
On what grounds do you believe that . . . ?
Doesn't what you say rest on the notion that . . . ?
Open questions to help people be consistent and keep to the point
How do you relate . . . to what you said earlier?
Are you making the same point now as you did earlier when you said . . . ?
I am not clear. Tell me why you think . . . is important to your earlier point . . . ?
Open questions to help people consider the implications of their views
So what do you think would be the outcome of what you're suggesting?
Are you suggesting that . . . ?
In view of what you've said, are you implying that . . . ?
Open questions to encourage a consideration of alternative views
Does anyone else have a different view?
What if someone were to suggest that . . . ?
Open questions to encourage general appraisal and outcome/solution
Could you give a summary of the points you are making and where you think we should go?
Can I sum up your solution as follows . . . ?

---

* Compiled and adapted from IMC Resource Material on 'Communications Skills'; Lipman, 1980; and Kendall, 1982.

Part III – key points

- The core leadership-team attitudes and skills are *learnable and not inborn*.
- Only by first developing the core collaborative skills will aspects of the higher level *team functions and related team roles* – a central plank of much leadership/team training today – be dealt with adequately.
- The *key* skills of managers and teachers are those of *collaborative leadership and teamwork*.
- With few exceptions, most courses in management and teacher training are too theoretical and neglect both the central importance of developing collaborative leadership-team skills, and the need for *practical skills* training.
- Learning the core skills is most effectively achieved by collaborative *'doing'*, ie *a collaborative consideration of theory centring on work-based experience*.
- Courses should only be considered as a *starting point* to an on-going process of *self-appraisal and development* of the core skills within the workplace.
- A collaborative organisational culture enables on-going *self-team appraisal and development*, where both management and non-management personnel can *learn* from, and be *supported* by, the open, honest, *'critical' feedback* of colleagues and customers.
- Self-team development requires a collaborative organisational culture which enables and *recognises and rewards* such development.
- Self-team development is best undertaken through *action research*, ie reflect/plan and act, incorporating group feedback and evaluation.
- The collaborative skills checklist and basic team format are the bare bones of what is needed to develop the core interpersonal skills essential for success and continuing success in both the learning and working environments.
- The checklist and basic team format provide useful aids for facilitating the action research process, and developing the core attitudes and skills in a reinforcing cycle.

Conclusion

Human relations are not just the surface froth of the workplace or the school, but are at the root of everything that goes on. Put simply, what we do cannot be separated from the way that we do it, style cannot be separated from substance. Attitudes towards people and oneself – interpersonal attitudes – such as respect, trust, honesty, love, etc, are the basis of collaborative interpersonal skills, such as listening, openness, non-judgemental tolerance, rationality, self-appraisal, etc; and this book has endeavoured to illustrate that these 'soft' attitudes and skills are the basis of ethical working practices, and form the core of effective management, effective teaching, effective teamwork, and effective learning. They are, therefore, the key to success, and continuing success, in both industry and education. In the increasingly competitive 1990s, there will be less room for the traditionally admired 'hard-headed' leader who operates independently of the human factor.

Evidence from industry and education has been considered to indicate that the ethos or culture of an organisation is set by the person at the top. It is essential, therefore, for top managers to initiate the process of developing these core collaborative attitudes and skills, in order to bring about enabling *collaborative organisational cultures*. In this way, instead of demotivating and disenabling the human resource as occurs in the prevailing pyramidal, hierarchical, power structures, *all* employees will be empowered and rewarded through a horizontal team structure that equally involves them in the decision-making process and that gives them responsibility for quality and other outcomes. Only in this way will people be able to continue to develop and lead creative and fulfilling lives – the bedrock of constant improvement in efficiency, quality, innovation and success. Top managers who do not initiate and support this collaborative development process will preside over uncaring, non-learning organisational cultures, with unethical and inefficient working practices, limited and inefficient training and development, and a consequent lack of fitness and innovativeness to survive increasing competition, diminishing resources, a growing socially and morally aware customer, and adverse 'non-collaborative' external pressures.

Collaborative skills development will not happen overnight – it involves changing deep-seated interpersonal attitudes that have shown a considerable resilience to best practice over many decades. The task, therefore, should not be underestimated. Time and again the author, along with others who propose a more participatory approach, has been met with the response from people both in industry and education that they are already aware of the 'human resource' message – 'there is nothing new in it'. And time and again it is either dismissed as not that important or, increasingly today as competitive and other forces are putting pressure on organisations to change their working practices, many managers and teachers attempt to delude people, and maybe even themselves, that they are already using a collaborative approach. As considered within the book, such delusion is the outcome of entrenched 'hierarchical' attitudes and skills, including arrogance, dishonesty, lack of genuineness, etc. Delusion and rhetoric abound, while action in the main remains unchanged. It is a dangerous situation for the well-being of individuals, organisations and the country as a whole. Concerned with the situation, management guru Peter Drucker relates his frustrated response when his clients tell him that he of course has not told them anything they did not know, which he now expects them to do: 'I turn nasty, I snarl, and I say, "For goodness sake why don't you *do* it then?!" ' (*Business Matters*, 5.9.91).

The answer, of course, is that 'the saying' and 'the deluding' is much easier than 'the doing', because, as this book has considered, 'the doing' requires a change in underlying attitudes towards people and their value. It is to be hoped that, armed with this awareness and the need *patiently* to develop more collaborative attitudes and skills, those managers, teachers, and others who have enough humility to recognise their own need to change, will have a better idea of *how* to go out and begin 'the doing' process.

Bibliography

Adair, J (1984) *The Skills of Leadership*. Gower, Aldershot.

Adair, J (1986) *Effective Teambuilding*. Gower, Aldershot.

Adams, R, Carruthers, J, and Hamil, S (1991) *Changing Corporate Values – A Guide to Social and Environmental Policy and Practice in Britain's Top Companies*. Kogan Page, London.

Anderson, W (1991) Forthcoming paper on stress in the workplace. Contact: Dr W Anderson, Faculty of Social and Health Sciences, Department of Psychology, Magee College, University of Ulster, Londonderry.

Beck, M (1989) 'Learning Organisations – How to Create Them'. *Industrial and Commercial Training*, vol21 (May/June), pp21–8.

Belbin, RM (1981) *Management Teams – Why and How they Succeed or Fail.* Heinemann, London.

Bennett, EB (1955) 'Discussion, decision, commitment and consensus in "group decision" ', *Human Relations*, vol8, pp251–73.

Blackburne, L (1990) 'NUT launches an action plan to combat stress', *The Times Educational Supplement*, 26 January, p3.

Blumberg, P (1968) *Industrial Democracy: The Sociology of Participation*, Constable, London.

Bocock, J (1989) 'The polytechnics – an independent assessment', *National Association of Teachers in Further and Higher Education Journal*, no6 (November/December), pp9–10.

BTEC (1989) Private Communication with Mr John Sellars, Chief Executive of the Business & Technician Education Council. For information on their publications contact: Central House, Upper Woburn Place, London WC1 0HH.

Burlingham, B (1990) 'This woman has changed business forever', *INC*, June issue, p34ff.

CBI (1989) *Towards a Skills Revolution – Report of the Vocational Education and Training Task Force*, Confederation of British Industry.

Chaney, FB and Teel, KS (1977) 'Participative management – a practical experience, in FJ Bridges and GE Chapman (eds) *Critical Incidents in Organizational Behaviour and Administration*, pp225–30, Prentice-Hall, New York.

Clarke, T (1990) 'Research: the missing agenda', *National Association of Teachers in Further and Higher Education Journal*, No1 (January/February), pp14–17.

Comer, J (1989) 'Grim reality at the margins', *Education Now*, No4, pp8–10.

Davies, J and Easterby-Smith, M (1984) 'Learning and developing from managerial work experiences', *Journal of Management Studies*, vol21, no2, pp169–83.

Deming, WE (1986) *Out of the Crisis*, Massachusetts Institute of Technology, Centre for Advanced Engineering Study.

Deming, WE (1988) Included in 'Keypoints of Deming's teachings' in the 'British Deming Association' pamphlet, Secretary General Tony Carter.

DES 385 (1990) 'Teacher training a priority area', Tim Eggar, Department of Education and Science, November, HMSO.

DES 389 (1990) 'Teacher appraisal to be compulsory', Kenneth Clarke, Department of Education and Science, December, HMSO.

Drew Smith, S (1991) 'Investors in people – The employer view', *TEC Director*, (Employment Department), December/January 1990/91.

Drucker, P (1991) Article in *Wall Street Journal*, Princeton, New Jersey, 11 January; taken from *Business Matters*, 5.9.91, *op cit*.

Elliott, L (1990) Article in *The Guardian*, 22 February, p12.

Erskine, S (1990) 'Staff appraisal and teaching as a career in Scotland', *Educational Management and Administration*, vol18, no1, pp17–26.

Freire, P (1972) *Pedagogy of the Oppressed*. Penguin, Harmondsworth.

French, JRP, Israel, J and Aas, D (1960) 'An experiment in participation in a Norwegian factory', *Human Relations*, vol13, pp3–10.

Garnett, J (1983) *The Manager's Responsibility for Communication*, The Industrial Society, London.

Gibbons, J (1989) 'Craft works', *The Times Educational Supplement*, 3 March, ppB1–B2.

Goldsmith, W and Clutterbuck, D (1984) *The Winning Streak – Britain's Top Companies Reveal their Formulas for Success*, Weidenfeld & Nicolson, London.

Golzen, G (1991) 'Is training out of touch with the 1990s?', *The Sunday Times*, Section 4, p9, 18 August.

Gray, HL (1989) 'Resisting change: some organisational considerations about university departments', *Educational Management and Administration*, vol17, no3, pp123–32.

Handy, C (1987) *The Making of Managers*, National Economic Development Office, London.

Handy, L (1987) 'Developing the high flier – a challenge for the future', *Journal of European Industrial Training*, vol11, no8, pp5–10.

Handy, L (1988) *Management for the Future*, Ashridge Management College and Foundation for Management Education, Berkhampstead.

Harber, C and Meighan, R (eds) (1989) *The Democratic School – Educational Management and the Practice of Democracy*, Education Now Publishing Cooperative.

Hellawell, DE (1990) 'Headteacher appraisal: relationships with the LEA and its inspectorate', *Educational Management and Administration*, vol18, no1, pp3–15.

Henry, C and Kemmis, S (1985) 'A point-by-point guide to action research by teachers', *The Australian Administrator*, vol6, no4, pp1–4.

HMI (1988) *The New Teacher in School – a Survey by HM Inspectors in England and Wales 1987*, Department of Education and Science, HMSO.

HMI (1989) *The English Polytechnics – An HMI Commentary*, Department of Education and Science, HMSO.

Honda (1990) Private communication with the plant manager and an associate manager at the Honda plant at Swindon, Wiltshire.

HSE (1990) *Managing Occupational Stress: A Guide for Managers and Teachers in the School Sector*, The Health and Safety Executive's Education Service Advisory Committee, HMSO.

Hyland, G (1990) 'Colleges: the natural focus for people development in their area', *PICKUP In Progress*, no 21, May, pp9–11, Department of Education and Science, HMSO.

ILEA (1986) *The Junior School Project – A Summary of the Main Report*. Inner London Education Authority.

Jenkins, J (1986) 'Those most powerful things on earth: a report on the use of *Harry Stottlemeier's Discovery*, 1984–1985', *Thinking*, no6, pp33–7.

JIT (1989) *Just in Time*, Training video, BBC Enterprises.

Jones, J (1990) 'The role of the headteacher in staff development', *Educational Management and Administration*, vol18, no1, pp27–35.

Jones, S (1988) 'The collaborative approach in health education and training', *Journal of the Institute of Health Education*, vol26, no4, pp153–60.

Jones, S (1989a) 'Training teachers by doing', *Education Now*, No4, pp11–12.

Jones, S (1989b) 'Quality training in theory and in practice', *New Era in Education*, vol70, no3, pp90–92.

Kemmis, S *et al* (1982) *The Action Research Planner*, Deakin University Press, Victoria 3217, Australia.

Kendall, R (1982) 'Active listening', *The Training Officer*, (May), pp109–11.

Lacey, C (1988) 'Towards a relevant curriculum in today's world', *Education Now*, no2, pp20–22.

Lane, NR, Lane, SA and Pritchard, MH (1986) 'Liberal Education and Social Change', *Educational Philosophy and Theory*, vol18, no1, pp13–24.

Lawrence, E (1990) 'The impact of reorganisations in HE institututions', *National Association of Teachers in Further and Higher Education Journal*, vol15, no4, pp28–9.

Levinson, H (1976) *Psychological Man*, Cambridge Levinson Institute.

Lewin, K (1947) 'Group decision and social change', in GE Swanson *et al* (eds) *Readings in Social Psychology*, Henry Holt, New York.

Lightfoot, SL (1983) *The Good High School: Portraits of Character and Culture*, Basic Books, New York.

Likert, R (1961) *New Patterns of Management*, McGraw-Hill, New York.

Lipman, M, Sharp, AM and Oscanyan, RS (1980) *Philosophy in the Classroom*, Temple University Press, Philadelphia. (See also note on p21.)

Locke, M (1989) 'Higher education – can collegiality and entrepreneurship exist together?', *Management in Education*, vol3, no4, pp6–7.

Lorenze, A (1991) 'Rover skids into losses', *The Sunday Times*, Section 4, p2 18 August.

Margerison, CJ (1987) *Conversation Control Skills for Managers*, WH Allen, London.

Margerison, CJ (1988) 'Conversation control in management development', *Journal of Management Development*, vol7, no3, pp68–73.

Margerison, CJ and McCann, R (1985) *How to Lead a Winning Team*. MCB University Press.

McGregor, D (1977) 'The human side of enterprise', in FJ Bridges and JE Chapman (eds) *Critical Incidents in Organizational Behaviour and Administration*, pp206–12, Prentice-Hall, New York.

McGregor, D (1987) *The Human Side of Enterprise*, Penguin, Harmondsworth.

Meighan, R (1988) 'Training teachers for democratic practice'. *Education Now*, no2, pp13–15.

Meighan, R and Harber, C (1986) 'Democratic learning in teacher education: a review of experience at one institution', *Journal of Education for Teaching*, vol12, no2, pp163–72.

Mintzberg, H (1973) *The Nature of Managerial Work*, Harper & Row, London.

Murray, G (1990) 'Opening up industry in Britain', *Intercity*, September issue, pp40–44.

NatWest (1991) 'The Body Shop International', *County NatWest WoodMac*, 3 September.

NFER (1990) *Enabling Teachers to Undertake In-Service Education and Training*, a report by the National Foundation for Educational Research for the Department of Education and Science, NFER, Slough.

Nissan (1985) From the Nissan Motor Manufacturing (UK) Company information sheets: 'Quality'; 'Employment'; 'Facts Against Fallacy'; 'Local Content and

Design'; 'Company Profile and Background'.

NUT (1990) *Health and Safety, Teachers, Stress and Schools*, National Union of Teachers.

OU (1991a) *Mastering Management*, Open University. Taken from BBC 2 broadcast 10 March 1991.

OU (1991b) *So You Want to be a Better Manager?*, Open University. Taken from BBC 2 broadcast 26 May 1991.

OU (1991c) *Managing in the Community*, Open University, Course Code B789. Taken from BBC 2 broadcast 22 September 1991.

Peters, T (1989) *The Tom Peters Experience – The Customer Revolution*, Training Video, BBC Enterprises.

Peters, T and Austin, N (1985) *A Passion for Excellence – The Leadership Difference*, Fontana/Collins, London.

Prideaux, G and Ford, JE (1988a) 'Management development: competencies, contracts, teams and work-based learning', *Journal of Management Development*, vol7, no1, pp56–68.

Prideaux, S and Ford JE (1988b) 'Management development: competencies, teams, learning contracts and work experience based learning', *Journal of Management Development*, vol 7, no3, pp13–21.

Revans, RW (1978) *The A.B.C. of Action Learning*, RW Revans, Manchester.

Reynolds, M (1980) 'Participation in work and education', in J Beck and C Cox (eds) *Advances in Management Education*, J Wiley, Chichester.

Ritchie, B and Goldsmith, W (1988) *The New Elite – the Secret of Britain's Top Chief Executives' Success*, Penguin, London.

Roddick, A (1991) *Body and Soul*, Ebury Press. Taken from extracts in *The Sunday Times*, 22 and 29 September, Section 3, p1 and p8.

Ruddock, J and Cowie, H (1988) 'Collaborative group work in schools', *Education Now*, no2, pp5–6; also from *Learning Together and Working Together*, BP Educational Service pamphlet.

Sampson, P (1990) 'Opinion', *Teachers' Weekly*, no127, p20.

Schumacher (1990) From the 1990 Schumacher lectures, The Schumacher Society, Hartland, Bideford, Devon.

Smith, EP (1969) *The Manager as Leader*, The Industrial Society, London.

Smithers, A (1991) *The Vocational Route into Higher Education*, University of Manchester.

Stenhouse, L (1969) 'Open-minded teaching', *New Society*, 24 July, pp126–128.

Stenning, R (1989) 'The conduct of industrial relations in schools: from collectivism to laissez-faire?' *Educational Management and Administration*, vol17, no4, pp225–31.

Utley, A (1990) 'Morale lowered by confrontation', *Times Higher Educational Supplement*, 22 June, p3.

Vroom, VH (1960) *Some personality determinants of the effects of participation*, Prentice-Hall, New York.

Wenham, M (1989) 'What about human values in curriculum?', *Education Now*, no4, pp14–16.

White, P (1983) *Beyond Domination – an Essay in Political Philosophy of Education*, Routledge & Kegan Paul, London.

White Paper (1988) *Employment in the 1990s*, HMSO.

Willie, E (1991) 'People development and improved business performance', *TEC Director*, (Employment Department), December/January, 1990/91.

Acknowledgement of sources

Individual

I would like to express my gratitude to the following for their kind help in providing material and/or for giving their permission to quote and reproduce material:

HRH The Prince of Wales; Anita Roddick, Managing Director of The Body Shop; Tony Webb, Director of Education and Training, the Confederation of British Industry; John Neilson, Press and Public Relations Executive, Nissan Motor Manufacturing (UK) Ltd; the Controller of Her Majesty's Stationary Office; and MCB University Press Limited.

Media

I am greatly indebted to the following for granting me permission to use short quotations, and also to all the programme editors/producers, presenters and production teams involved:

Glyn Mathias, Controller of Public Affairs, Independent Television News.

Channel Four Television for: *Check Out*, by Diverse Production for Channel 4; *Opinion* by Clark Production Ltd for Channel 4; *The Thatcher Audit* II (28.8.90, Mary Goldring) by Juniper Communications for Channel 4, and III (4.9.90, Will Hutton) by Realtime Television Ltd for Channel 4.

Andrew Clayton, Editor *Business Daily*, by Business Television Ltd for Channel 4.

Nick Hayes, Editor *World in Action*, Granada Television.

Jeremy Bugler, Director Fulmar Television & Film Ltd for 'There's no business like green business' for *Nature* (5.11.90) BBC TV (2).

I am also much indebted to the programme editors/producers, presenters, production teams, and the various third party contributors who kindly gave me permission to reproduce their comments, of the following British Broadcasting Corporation programmes:

BBC 1 *Great Expectations, Panorama, Question Time, State of Training, Tomorrow's World, Walk the Talk* (Scotland), News bulletins.

BBC 2 *Business Matters, The Great Education Debate, Fighting Talk, How Euro Are You?* (Midlands), *The Midlands Report, The Money Programme, Newsnight, Nature, Nippon, Public Eye, Top Gear, Troubleshooter, Where on Earth are We Going?*, News Bulletins.

BBC RADIO 4 *Analysis, Enterprise '90, In Business, Medicine Now, Money Box, Money Box Live, Open Mind, The State in Question, Whose Fault is it Anyway? (An Abuse of Power), The World at One.*

Index